Reach without Grasping

Studies in Body and Religion

Series Editor: Richard M. Carp, Saint Mary's College of California

Studies in Body and Religion publishes contemporary research and theory that addresses body as a fundamental category of analysis in the study of religion. Embodied humans conceive of, study, transmit, receive, and practice religion, with and through their bodies and bodily capacities. Volumes in this series will include diverse examples and perspectives on the roles and understandings of body in religion, as well as the influence and importance of religion for body. They will also move conversation on body and religion forward by problematizing "body," which, like "religion," is a contested concept. We do not know exactly what religion is, nor do we know exactly what body is, either; much less do we understand their mutual interpenetrations. This series aims to address this by bringing multiple understandings of body into an arena of conversation.

Recent Titles in Series:

Reach without Grasping: Anne Carson's Classical Desires, by Louis A. Ruprecht Jr.
Religion, Climate Change, and Our Bodily Future, by Todd LeVasseur
Quatremère de Quincy's Moral Considerations on the Place and Purpose of Works of Art: Introduction and Translation, by Louis A. Ruprecht Jr.
Creative Encounters, Appreciating Difference: Perspectives and Strategies, by Sam Gill
Religion and Technology into the Future: From Adam to Tomorrow's Eve, by Sam Gill
Sensing Sacred: Exploring the Human Senses in Practical Theology and Pastoral Care, edited by Jennifer Baldwin
Body of Christ Incarnate for You: Conceptualizing God's Desire for the Flesh, by Adam Pryor
Sacred Scents in Early Islam and Christianity, by Mary Thurlkill
Dancing Bodies of Devotion: Fluid Gestures in Bharata Natyam, by Katherine C. Zubko
Early Daoist Dietary Practices: Examining Ways to Health and Longevity, by Shawn Arthur

Reach without Grasping

Anne Carson's Classical Desires

Louis A. Ruprecht Jr.

LEXINGTON BOOKS
Lanham • Boulder • New York • London

Published by Lexington Books
An imprint of The Rowman & Littlefield Publishing Group, Inc.
4501 Forbes Boulevard, Suite 200, Lanham, Maryland 20706
www.rowman.com

86-90 Paul Street, London EC2A 4NE

Copyright © 2022 by The Rowman & Littlefield Publishing Group, Inc.

All rights reserved. No part of this book may be reproduced in any form or by any electronic or mechanical means, including information storage and retrieval systems, without written permission from the publisher, except by a reviewer who may quote passages in a review.

British Library Cataloguing in Publication Information Available

Library of Congress Cataloging-in-Publication Data

Names: Ruprecht Jr., Louis A., author.
Title: Reach without grasping : Anne Carson's classical desires / Louis A. Ruprecht Jr.
Description: Lanham : Lexington Books, [2021] | Series: Studies in body and religion | Includes bibliographical references and index.
Identifiers: LCCN 2021036056 (print) | LCCN 2021036057 (ebook) | ISBN 9781793637666 (cloth ; alk. paper) | ISBN 9781793637673 (epub)
Subjects: LCSH: Carson, Anne, 1950—Criticism and interpretation. | American literature--Classical influences. | LCGFT: Literary criticism.
Classification: LCC PS3553.A7667 Z86 2021 (print) | LCC PS3553.A7667 (ebook) | DDC 811/.54—dc23
LC record available at https://lccn.loc.gov/2021036056
LC ebook record available at https://lccn.loc.gov/2021036057

ISBN 9781793637680 (pbk. ; alk. paper)
ISBN 9781793637666 (cloth ; alk. paper)
ISBN 9781793637673 (epub)

The paper used in this publication meets the minimum requirements of American National Standard for Information Sciences—Permanence of Paper for Printed Library Materials, ANSI/NISO Z39.48-1992.

This book is dedicated to my brother
Thomas Holt Ruprecht

Being surer of himself, Tom was more open about it, where Ernest and I hide behind the cover of art and irony. At heart Tom possessed a religious feeling for the country and his best work has an ecstasy that can't be manufactured.

Stewart O'Nan, *West of Sunset*, 203

He stood in my living room and spoke
without looking at me. Not enough spin on it,
he said of our five years of love.
Inside my chest I felt my heart snap into two pieces
which floated apart. By now I was so cold
it was like burning. I put out my hand
to touch his. He moved back.
I don't want to be sexual with you, he said. Everything gets crazy.
But now he was looking at me.
Yes, I said as I began to remove my clothes.
Everything gets crazy. When nude
I turned my back because he likes the back.
He moved onto me.
Everything I know about love and its necessities
I learned in that one moment
when I found myself
thrusting my little burning red backside like a baboon
at a man who no longer cherished me.
There was no area of my mind
not appalled by this action, no part of my body
that could have done otherwise.
But to talk of mind and body begs the question.
Soul is the place,
stretched like a surface of millstone grit between body and mind,
where such necessity grinds itself out.
Soul is what I kept watch on all that night.

Anne Carson, "The Glass Essay" (1995)

Contents

Permissions	xi
Preface	xiii
Acknowledgments	xix
Introduction	1
Chapter 1: *Eros the Bittersweet*, or, *The Poetics of Desire*	7
Chapter 2: Translation as Modern Criticism, Creation and Conjuring, or, The Musing Scholar	35
Chapter 3: Poetry, Madness and Markets, or, The Ancients and the Moderns	77
Chapter 4: Hybrid Genres Between Body and Spirit, or, Righting the Self and Writing God	105
Conclusion	149
Epilogue: Six Questions and an Afterword	169
Appendix	175
Bibliography	177
Index	193
About the Author	197

Permissions

The author wishes to thank the following for their permission to reproduce material here.

Chapter 1 originally appeared in *Arion, a Journal of Humanities and the Classics*, in a somewhat different format [Volume 27.2 (2019): 137–167]. The editors of *Arion* have long supported my work in a variety of ways, and I am most grateful to them.

Portions of "The Glass Essay" by Anne Carson, from GLASS, IRONY, AND GOD, copyright ©1995 by Anne Carson. Reprinted by permission of New Directions Publishing Corp.

Excerpt(s) from AUTOBIOGRAPHY OF RED: A NOVEL IN VERSE by Anne Carson, copyright © 1998 by Anne Carson. Used by permission of Alfred A. Knopf, an imprint of the Knopf Doubleday Publishing Group, a division of Penguin Random House LLC. All rights reserved.

Excerpt(s), "1 [Deathless Aphrodite of the spangled mind]," "16 [Some men say an army of horse and some men say an army on foot]," "105b [like the hyacinth in the mountains that shepherd men]," "168B [Moon has set]," "38 [you burn me]," "105a [as the sweetapple reddens . . .]," "103CB," and "146 [neither for me nor the honey bee]" from IF NOT, WINTER: FRAGMENTS OF SAPPHO, translated by Anne Carson, copyright © 2002 by Anne Carson. Used by permission of Alfred A. Knopf, an imprint of the Knopf Doubleday Publishing Group, a division of Penguin Random House LLC. All rights reserved.

Excerpt(s) from WEST OF SUNSET: A NOVEL by Stewart O'Nan, copyright © 2015 by Stewart O'Nan. Used by permission of Viking Books, an imprint of Penguin Publishing Group, a division of Penguin Random House LLC. All rights reserved.

Excerpts from GRIEF LESSONS by Anne Carson © 2006 by Anne Carson. Reprinted by permission of Anne Carson and Aragi Inc. All rights reserved.

"III. And Finally a Good Dedication Is Indirect (Overheard, etc.) as if Verdi's '"La Donna è Mobile' Had Been a Poem Scratched on Glass" and "VIII. It Was Just Night Laundry Snapping Its Vowels on the Line When Mother Said What's That Sound," from THE BEAUTY OF THE HUSBAND: A FICTIONAL ESSAY IN 29 TANGOS by Anne Carson, copyright © 2001 by Anne Carson. Used by permission of Alfred A. Knopf, an imprint of the Knopf Doubleday Publishing Group, a division of Penguin Random House LLC. All rights reserved.

"Decreation Aria," and "L' (Ode to Monica Vitti)" from DECREATION: POETRY, ESSAYS, OPERA by Anne Carson, copyright © 2005 by Anne Carson. Used by permission of Alfred A. Knopf, an imprint of the Knopf Doubleday Publishing Group, a division of Penguin Random House LLC. All rights reserved.

"Drop't Sonnet," and "Wildly Constant" from FLOAT by Anne Carson, compilation copyright © 2016 by Anne Carson. Used by permission of Alfred A. Knopf, an imprint of the Knopf Doubleday Publishing Group, a division of Penguin Random House LLC. All rights reserved.

Finally, I am grateful to Taylor & Francis Group Academic Books for permission to quote from pages 638–639 of THE NOTEBOOKS OF SIMONE WEIL.

Preface

Umberto Eco describes a somber and strangely spiritual scene in his artful debut novel, *The Name of the Rose*, when his neophyte reporter, Adso, first comes to the comprehension of a medieval *scriptorium*.

> Until then I had thought each book spoke of the things, human or divine, that lie outside books. Now I realized that not infrequently books speak of books: it is as if they spoke among themselves. In the light of this reflection, the library seemed all the more disturbing to me. It was then the place of a long, centuries-old murmuring, an imperceptible dialogue between one parchment and another, a living thing, a receptacle of powers not to be ruled by a human mind, a treasure of secrets emanated by many minds, surviving the death of those who had produced them or had been their conveyors.[1]

"Books speaking to books." That description, for all of its marvelous and mournful evocation, can seem like the very thing that makes Classics and classical learning seem so dated and so often irrelevant. If all ancient books do is to reference one another, and to inspire deadening conversation among classicists, then what is their use? Friedrich Nietzsche, who did his graduate work in Classics and taught as a Classics professor for over a decade, felt that promoting this bookish image was the mistake most Classicists made, hiding their classical lights under scholarly bushels. "It would be a shame if the Classics spoke less clearly to us," he quipped in 1876, "because a million words stood in the way."[2] Nietzsche also condemned most of his classical colleagues for promoting an image of the scholar as a disembodied brain, and an image of the discipline of Classics as brains speaking in and to books, as it were. What was missing, he insisted, was body, and soul, and spirit. If his colleagues refused to *embody* classical wisdom, refused to aspire to *live* classically, then the transformative power of the literary material entrusted to their care would be lost, perhaps irrevocably, he feared.

Anne Carson positions herself within the realm of classical literatures in much the same way. She does not want her words to stand in the way. She does not want to participate in, nor to cultivate, the image of the classicist as disembodied intellect. Her conversation with the Greek books she loves issues in a mode of writing that is luxurious, sensual, lusciously material. From the beginning of her career, Carson anticipated many of the themes and insights we associate with the "new materialism" in comparative religion today. In her more recent work, Carson also refuses the tired (and falsifying) dichotomy that separates Classical and Christian learning. To her way of seeing, Sappho's lyric fragments represent one chapter in the very long history of Greek religion. They gesture backward to the Homeric poems, as well as forward to Plato's dialogues . . . as well as further on to the New Testament. The discipline of Classics has come around only lately to this indubitable spiritual assessment.

Bodily language is often applied to classical works. We speak of an author's *corpus*, and indeed, the same term is often applied more broadly to the entirety of a library, or a collection from antiquity, what we tend to conceive of today as a *tradition* of inquiry. Take, for example, the *Corpus Hermeticum*, edited and translated into Latin by Marsilio Ficino in 1471, inspiring a wave of neo-gnostic speculation in the early years of the Florentine Renaissance.

Ficino was even more influential as the author of lectures on "Platonic theology," and here we come upon a paradox that will recur throughout this book. How could an interest in highly speculative and esoteric Greek themes, especially those inspired by Plato's rigid and hierarchical dichotomy between the body and the soul, have served to inspire the visual fleshiness and artful corporeality of the North Italian Renaissance? One answer to this dilemma is that Ficino and his ilk did not read Plato that way. If anything, they saw him as one of the great theorists of embodiment, passion, desire, and inspiration. Transcendence began with the body, they believed, and the extensive body of Plato's literary leavings were an excellent means with which to step onto the ladder of spiritual ascent he so eloquently described in his *Symposium*.

We would do well to notice the lush tones of Eco's description of the Late Medieval *scriptorium*, his deep appreciation for the materiality of books, and of the word.

Too many words, or words of the wrong kind, tend to cover over the fact that most of these classical words were concerned with matter, with bodies. The classical tradition mattered to them in large part because of its creative concern with matter and materiality. Words, manuscripts, codices, and print books were, all of them, lush material artifacts. They were also, for this very reason, fragile, fungible, and mortal. Death, as the Greeks understood very well, was a bodily matter—hence the essentially corporeal concerns of their vast corpus. But their conception of materiality was more capacious than most modern ones. We moderns, and not just the kind of classicist Nietzsche condemned, speak of books and bodies as if they are utterly different types of things. That is not the classical view of the matter; where we set boundaries, they built bridges. The links that Greek writing established between sentient bodies and written texts may seem "merely" metaphorical, but metaphors are what we live by. That was a canon of Plato's Middle Period dialogues, most notably in the *Phaedrus*, where metaphors of desire, body, soul, and writing were joined with great artistry.

This same corporeal semantics offers one way into an understanding of Anne Carson's challenging and inspiring corpus. Like Nietzsche, Carson was trained as a classicist. Like him, she draws deeply on classical literatures, including philosophy, both ancient and modern. Like Ficino, Carson sees deep spiritual questions broached by the classical canon, and like him, she sees no necessary disjuncture between Classical and Christian themes. They both reject the alleged division of labor whereby the Greeks spoke of bodies and the Christians spoke of souls and spirits. For Carson, Plato was a speculative theologian, and he was also, like Sappho, an erotic thinker. There is no division of labor here.

What is unique in Carson's corpus is the close attention she pays to the art of translation, especially the translation of Greek lyric and stage drama, both of these embodied, *performative* genres. Carson is also an award-winning poet, herself. This rare combination of poetic skills and literary interests has produced a body of work that is unique in contemporary North American letters.

Carson inclines more toward Greek than Latin literature, although, as I will demonstrate in the final chapter, Ovid may provide a unique comparative point of entry into her body of work, given his mingled interests in the arts of love, bodily metamorphoses, soulful desire, and physical exile. Carson inclines more toward Greek lyric and Athenian drama than to any other classical genres. Carson inclines more toward Sappho than to any other Greek lyricist—Sappho, whose poetic fragments she has been reading since she was in high school, and which she published in a stunningly original translation in 2002. For many, the fragmentary state of Sappho's poetry has been an invitation to fill her out, to make wholes out of her fragments, and to construct a personality as allegedly found within that poetry. Carson is tempted by that work of poetic reconstruction, though more circumspect. Making wholes out of fragments is not unique to Sappho, she knows. That *just is* the work of the Classics. Most classical literature is lost to us. Umberto Eco's characters were in search of Aristotle's lost manuscript discussion of Greek comedy. There are many such losses in a library, or in a literary tradition. We are creatures of, and in, time.

What Carson revels in, uniquely, is the sheer materiality of the problem that Sappho's fragments present. The fragments are textual, reliant on the same materiality that Eco's character savored in the *scriptorium*. What we have of Sappho is preserved mostly by classical tradition, through quotation by other authors in antiquity, quotations that were dutifully copied over by monastic scribes across the millennia; we might view this tradition as constituted by a multiplicity of human hands joined in a sort of textual communion. Each hand adds its mark to the manuscripts.

We also have a number of newer Sapphic (and other) fragments, read off of scraps of Egyptian papyri. Some were glued together to form the cover of new codices; unglued and separated, they may reveal much older layers of text. Others were torn into strips, or already shredded, and then caulked, paper-mache style, into "mummy cartonnage" for cats and other pets, as well as for human bodies. But most of them have been discovered in an enormous garbage dump at Oxyrhynchus, Egypt, which has been producing new Classical and Christian manuscripts for over a century.[3] In fact, two new poems and some exciting new Sapphic fragments have been discovered and published in just the last decade, subsequent to the publication of Carson's edition of Sappho.

The corpus, like the canon, can change.

Zeroing in still more closely, we will notice that Carson inclines toward one Sapphic fragment more than any other piece in the entire body of classical poetry, one describing a singular kind of poetic love triangle. What Carson discerned in that poetic description of the love triangle in her very first book (*Eros the Bittersweet*, 1986) has been with her ever since. And she later applied the insight to conceive of spiritual aspiration as a love triangle in the works of three religious women. I will suggest that this book (*Decreation*, 2005) has been her most underappreciated work.

What Carson sees in the love triangle is a *geometry* of the hallowed hollow, such that the would-be lover discovers an emptiness, "the hole in him, unnoticed before." The points of the triangle actually serve to define a space, an emptiness within. The never-ending attempt to fulfill the lover's destiny within such an emptiness is the task that Carson believed links three decisive women who were also spiritual adepts. One of them was Sappho; the others were Marguerite Porete and Simone Weil.

Their lesson is this: one may reach, but one may not grasp; one may passionately desire, but one may not aim to possess. That goes for the beloved as well as for God. In sensing this, Carson tells us—and such knowledge is intimate, sensual, intense—that *eros* inscribes the poetic metaphor free spirits live by.

In the excruciating poem which I quote in the frontispiece, Carson distinguished between her body, which passionately desires a lover it is losing, and her mind, which resists the action and is appalled. But then she stops, starts again, and rejects the dichotomy as begging the question. "Soul," she says, "is *the place*." We will need to consider what kind of place that is.

This book's title, *Reach without Grasping*, is taken from the prefatory discussion in Carson's first book, *Eros the Bittersweet*. The distinction is philosophical and its resonance is spiritual, but we should not let this distract us from the fact that the metaphors are physical. Hands, not just minds, reach and grasp. It is one of the distinguishing characteristics of Carson's poetics that she refuses such dichotomies, preferring to keep the matter open. I will not belabor this point in what follows, since I do not want my own words to get in Carson's way, but I encourage the reader to notice how shot through with bodily and material concerns the entirety of her corpus actually is.

Here at the outset, it is enough to say that reaching and grasping both involve the passionate pretense, and the erotic promise, of touch.

NOTES

1. Umberto Eco, *Il nome della rosa* [The Name of the Rose] (Milano: Gruppo Editoriale Fabri-Bompiani, 1980). The book was published in an English translation by William Weaver in 1983, and made into a feature film by the same name in 1986.
The quoted text appears in *The Name of the Rose*, William Weaver trans. (New York, NY: Harcourt, Brace, Jovanovich, Inc., 1983), 342–343.

2. The comment appears in notes Nietzsche drafted for an "Untimely Meditation" he never published, one entitled *Wir Philologen*. These notes were published as "We Classicists," William Arrowsmith, trans., in his edition of *Nietzsche: Unmodern Observations* (New Haven, CT: Yale University Press, 1990), 307–387. The German text may be found in Giorgio Colli and Mazzino Montinari, eds., Friedrich Nietzsche, *Samtliche Werke: Kritische Studienausgabe* (Berlin: Walter de Gruyter, 1967–1977) [hereafter KSA] KSA VIII: 1–120.

3. A superb summary of the cartonnage, the Oxyrhynchus excavations and a wealth of other manuscript discoveries spanning the last 150 years, may be found in Brent Nongbri, *God's Library: The Archaeology of the Earliest Christian Manuscripts* (New Haven, CT: Yale University Press, 2018), esp. 216–246 on Oxyrhynchus, and 269–270 on a singular example of mummy cartonnage. The chief virtue of Nongbri's book for the purposes of this series is its identification of a new perspective with which to supplement traditional papyrology and biblical studies—namely, the new materialism, that calls for closer attention "to the books themselves as three-dimensional archaeological artifacts worthy of study in their own right" (11). I am suggesting that Anne Carson approaches the classical tradition much as Nongbri approaches the Christian, that is, with this same historical attention and virtually museological sensibility.

Acknowledgments

It is as sensually pleasurable as it is intellectually daunting to attempt to write about Anne Carson in a way that will communicate my deep admiration for her and for her work, and to do so in a manner that suits *her* purposes. I hope that I have managed to do at least some of that here. And, in any case, the first necessary word of gratitude belongs to her, for a dazzling body of work in both poetry and prose that continues to inspire and provoke delight.

Having the privilege of doing so amid the rich resources and rare beauty of the Vatican Library certainly added a boost of inspiration to the attempt to write about her. I am deeply grateful, as I have been for more than a decade now, for the extraordinary hospitality and support of the administration and staff of that truly remarkable, and remarkably cosmopolitan, scholarly institution.

Rome is a city of rare and enduring hospitality, and I've long reveled in that fact as well. Anne Carson pays homage to the city in her 1995 poem, "The Fall of Rome: A Traveler's Guide." As long as I have been working in the Vatican Library, I have been staying in an apartment provided to me by Carolina Olcese, boasting one of the finest views and decidedly the most enchanted terrace garden I've yet encountered in that most enchanting of cities. Carolina has become a dear and cherished friend over the years; one wise in the arts, in history, and in humanity, she brings a singular passion to all she does. It is she who has done the most to make Rome feel like home to me. And in the past two years, Carla Canonera has joined our circle of late-night garden conversations, contributing her boundless energy and good cheer to the company.

So too have a close circle of friends who continue to make my daily life in Rome an adventure and a benediction—with shared meals, sparkling conversation, rich humor, and travels both local and long. I am grateful, well past the ability of words to say or repay, for the friendship of Elisabetta Calderoni, Tiziana Checchi, Mauro Corso, Marika Favre, Ludovica Lanini, Gabriella Milea, Sara Millozzi, Emma Mintrone, Alice Rinaldi, Gabriele Santoro, Irma Storti, and Begoña Zubero.

The administration of Georgia State University has enabled me to carve out a regular work schedule in Rome, through the resources provided by the William M. Suttles Chair in Religious Studies, which I am the first scholar to have occupied. I wish to thank Parris Baker, Isra Hassan, Jill Jantosciak, Kathryn Kozaitis, William Long, the late Fred Mote, Provost Risa Palm, Esther Prince, Dean Sara Rosen, Sabrina Smith, James Taylor Jr., Felicia Thomas, Chrislyn Turner, and Carol Winkler each for their role in ensuring that I am able to do what I want, when I want, all with quite amazing grace and good cheer. That they continue to do so when all they ever get from me are postcards from the same old Roman landmarks speaks to a rare combination of generosity and humane sensibilities of which I continue to be the beneficiary. I'm truly grateful to them all.

In the US and abroad, I have also been blessed for many years with dear friends who are stunningly perceptive readers, as well as widely accomplished writers on their own. Sarah Ahrens, Wesley Barker, Mauro Corso, Mary Grace DuPree, Lori Anne Ferrell, Aikaterini Grigoriadou, Pauline Jaccon, Laura Jansen, Andrew Lee, Sarah Levine, Laura McKee, Michelle Miles, and the late John Rivenbark each read this manuscript in its entirety, saving me from countless mistakes and infelicities, and boosting my confidence whenever it wavered (which was often enough). Their generosity of spirit is matched by their generosity with time, and I'm deeply touched by the gift of both.

My thanks also go to the production team at Lexington Books and to the editors for their decision to include this title in their wonderful Body and Religion series. The series editor, Richard Carp, has been my friend and teacher for virtually the entirety of my professional career. We met in the summer of 1993 at the University of Hawai'i at Manoa, when I was selected to participate in an NEH seminar that he co-taught there with Mark Juergensmeyer. The seminar was entitled "Beyond the Text: Teaching Religion and Material Culture," a stunningly original and far-reaching seminar that took me many years to understand properly. At the time, I was working on a translation of Sappho's poetic fragments; to that end, I first read Carson's *Eros the Bittersweet* under the palm trees near Waikiki. Over the years, Richard has taught me how to integrate art history, studio production, dramatic performance and materiality into these forms of scholarly and aesthetic engagement. He knows better than anyone how much I owe to him, and I know to say at least this much in gratitude.

And now a final, more personal word of thanks. I don't recall how my family's love of literature expressed itself in my early childhood, apart from the books that were always in hand or by the bedside: *The Cat in the Hat, One-Fish-Two-Fish-Red-Fish-Blue-Fish, A Fly Went By, Good-Night Moon, The Little Engine That Could, The Little Red Caboose*, each of which I'd committed to memory by the time Kindergarten came a-calling.

But there must have been more to it than that, as my and my two brothers' careers will attest. We have all three spent much of our lives in and among written words. My younger brother, Cliff, completed his PhD, and an ambitious thesis on Kierkegaard and Lacan, before going on to law school. His professional life is built largely upon words, and ideas, and their artful combination.

But it is my youngest brother, Tom, whose literary career takes the palm. A tremendously talented comic writer who has enjoyed a span of remarkable successes in books and on television—that most unfunny and unforgiving medium—Tom started early . . . and here again, I don't recall the clues that would have alerted us to what was coming. He was already performing one-man stand-up routines at high school assemblies, and after graduating from college, he initiated a staggering pace of producing articles, short bits and screenplays that has never eased. At the same time, he is as devoted (and as funny) a husband and father as any I've known—to his wife, Lorraine, and to his two children, Sally and Zach. Tom was ten years old when I headed off to college, just discovering the joys of toy trucks and baseball. With sibling age differences of that size, friendships, when they come, tend to come later in life. I'm deeply grateful to him for his. So this book, a study of the relationship between an especially creative body of ancient words and their poetic adaptation by a contemporary writer, is fittingly dedicated to him.

LAR
Atlanta
June 2020

Introduction

THE QUEST FOR A GENRE, OR, WHERE BOUNDARIES TOUCH THEN BLUR

You know that poetry (*poiêsis*) is many-faceted. For anything that passes from not-being into being has poetry (*poiêsis*) as its fundamental cause, such that all the works of all the arts and crafts are poetries (*poiêseis*) and all their creators are poets (*poiêtai*).

What you say is true.

Nevertheless, she said, you know that they are not all called poets (*poiêtai*), but they have other names, and from out of all the poetries (*poiêseôs*) one of them is set apart—the part involving music and meter—and given the name. This alone is called poetry (*poiêsis*) and only those who take up this part of poetries (*poiêseôs*) are called poets (*poiêtai*).

—Plato, *Symposium* 205b–c

In this book, I intend to explore the robust engagement with classical literatures, classical themes, classical aspirations and, most of all, hybrid genres in the works of Anne Carson, a writer and luminary who explores as many and as diverse a range of genre choices as the classical authors from whom she has drawn so richly throughout her career. She does so in Greek and in Latin. She does so in poetry, plays, and prose. She does so with a dazzling sense of poetry's creative powers (as enunciated in Plato's expansive conception of the term with which this Introduction begins), attending to the supreme musicality and meter of language and delighting in the alchemical passage from empty pages to script, from pre-poetic emptiness to fuller being. I wish to begin here by reflecting on her prosodic range and genre-bending virtuosity.

On the 19th of May in 1603, the Letter of Patent for the King's Men (formerly called the Lord Chamberlain's Men) gave the group permission to present at court "Comedies, Tragedies, histories, Enterludes, moralls, pastoralls, Stage-plaies and Suche others like as theie haue alreadie studied or hereafter shall vse or studie, aswell for the recreation of our lovinge Subjectes, as for our Solace and pleasure when wee shall thincke good to see them, duringe our pleasure."[1] Twenty years later, in the first print folio edition of Shakespeare's complete plays (1623), the suggestive list of genres had been reduced to three: "Comedies, Histories & Tragedies." This scattershot approach to dramatic genre is suggestive, doubly so in relation to the man who could claim "that which we call a Rose / by any other name would smell as sweet."[2] Genres are very loose outfits that poetic languages wear, and they ought not be too confining. The question of what to *call* certain works is not necessarily the most fruitful question to place in the foreground when studying them.

In Anne Carson's case, the question of genre is best left in question; most of her career has been defined by the attempt to push against the strictures of generic expectations, in the name of taking calculated rhetorical risks aimed at generating new insights which can inspire delight.[3]

If there is any truth to the idea that Mark the evangelist essentially created a new genre, the gospel, by expanding expectations and combining the rhetorical field of several genres available to him in the Greek-speaking Roman Mediterranean (like tragedy and gnomic wisdom-sayings),[4] then I will suggest that something similar has been at work throughout the course of Anne Carson's astonishing literary career. She has been playing within and between genres in the attempt to create hybrids and new genres uniquely suited to the cultivation of new insight and perennial delight. It is also suggestive that the two texts most clearly identified by their genre-bending experimentalism (*Decreation* and *Nox*[5]) are both aimed at traditionally religious themes, where traditional dichotomies tend to break down: the blurring of the borders of self in the former text; the love-work of mourning and remembering in the latter; the ellipsis between body and soul in both. That Sappho is a lodestar in the former text, and that Catullus, a poet who occasionally aspired to be her Latin mirror-image, is a lodestar in the latter, is also suggestive. Whatever else she is, Anne Carson is a lyric poet with an ancient pedigree.

That Carson will recall Sappho as priestess, as well as poet, in *Decreation* also highlights a little-remarked dimension of Carson's lifelong engagement with classical texts: namely, her interest in *religious* themes. This may seem an odd-sounding claim to make on Carson's behalf, but it will become clearer if we permit our conception of "religion" to be as elastic as our expectations of genre must be in any reading of her work. I will return to this dense issue in the fourth chapter and again in the Conclusion.

* * * * *

Anne Carson was born in Toronto, Canada,[6] on June 21, 1950, and is one of the most versatile of those living writers in the English language who have drawn deeply from the well of Classical waters. She trained as a classicist, but is far better known as an accomplished poet and translator. Anne Carson burst on the scene in 1986 with the publication of her first book, *Eros the Bittersweet: An Essay*. What this book announced most clearly (in addition to Carson's complex identity as a poet-classicist-philosopher, all in one[7]) was her unique ability to work across the expectations and the loose boundaries which define a genre, and thus to create new genres along the way. It is an *essay*, in the purest sense given to the term by Montaigne, a steadfast attempt at honest and more self-aware thinking.[8] As Carson herself puts the matter later, "calling [my writing] an essay means that it's not just a story but a reflection on that story."[9] I will devote the first chapter of this book to a close reading of the stunning literary and philosophical achievement that is embodied in her first book.

In this book about her, I also hope to explore the role played by generic transgressions (in poetry, in prose, in essays, and even libretto), and by the spiritual coupling (speaking very loosely) of both Classical and Christian texts, throughout Carson's long career of re-staging the classical legacy in creative and more contemporary literary terms. Placed at the historical crossroads from which the Classical and Christian religions slowly parted company were Roman writers such as Ovid, whose encyclopedic knowledge of Greek literary forms, and whose decidedly transgressive sensual-spiritual interests, culminated in an astonishing new genre: the "Metamorphoses." Ovid rarely appears in Carson's work, but I suspect that he is one of the classical writers closest, within important limits, to Carson's own transgressive work betwixt and between genres and religious inclinations. In a word, both of these strikingly original conceptual poets *strive to enact continuous changes*.

Anne Carson has produced a body of work that is as difficult to characterize as it is thrilling to read and to ponder. Her early essays on classical themes—leavened by her own deep interest in poetic expression, and her remarkable gifts as a poet—have inspired a larger body of work that possesses two centers of gravity, or pivot points: her own lyrical poetic production; and her lifelong engagement with the Greek language as a translator[10] of rare insight and grace. Her translation work has focused almost exclusively on Greek lyric poetry (Sappho, preeminently) and on Greek tragedy; her relatively recent move to New York City appears to have been inspired in part by her resolve to commit herself almost entirely to matters of public performance.[11] She now designs all of her poetry and translation for staged performance, largely in collaboration with other artists in the visual, textual, and more hybrid media arts. It is worth noting that theatrical performance requires the living presence of bodies joined in time and space; a play cannot only be a book. Hybridity, in any case, increasingly defines the aesthetic landscape Carson inhabits most comfortably, and this is one of the main reasons why the question of her playful work within and between genres is best left in question, a means of re-opening rather than foreclosure.

It makes a kind of aesthetic sense, then, that Anne Carson has achieved a decidedly unique place in the realm of North American letters, as symbolized by the award of some of the most prestigious academic and creative grants in the Arts and Humanities,[12] including: the Lannan Literary Award in 1996; the Pushcart Prize in 1997; a John Simon Guggenheim Fellowship in 1998; the MacArthur Foundation "genius grant" in 2000; the Griffin Poetry Prize in 2001 (she was the first woman to be so recognized); the T.S. Eliot Prize, also in 2001; the PEN Award for Poetry in Translation in 2010; and a second Griffin Poetry Prize in 2014 (she is the only person to receive this award twice). And she has been a Writer-in-Residence at countless prestigious posts over the years. It is my hope that this book will do justice in some small way to the classical wisdom, the emotional depth, and the sheer audacity of her work.[13]

NOTES

1. The Letter is quoted in Peter Thomson, *Shakespeare's Theatre*, 2nd Edition (New York, NY: Routledge, 1992), 73.

2. William Shakespeare, *Romeo and Juliet*, II.ii. This idea inspired the title for Eco's debut novel, of course.

3. Taking note of Anne Carson's heterodox disregard for normal generic expectations has provided the starting point for many excellent studies of her challenging body of literary work. I note, as exemplary, the following: John D'Agata, "Review of *Men in the Off Hours* by Anne Carson," *Boston Review* 25.3 (Summer 2000) [http://bostonreview.net/BR25.3/dagata.html]; Guy Davenport, "Introduction" to *Glass,*

Irony and God (New Directions, 1995) vii–x; Ian Rae, "'Dazzling Hybrids': The Poetry of Anne Carson," *Canadian Literature* 166 (2000): 17–41; Ian Rae, "Verglas: Narrative Technique in Anne Carson's 'The Glass Essay,'" *English Studies in Canada* 37.3/4 (2011): 163–186; Melanie Rehak, "Things Fall Together," *New York Times Magazine* (26 March 2000): 36–39; and "An Interview with Michael Ondaatje," in Sam Solecki, ed., *Spider Blues: Essays on Michael Ondaatje* (Montreal: Vdhicule, 1985), 329.

Her heterodoxy has generated criticism as well—for demonstrating a genre-averse poetics, or else for creating a hopeless mish-mash—from those less willing to let her float free of expected literary constraint. See, for example, Jeet Here, "Poet or 'Prize-Reaping Machine?'" *National Post* 31 (January 2002): B5+; Kathleen Kuiper's entry on "Anne Carson" in the *Encyclopedia Brittanica*; Robert Potts, "Neither Rhyme nor Reason," *Guardian UK* (26 January 2002): 1–3; and David Solway, "The Trouble with Annie," *Books in Canada* 30.1 (July 2001): 24–26.

In this book, I side with the yea-sayers, since the naysayers seem deliberately to refuse the lessons Carson has patiently (and even relentlessly) tried to render discernable by writing in the manner she chooses. What is unique in my approach is: first, to note the way that genre-bending was itself a hallmark of the ancient Greek lyric tradition which Carson so often adapts to her own purposes; and, second, to highlight the religious implications of Carson's generic choices, especially the transgressions.

4. For more on this idea of Christian genre bending-and-blurring, see Louis A. Ruprecht Jr., *Tragic Posture and Tragic Vision: Against the Modern Failure of Nerve* (New York, NY: Continuum, 1994), and *This Tragic Gospel: How John Corrupted the Heart of Christianity* (San Francisco, CA: Jossey-Bass, 2008). A superb extension of this idea to Mediterranean Late Antiquity is Robert Shorrock, *The Myth of Paganism: Nonnus, Dionysus and the World of Late Antiquity* (London: Bloomsbury Academic, 2011, 2013).

5. The entirety of Carson's major published work, with full bibliographic references, may be found listed in chronological order in the Appendix to this book.

6. Carson's questionable Canadian pedigree has also generated discussion, much of it frankly perplexing to me. The issues are nicely laid out by Ian Rae, in a chapter dedicated to Carson's work, in *From Cohen to Carson: The Poet's Novel in Canada* (Montreal: McGill-Queen's Press, 2008), 223–260, esp. 243–244 and 256–258, as well as in "Verglas: Narrative Technique in Anne Carson's 'The Glass Essay,'" esp. 179–182.

While Carson was born in Canada, she has worked primarily in the United States by choice. English is her first language as well as the language in which she writes, but she clearly knows French well. The nationalist questions driving this discussion seem to miss the centrality of the Classics in the entirety of her literary formation and of translation in her literary production; the Classics, in her view, knows no modern border, whether national or linguistic or generic.

7. In the words of Lee Upton, "[w]hile Carson has the philologist's and the classicist's authority, I'm not sure that her authority as a poet resides in intellection, in research itself, in the materials which tend to be unstable for her. . . . Her authority may more fully reside in a bold act of ligature between scholarship and at least the tonal quality of confession as her scholarship protects the story of romantic triangulation from closure" [*Defensive Measures; The Poetry of Niedecker, Bishop, Glück, and Carson* (Lewisburg, PA: Bucknell University Press, 2005), 113].

8. For more on the play with Montaigne's concept of the *essai*, see Ian Rae, "Verglas: Narrative Technique in Anne Carson's 'The Glass Essay,'" 164–166.

9. Anne Carson, *The Beauty of the Husband: A Fictional Essay in 29 Tangos* (New York, NY: Alfred A. Knopf, 2001), 33. She adds that this "is also a way of making it less personal or not only personal. But I also just like the absolute inanity of calling anything a fictional essay. Something about that appeals to me."

10. Chris Jennings goes so far as to call translation "her master trope," in an essay devoted primarily to the concept of "triangulation" she first developed in *Eros the Bittersweet*. See Chris Jennings, "The Erotic Poetics of Anne Carson," *University of Toronto Quarterly* 70.4 (2001): 923–936, esp. 923–926.

11. Carson most recently collaborated with Claudia Rankine on "The Mile-Long Opera," which was performed on the High Line in New York City in the fall of 2018, and staged a new adaptation of Euripides's *Helen* off-Broadway at "The Shed" on April 9, 2019. The latter text was published as *Norma Jeane Baker of Troy* (Oberon Books Ltd., 2019).

12. Roy Scranton notes that this impressive recognition came shortly after "she erupted onto the contemporary American poetry scene with two books" in 1995, granting Carson "that rarest place in American culture: an experimental poet whom people actually read." See Roy Scranton, "Estranged Pain: Anne Carson's *Red Doc>*," *Contemporary Literature* 55.1 (2014): 202–214, quote at 205. Finally, Carson collaborated with the visual artist, Rosanna Bruno, on *Euripides: The Trojan Women, A Comic* (New York, NY: New Directions Publishing Corporation, 2021).

13. Craig B. Hannaway's *Anne Carson: A Brief Introduction* (Coppell, TX: Erimus Books, 2021) appeared after this book had gone into production. As he admits, "I have tried to provide a key to her work rather than a comprehensive survey of it, which would take a much longer book. Not all her work is interpreted here. Rather, I have focused on the remarkably interesting relationship between Carson the Classicist and Carson the Writer/Artist/Maker" (9). While I do not agree with all of his critical judgments, some of which seem unduly negative, I read the book with great interest.

Chapter 1

Eros the Bittersweet, or, *The Poetics of Desire*

> I take this evanescence and lubricity of all objects, which lets them slip through our fingers when we clutch hardest, to be the most unhandsome part of our condition.
>
> —Ralph Waldo Emerson, "Experience" (1844)

On rare occasions, a first book may give us a telling insight into everything that is to follow. Anne Carson's *Eros the Bittersweet: An Essay*[1] is such a first book. What the book does best is to announce itself, and its author, as the bearer of unconventional news, reported in an unconventional manner, all of it expressed in uncommonly luminous prose. It is a book that refuses to be categorized, a book that refuses genre—strangely enough, virtually by creating one for itself. And along the way of creating—that is, of poeticizing—in its singular way, this book generates new desires entirely of its own creation.

There is a history to such literary and generic non-conformity.

When Friedrich Nietzsche (1844–1900) was invited to take up a professorship at the University of Basel, at the astonishingly young age of twenty-four and without having yet produced his dissertation, the expectations surrounding his first book were elevated, to say the least. Well aware of this, aware too of having been described by his mentor, Friedrich Wilhelm Ritschl (1806–1876) as bearing the future of Classics in Germany on his shoulders, Nietzsche published *The Birth of Tragedy Out of the Spirit of Music* in 1872.[2] He was still just twenty-six years old, and very few classicists knew what to make of it; even his strongest boosters, like Ritschl and Erwin Rohde (1845–1898), regretted the rashness of the thing. Meaner spirits mockingly called it a work of "future-philology!" suggesting that, while Nietzsche was free to pen whatever sort of "gospel" he wished, he was not free to call such evangelizing "classics."[3] Nietzsche would leave the university, and the profession, just seven years later, and suffered a complete mental collapse one decade after that. The genius of the book was not really appreciated until shortly after his death. I have often had this story in mind as I have contemplated the intricate twists and turns in Anne Carson's career.

There have been other such noteworthy idylls of the unconventional scholarly mind. One thinks of Walter Benjamin's (1892–1940) dissertation, *On the Origin of German Tragic Drama*,[4] which was completed in the spring of 1925, then promptly ignored and forgotten. After his tragic suicide in flight from the Nazi occupation of France, Benjamin's text soon came to be considered, in the words of George Steiner, as "one of the most original books of philosophical and literary criticism of the twentieth century."[5] As one of Benjamin's later supporters quipped, "*Geist kann man nicht habilitieren*, You cannot credential spirit."[6]

One thinks as well of Carlo Michelstaedter's (1887–1910) dissertation, *Persuasion and Rhetoric*,[7] a work of similarly audacious range and philosophical scope. Grappling with the relationship between the pre-Socratic philosophers' own claims about their intentions and what creative use Plato was to make of their legacy, Michelstaedter insisted on viewing philosophy as the seizure of (or by?) a *belief too strong to shake*. In short, it was not as rational as its pretenders claimed it to be. Michelstaedter punctuated the completion of that daunting work by committing suicide. You can't credential spirit.

It is striking that each of these books attempted its essay in near impossibility by grappling with classical thought. Occasioned by a new look in a new way, these exercises in reading the Classics obliquely were written for an audience that had arguably not yet been born. Their successes were mostly posthumous. And each of their authors came to a relatively tragic end.

We might consider Martha C. Nussbaum's *The Fragility of Goodness* in a similar light.[8] And in this case, the gendered body of the non-conforming author is material. Nussbaum, like Carson, elected to enter two of the most male-dominated disciplines in the Humanities: Classics and Philosophy. More audaciously still, she insisted on being credentialed in both. Admittedly, Nussbaum established her *bona fides* with a far more traditional first book, a more recognizable essay in philosophical classics. This was her impressive philological-and-philosophical study of Aristotle's "On the Motion of Animals."[9] Having established her classical credentials, however, Nussbaum next produced a massive, and exquisitely creative study of virtually everything Athenian, from Aeschylus through Aristotle, all of it unified by a thesis as simple as it was profound: Greek tragedy offers an emphatic interrogation of the inescapable fragility of human life, the moral life especially; Plato wishes to make the life of virtue invulnerable (and relatively unfeeling as well); Aristotle retrieves fragility (and feeling) as a central moral value and tragedy as therefore essential for philosophical understanding. Unsurprisingly, eros was a central theme in Nussbaum's book. What offered surprise was that a female classicist so recently credentialed would dedicate nearly a decade to writing about erotic matters, with all the invitations to dismissal as little more than academic sentimentality that such a publication risked. If Nietzsche dared a gospel, then Nussbaum dared to write a lyrical epic. Remarkably, such Nietzschean dismissals were not the driving spirit behind the book's reception: *The Fragility of Goodness* launched Nussbaum's meteoric rise to academic stardom as a public intellectual.

Anne Carson's career may be understood within this same general framework, inspired by the devilish daring of dipping into suspect or unprecedented hybrid genres. In a word, Carson made herself a part of this *nonconformist* classical tradition, one largely Nietzschean in inspiration, and she intended to supplement the daring with feminine and feminist sensibilities that would take years to clarify. Unlike Nussbaum, Carson played her trapeze act without a net, publishing her first book in the very same year that saw *The Fragility of Goodness* into print. Equally at home in Classics and philosophy and poetry, Carson played breezily with all three, and produced a first book—the book that would normally be assessed to grant an Assistant Professor of Classics tenure (or not)—that managed more in 173 aphoristic pages than many poets or scholars manage in a lifetime.[10]

* * * * *

The short, one-page Preface to *Eros the Bittersweet* makes very plain that something strange is afoot.[11] The mention of eros in the title, coupled with the cover image of an erotic Greek vase painting, creates classical (and more subtly philosophical) expectations. Yet the Preface begins, *sans* explanation, with a reading of Franz Kafka's short story, "The Top."[12] The story involves a "philosopher" who loves to watch children playing with tops; his passionate obsession is due to a belief that eventually issues in an action. He believes that close study of any single thing will result in the knowledge of all things. The small thing he has chosen is a child's top "in spin." He dares to snatch them up in mid-spin; he believes that he is going to see something in that unique moment of capture. But of course he never does; the capture serves only to freeze the scene and stop the top. Delight turns almost immediately to despair, and hope turns to nausea. Thus, the doomed philosopher wavers endlessly between the reach of hope and the grip of despair.

Much like a lover.

Carson introduces a whole range of words in her summary of Kafka's story that will carry the burden of heavy argument throughout the essay: delight; impertinence; understanding; love. She claims, inexplicably, that this is a story about "the delight we take in metaphor" (metaphor, as we will see, is a central topic in Plato's *Phaedrus* as well). She suggests, inexplicably, that the story concerns "why we love to fall in love" (falling in love, as we will see, is a central poetic preoccupation for Sappho as well). Narrowing her focus now to that elusive (and Kafka-esque) idea of love, Carson carves a new metaphor out of the story, as a talented poet may. She concludes that beauty, the beauty of the lover, just *is* that spinning top, and that grasping it would allow us to understand "that impertinent stability in vertigo is possible." Before we will be able to make sense of that strange-sounding claim (to gain our sea-legs, if you will), we will need some time to digest the difference between reaching and grasping and the space between the two. This Kafka's philosopher failed to do.

Carson observes that lovers do not want *to suppress* impertinence (arguably, if only implicitly here, it may be her measured judgment that academic classicists and philosophers do that—there are shades of Nietzsche's startling and self-critical practice of the Classics already in this alternately-cautious-and-audacious first book). And now she offers her striking conclusion to this staging of Kafka's "The Top." A real philosopher, she tells us, is one "whose profession is to delight in understanding," not to *grasp* after it. A real philosopher, she implies, is a philosopher only insofar as he or she is also a lover: one who has come to see that becoming a philosopher is merely a ruse, a pretext for chasing vertiginous spinning tops. The whole point and purpose of the exercise is to *chase* them, not to *catch* them. As we will learn, that simultaneously intellectual and emotional space—the space *in between* reach and grasp—also inscribes the moment when the lover really lives *in hope*. Such is the unhandsome condition of the genuine philosopher.

Carson utilizes this intriguing story in order to gesture to the paradoxes of a philosopher who is a lover, and a lover who is a philosopher. She appears to have Socrates and Sappho in mind (though we might well add Nietzsche to the list). Both of them are top-chasers. And it will take poetry as well as philosophy to render this central paradox legible. Of paradox, Carson will later observe the following: "What is a paradox? A paradox is a kind of thinking that reaches out but never arrives at the end of its thought."[13] Now we arrive at the literary pretense that gives rise to this entire book: Anne Carson will turn to Sappho's poetic fragments, together with Plato's dialogue, the *Phaedrus*, as a sort of erotic lodestar. She will read them together in order to take eros apart. If philosophical top-chasing creates the space where despair and hope commingle, then eros creates the moment when pain and pleasure commingle. Sappho helps us to understand desire spatially; Plato situates desire squarely in human (and divine) time. Carson combines the two to produce a dazzling, distinctively modern, and decidedly post-Einsteinian reflection on the difficult relativity of desire.

To understand how this all works, she begins with Sappho. It is one of this ancient poet's finest reputed insights to have coined the word "bittersweet" in reference to eros:

> Eros once again limb-loosener whirls me
> sweetbitter, impossible to fight off, creature stealing up.[14]

Carson notes that the word Sappho coins (γλυκύπικρον, *glukupikron*) has been strangely inverted in English translation: as bitter-sweet, rather than sweet-bitter. The ordering of emotional affect matters, Carson suggests, especially "in poetry, where most love ends badly."[15] That is to say, for most love poets, as for most Romantics, love begins sweetly and ends in bitter agony; it shape-shifts through the course of time. But even to say it this way is not quite right.

> Her poem begins with a dramatic localization in time (*deûte*) and fixes the erotic action in the present indicative tense (*donei*). She is not recording the history of a love affair but the instant of desire. One moment staggers under pressure of eros; one mental state splits. A simultaneity of pleasure and pain is at issue.[16]

From Homer, to Aeschylean tragedy and Aristophanic comedy, through Hellenistic epigrams, and even into the Latin rehearsals of Sappho by Catullus, the sweet and bitter aspects of passionate desire are emphasized by the poets whom they perplex. *Odi et amo*, says Catullus; "I love and I hate."[17] But why, Carson wonders, should that simultaneous and contradicting affect constitute eros's primary effect?

It is instructive that Carson begins her analysis of Sappho's Bittersweet Fragment by attending to tense and temporality. She gestures in this direction, the oblique and evanescent direction of time, but she will not pick up this issue directly until we come to her crucial discussion of the adverb, *deûte*, at the mid-point of the book, when she transitions from an analysis of Sapphic poetry to Plato's erotic philosophy as enunciated in the *Phaedrus*.[18]

We want to know more about this strange issue of simultaneity and self-contradiction ("I don't know what to do / two states of mind in me," Sappho will say in Fragment #51). Desire is deferral. In fact, this deliberate delay in attending to the question of time will enable Carson to illuminate the ways in which Sappho's poetic genius is primarily spatial, geometrical even, rather than temporal. It is almost as if there were an ancient division of labor in play here, such that philosophers tend to erotic time, whereas poets tend to erotic space; Carson will attend to both, in series.

From the Renaissance and the first print editions of Sappho's poetry,[19] Sappho had been known primarily for four poems: the justly famous Ode to Aphrodite (#1, the only complete poem in our possession until quite recently[20]); the Bittersweet Fragment (#130) I have just rehearsed; another fragment (#168B) that I will refer to as the Pleiades Fragment, in which a sleepless lover gazes at the setting moon and stars; and what I will refer to, a bit crudely, as the Love Triangle Fragment (#31). It is to the fourth of these ("one of the best-known love poems in our tradition"[21]) that Carson turns our attention now.

> He seems to me equal to gods that man
> who opposite you
> sits and listens close
> to your sweet speaking
>
> and lovely laughing—oh it
> puts the heart in my chest on wings
> for when I look at you, a moment, then no speaking
> is left in me
>
> no: tongue breaks, and thin
> fire is racing under skin
> and in eyes no sight and drumming
> fills ears
>
> and cold sweat holds me and shaking
> grips me all, greener than grass
> I am and dead—or almost
> I seem to me.[22]

It is easy to see why this evocative poetic fragment is so popular, though it remains a point of heated contention what precisely the poet was really up to.[23] For Pseudo-Longinus, who quotes it in his essay *On the Sublime*, the fragment is a marvel of symptomatology. Sappho, he feels, has perfectly captured the limb-slackening, near-death experience of the lover in the raw grip of fresh desire. According to Carson, two of the primary interpretive means of grappling with this complex poem (she calls it a "ruse") have emphasized either the role of jealousy in the set-up, or else the rhetorical manner in which the third person ("that man," who *seems* like a god) is the necessary figure created (that is, invented) by Sappho's virtuoso word-play.

Carson sees something else at work here, something decidedly spatial, geometric even. "It is not a poem about the three of them as individuals, but about the geometrical figure formed by their perception of one another, and the gaps in that perception. It is an image of the distances between them."[24] But why a *triangle*? What is the meaning of that trite erotic truism, suggesting that some third thing (not always, or only, a person) necessarily intrudes upon the erotic couple in ways that make the loving more dynamic?

> We may, in the traditional terminology of erotic theorizing, refer to this structure as a love triangle, and we may be tempted, with post-Romantic asperity, to dismiss it as a ruse. But the ruse of the triangle is not a trivial mental maneuver. We see in it the radical constitution of desire. For, where eros is lack, its activation calls for three structural components—lover, beloved, and that which comes between them.[25]

The interference creates the dynamic. Such dynamism is the very crux of eros, Carson surmises: "For in this dance the people do not move. Desire moves. Eros is a verb."[26]

It will take some time to work this spatial reasoning through, and when Carson has done so, a surprising conclusion suggests itself:

> Eros is an issue of boundaries. He exists because certain boundaries do. In the interval between reach and grasp, between glance and counterglance, between "I love you" and "I love you too," the absent presence of desire comes alive. But the boundaries of time and glance and I love you are only aftershocks of the main, inevitable boundary that creates Eros: the boundary of flesh and self between you and me. And it is only, suddenly, at the moment when I would dissolve that boundary, I realize I never can. . . .
>
> Like Sappho's adjective *glukupikron*, the moment of desire is one that defies proper edge, being a compound of opposites forced together at pressure. Pleasure and pain at once register upon the lover, inasmuch as the desirability of the love object derives, in part, from its lack. To whom is it lacking? To the lover. If we follow the trajectory of eros we consistently find it tracing out this same route: it moves out from the lover toward the beloved, then ricochets back to the lover himself and the hole in him, unnoticed before. Who is the real subject of most love poems? Not the beloved. It is that hole.[27]

In the end, love and desire are not at all what we thought they were. The dilemma is not temporal; the temporal problem is only an "aftershock." The real problem is spatial, and bodily. We have physical boundaries, fleshed edges, hidden hearts. There is a hole at the heart of our desire, and the radical incompleteness that comes upon the lover in love, once recognized, will never vanish. Other types of thinking and speaking will be necessary to make sense of this strange condition.

One aspect of desiring ruses are puns. This too may seem very strange at first glance.

To think about one's own tactics is always a tricky business. The exegesis measures out three angles: the lover himself, the beloved, the lover redefined as incomplete without the beloved. But this trigonometry is a trick. The lover's next move is to collapse the triangle into a two-sided figure and to treat the two sides as one circle. "Seeing my hole, I know my whole," he says to himself. His own reasoning process suspends him between the two terms of this pun.[28]

The lover who has come this far in thinking about his desire (and his lacking) now discovers a new problem; he cannot even speak clearly about this desire. That Carson uses the masculine pronoun here is suggestive, though the register is not primarily homoerotic. We will return to that point. But here, we can see that the poetic language necessary for eros is pressed past the normal semantic range of words. Puns enable the lover to reach for more than normal speech can say. His hole-y nature is also holy. The lover in love, radically and spatially incomplete, is nonetheless a spiritual being, involved now in a new quest, and in a new way. The pun makes the language more dynamic, ensuring that eros remains a verb, in motion.

But such puns take us well beyond where Archaic Greeks such as Sappho were prepared to go. For them, there is nothing good about desire of this intensity or the soulful transformations it enacts. "Change of self is loss of self to these poets. Their metaphors for the experience are metaphors of war, disease and bodily dissolution."[29] But something clearly happened to the Greek experience of loving, their relentless thinking about desiring, attaining and losing. On the one hand, an oral culture was to become a literature culture, first inventing and then expanding the role of writing in the evolving culture of the Greeks. "Oral cultures and literate cultures do not think, perceive, or fall in love in the same way,"[30] Carson observes. Next came the astonishing innovation that would render the Greeks decidedly different from the love poets and all the other literate-erotic acolytes who preceded them. This linguistic revolution comes in a surprisingly simple form: the Greek language was the first and only one to generate an ancient writing system with vowels.[31] Consonants, which most writing systems possessed, constitute the sound; the vowel represents the empty space between two sounds, and it is that empty space in the middle that paradoxically defines the words with greater clarity and specificity. A Semitic alphabetic system may write a word such as S-T, but once the vowels come into being, then the words may flower into their full diversity. The word may now be "sat" or "set" or "sit" or "sot." The attention of the written Greek language was unique, in that for the very first time, literate people became interested in the empty space between things.[32] The love triangle, in other words, had been inscribed into the very form of the written Greek language; their very grammar was erotic. Sappho's Love Triangle fragment had come to rest in (Greek) writing.

This technological innovation, the way words might now possess clear and distinct vocalization, enabled the Greeks to do many new things with their writing. Poetry would eventually have to make room for novels[33] and letters of the epistolary kind.[34] But it was philosophy that would eventually emerge, in Plato's hands, as the new erotic genre *par excellence*.

> There would seem to be some resemblance between the way Eros acts in the mind of a lover and the way knowing acts in the mind of a thinker. It has been an endeavor of philosophy from the time of Sokrates to understand the nature and uses of that resemblance. But not only philosophers are intrigued to do so. I would like to grasp why it is that these two activities, falling in love and coming to know, make me feel genuinely alive. There is something like an electrification in them. They are not like anything else, but they are like each other. How?[35]

The answer to that question will necessitate a movement from the consideration of space to the contemplation of time. "The blind point of Eros is a paradox in time as well as in space."[36] The temporal paradox has something essentially to do with the difference between reaching and grasping, the central issue with Kafka's philosophy-inspiring spinning tops. "[Y]ou are aware that as soon as 'then' supervenes upon 'now,' the bittersweet moment, which is your desire, will be gone. You cannot want that, and yet you do. Let us see what this feels like."[37]

The key to this paradox, for Carson, involves the unique tense (and tension) of erotic desire, one captured in a single adverb that is shot through a great many of Sappho's surviving fragments:[38] *dêute*, or δηὖτε, a word which manages to combine the idea of "now" and "then" in a single, sensual, shocking moment, virtually an eternal affective now. The word is called a *crasis*, a mingling of two words, one particle (*de*) and one adverb (*aute*); joined together, they come to mean something like the paradoxical phrase, "now and then, again."

This adverb, utterly pervasive in Greek erotic poetry,[39] does very particular work in some of Sappho's most famous fragments. The first case we may consider is the Bittersweet Fragment Carson already introduced to us:

> Eros–here it goes again [*dêute*]–the limbloosener whirls me,
> sweetbitter, impossible to fight off, creature stealing up[40]

This same adverb does even more subtle work in the only complete poem in the Sapphic corpus, her Ode (or Hymn) to Aphrodite. In 2002, Carson had come to believe that placing "(now again)" in parentheses was the best way to translate—and to set apart—this unique and well-nigh impossible erotic tense:

> Deathless Aphrodite of the spangled mind
> child of Zeus, who twists lures, I beg you
> do not break with hard pains,
> > O lady, my heart
>
> but come here if ever before
> you caught my voice far off
> and listening left your father's
> > golden house and came,
>
> going to your car. And fine birds brought you,
> quick sparrows over the black earth
> whipping their wings down the sky
> > through midair—
>
> they arrived. But you, O blessed one,
> smiled in your deathless face
> and asked what (now again) I have suffered and why
> > (now again) I am calling out
>
> and what I want to happen most of all
> in my crazy heart. Whom should I persuade (now again)
> to lead you back into her love? Who, O
> > Sappho, is wronging you?
>
> For if she flees, soon she will pursue.
> If she refuses gifts, rather will she give them.
> If she does not love, soon she will love
> > even unwilling.
>
> Come to me now: loose me from hard
> care and all my heart longs
> to accomplish, accomplish. You
> > be my ally. (#1)[41]

There is subtle playfulness here, perceptible in the juxtaposition of a deathless (and hence, timeless) goddess with the poet who is locked in her desire, and thus in time. Her existential experience of time's suspension is reminiscent of the symptomatology in the Love Triangle Fragment (#31); the poet cannot move, she cannot speak, she cannot escape an overwhelming tide of erotic desire. But this has all happened before, and likely will repeat itself at some other time ("now again"). Such a moment of shattering desire seems like it will never end. And yet the goddess smilingly reminds us that it will pass, one way or another, with time . . . as it has done many times before. Desire is little else than this vast temporal paradox, a perennial filling-and-emptying-and-on-again.[42]

> The experience of eros is a study in the ambiguities of time. Lovers are always waiting. They hate to wait; they love to wait. Wedged between these two feelings, lovers come to think a great deal about time . . .[43]

And so, just like that, Carson is poised to make the crucial transition in the book:[44] from Sappho to Socrates, from poetry to prose, from love verses to erotic philosophy, and finally, from space to time.

* * * * *

The *Phaedrus* is a very complicated dialogue, one of the subtlest and most complicated in the Platonic corpus. It begins where the *Symposium* left off, with competing love speeches (*erôtikoi logoi*). Phaedrus tempts Socrates to take a stroll outside of the city walls, something this decidedly non-natural philosopher rarely does. The temptation takes the form of a speech, one that Phaedrus heard the great orator, Lysias, deliver earlier in the day. Having borrowed a copy of the speech, Phaedrus reads it to the rapt Socrates. Whether his attention is captured by Lysias's words, or by Phaedrus's shining beauty, will remain unclear throughout the day. It is enough to say that the entire dialogue may be read as a flirtatious scene of philosophical seduction.[45]

Socrates is not overly impressed by Lysias's clever speech. The pretense of it is this: the speech is written on behalf of a lover (*erastês*) who does not love (*erân*) a potential beloved (*erômenos*), and the thrust of the argument is that this weird and unexpected fact is what will make him the ideal lover for the boy. Such loveless love promises an escape from the disruptions of jealousy and other forms of impassioned, grasping desire. It promises the sweet grasp without the bitter reach (and thereby gets the erotic ricochet entirely backwards). This is not erotic desire, so much as it is dueling narcissism.

Socrates yawns when the speech concludes, and tells Phaedrus that he has heard much better erotic writing than this by other writers. Phaedrus challenges his friend for the name of one; "the lovely (*kalê*) Sappho" is mentioned, as is "the wise (*sophos*) Anacreon" (both poets, not speechwriters). When pressed, Socrates agrees to offer a rival speech of his own, and so he does. Phaedrus is delighted but, as the two prepare to leave the private grove where they have been flirting with erotic speech, and with each other, Socrates's *daimôn* informs him that he has sinned against the god, Eros. Thus Socrates offers a second speech—a retraction, or *palinode*, which is to say, a "(now, again) song"—to rectify his falsifying first speech and to purify the erotic scene. His rhetoric here rises to a feverish pitch, and we gradually come to see that Socrates has overturned the two primary assumptions of the first two speeches with this Palinode. Now, we are informed that erotic pain cannot be separated from erotic pleasure[46] and that, while eros is indeed a form of madness, it is a blessing sent to us by the gods (there are other things on the list of manic blessings as well, including prophecy and poetry, both).

Phaedrus, who has shown himself to be positively insatiable for love speeches, now begins to discuss this second speech with his friend. Yet this customary Socratic back-and-forth (called an *elenchus*) takes the dialogue in new and unexpected directions. We meet one of the most extended arguments for the immortality of the human soul, and its loose memory across incarnations. We confront one of the longest and most moving of Socrates's many metaphors for the human soul: that of a chariot being drawn by two competing and contradictory horses. And we meet an extended meditation on the limits and the corrupting power of writing. Thus, a dialogue about love becomes a dialogue about psychology, which then becomes a dialogue about rhetoric and writing. How can these themes be reconciled?[47]

Carson offers some unexpected and rather startling observations about this winsome dialogue, in order to supplement her spatial Sapphic reflections with Plato's temporal ones. She begins by noting that eros and logos have been joined in this dialogue ("as closely as two halves of a knucklebone"[48]) in ways that will complicate our erotic musings before they may clarify. Her conclusion is as profound as it is jarring:

> Damage is the subject of this dialogue. Plato is concerned with two sorts of damage. One is the damage done by lovers in the name of desire. The other is the damage done by writing and reading in the name of communication. Plato appears to believe that they act in the soul in analogous ways and violate reality by the same kind of misapprehension. The action of eros does harm to the beloved when the lover takes a certain controlling attitude, an attitude whose most striking feature is its determination to freeze the beloved in time. It is not hard to see that a similar controlling attitude is available to the reader or writer, who sees in written texts the means to fix words permanently outside the stream of time.[49]

Lysias's speech, Carson believes, mistakenly begins at the end,[50] taking on the perspective of a relationship when it is over . . . which is as much as to say that it never really began. His promise of a loveless love is just that, *love-less*. It determines a fixed erotic point from which the beloved boy will not need to change, nor should. There is something frozen and frightening about a love of that kind. It is the love of a philosopher who cannot stop grasping children's tops in mid-spin, and who fails to understand what his grasping has done to them.

As for eros, so too for logos. Socrates will refer to logos as "living" in this dialogue, precisely when he wishes to distinguish the dynamic back-and-forth of two people speaking from the frozen soliloquy of written speeches. Writing is literally a "dead letter."[51] "Change is essential to it, not because wisdom changes, but because people do, and must."[52] And now we begin to see the contours of the connection Socrates wishes to make: "wooing" is the same kind of action for the lover and the knower. Reaching for wisdom is an erotic art.

When he begins to describe the nature (rather than the immortality) of the human soul, Socrates makes a casual observation that is crucial to the entire Platonic corpus, in my view. He confesses that it would take a god to say what a soul actually is. But human beings, he adds with marked appreciation, are especially adept at saying what things are like. We live, and love, and think, in the realm of metaphors, similes, image-making.[53] Carson proceeds next to rehearse the meaning of three poignant images, or likenesses, from Socrates's extended *logos*: "a Lysian theory of love violates those natural currents of physical and spiritual change that constitute our human situation in time. What happens when you choose to abstract yourself from participation in time? Plato gives us three different images of the answer."[54]

These three images involve the tomb of King Midas, the myth of the creation of cicadas, and the gardens of Adonis. It is a striking and startling list. Midas, Carson reminds us, was Aristotle's token for "the absurdity of want in the midst of wealth."[55] Carson takes the myth much further, however; she sees it as a spatial and temporal absurdity. "Midas is an image of someone stranded in his own desire, longing to touch and not touch at the same time . . . Midas's golden touch would be a powerful symbol of perfect, self-extinguishing, self-perpetuating desire."[56] Midas begins in desire and he ends in isolation. *No change*.

The myth of the creation of cicadas appears to be Socrates's own invention. The two lovers hear their buzzing in the trees overhead, and Socrates pauses to reflect on the music they make. He claims that cicadas were people who lived on the earth in the time before the Muses were created. When the Muses came on the scene, and began to create music, these people were so mesmerized that they neglected all nourishment, content simply to hear this celestial music until they died. The Muses rewarded them for this passion with reincarnation as cicadas, animals who do not eat, and really do not do anything except make music. *No change*.

The "gardens of Adonis" refer to an intriguing fifth century BCE Athenian ritual. Plants were cultivated quickly in small pots, such that they bloomed very fast and, lacking roots, withered immediately. They were then cast away. In this, they symbolized the Romantic evanescence of Adonis, the idealized erotic Greek youth, and mortal lover of the deathless Aphrodite. When he changes (that is, withers), their love relationship is over. The mythic-erotic-divine ideal is still one in which *no change takes place*. "So Sokrates describes the manipulative tendencies of the conventional *erastês*. This lover prefers to play his erotic games with a partner who has neither roots nor future."[57]

Lysias is obsessed with control, self-control and control of the beloved in equal measure. Socrates cautions us to realize that eros cannot be so controlled, anymore than wisdom (or spinning tops) can be.

> As soon as eros enters his life, the lover is lost, for he goes mad. But where is the point of entry? When does desire begin? That is a very difficult moment to find, until it is too late. When you are falling in love it is already too late: *deûte*, as the poets say. To be able to isolate the moment when love begins, and so block its entry or avoid it entirely, would put you in control of eros. Lysias's nonlover claims to have achieved such control. He does not say how and the claim remains psychologically incredible. His *logos* simply ignores the moment when eros begins; he speaks from the end of the love affair as one who has never been taken over by desire at all. Nonlovers are people who remain "masters of themselves" (232a).
>
> Sokrates denies that such control is ever possible, or even desirable, for human beings.[58]

This realization—of the critical importance of admitting the limits of control in the lover and the knower, alike—constitutes the challenging heart of this dialogue, as well as of Carson's remarkable book. Here is her rousing conclusion to this arousing connection:

> As Sokrates tells it, your story begins the moment Eros enters you. That incursion is the biggest risk of your life. How you handle it is an index of the quality, wisdom and decorum of the things inside you. As you handle it you come into contact with what is inside you, in a sudden and startling way. You perceive what you are, what you lack, what you could be. What is this mode of perception, so different from ordinary perception that it is well described as madness? How is it that when you fall in love you feel as if suddenly you are seeing the world as it really is? A mood of knowledge floats over your life. You seem to know what is real and what is not. Something is lifting you toward an understanding so complete and clear it makes you jubilant. This mood is no delusion, in Sokrates' belief. It is a glance down into time, at realities you once knew, as staggeringly beautiful as the glance of your beloved (249e–250c).[59]

His gleaming metaphor for that dazzling burst of insight, that revelatory now, is the soul growing wings, and taking to the air.[60] It is an image, we should be sure to note, of bodily motion as well as of ascent; there is nothing static or literary about it. "No difference: no movement. No Eros."[61]

The final section of this remarkable book is entitled "Mythoplokos"; it is a Greek word which means roughly "weaver of stories." According to Maximus of Tyre, Sappho coined the word in reference to Eros:

> τὸν Ἔρωτα Σωκράτης σοφιστὴν λέγει, Σαπφὼ μυθοπλόκον.
> ---
> Socrates calls Eros a sophist, Sappho a storyteller.[62]

This curious juxtaposition (or is it a commingling?) of philosophy and poetry, sophistry and storytelling, inspires Carson to pose an interesting question. What would a city with no *eros* in it lack? Carson's list of the missing items is long: imagination, fiction, wings, movement, poetry. Such a city could never be home to a Sappho or a Socrates; there would be no need for what they have to offer.

> Eros is a story in which lover, beloved and the difference between them interact. The interaction is a fiction arranged by the mind of the lover. It carries an emotional charge both hateful and delicious and emits a light like knowledge. No one took a more clear-eyed view of this matter than Sappho. No one caught its features more accurately in adjectives.[63]

Why, then, would Maximus of Tyre link Socrates and Sappho as erotic thinkers? Carson has already hinted at one answer for us. In short, because of "the ancient analogy between the wooing of knowledge and the wooing of love."[64] The poet woos a lover the way the philosopher woos wisdom (and students). Both must learn how to reach without grasping. Both must consent to live in flux.

Carson's book is a primer on how to think and to feel, in tandem. The thinker must be a lover, and vice versa.[65] To extend Carson's juxtaposition further, I wish to recall a lengthier comparison which Maximus of Tyre draws in this same context:

> What else may we call the eros of this Lesbian woman (τῆς Λεσβίας) other than the erotic art of Socrates (ἡ Σωκράτους τέχνη ἐρωτική)? For they both seem to me to have had close friendships (φιλίαν) in their own way, she with women and he with men. For it is said that they loved many (πολλῶν ἐρᾶν ἔλεγον), and were captivated by all the beauties (πάντων . . . τῶν καλῶν). What Alcibiades and Charmides and Phaedrus were to him, Gyrinna and Atthis and Anaktoria were to the Lesbian. And just as Socrates was a rival in the art (ἀντίτεχνοι)

to Prodicus and Gorgias and Thrasymachus and Protagoras, so Sappho was to Gorgo and Andromeda. Sometimes she rebukes (ἐπιτιμᾷ"), them, sometimes she cross-examines (ἐλέγχει) them, and sometimes she ironizes (εἰρωνεύεται), all in the Socratic manner.[66]

This is an altogether remarkable comparison. Its frank admission of an "erotic art" which Sappho and Socrates shared would seem to admit to the essentially homoerotic dimension of that "art."[67] Much as Plato depicts the hapless Socrates, so Maximus sees Sappho: repeatedly subject to passionate "crushes," desperately wooing these crushes away from her poetic rivals. Maximus's comparison seems to take Greek homoerotic *desire* for granted, yet it turns away from sexuality altogether. However subtly, the last sentence undercuts this only apparently sexualized landscape. For Sappho's methods, like Socrates's, are entirely verbal; she does things to the girls in her orbit *with words*, much as Socrates did to the boys in his: with elenchic questioning, with bewildering poetic challenges, and with withering irony. If there is seduction here, then it is seduction into the desire for greater wisdom and increasing excellence. The Greek erotic art is—now, again—a manner of knowing as well as of wooing.[68]

To appreciate Anne Carson's remarkable achievement in this unique and unprecedented first book, it is important to recall that a great many Classical scholars were returning to these same Greek texts with renewed vigor in the early-to-mid-1980s. Sir Kenneth Dover's *Greek Homosexuality* (1979),[69] John Boswell's *Christianity, Homosexuality and Social Tolerance* (1980),[70] and the first two volumes of Michel Foucault's *History of Sexuality* (1976–1984)[71] all contributed to what would become a virtual cottage industry of exploring Greek sexualities and sexual identities, mostly (but not always) from the perspective of a progressive social politics intent on promoting acceptance of greater sexual diversity. Sidney Abbott and Barbara Love's *Sappho Was a Right-On Woman* announced this new literary approach already in 1972.[72]

Anne Carson mentions "homosexuality" only once in the entirety of *Eros the Bittersweet*.[73] The word appears once near the beginning of the book, then never again; like the erotic heart of a paradox, it simply "folds into itself and disappears." Sexuality simply does not constitute the heart of the matters Carson wishes to explore. Working very much against the grain—and very much like Friedrich Nietzsche, Walter Benjamin, Carlo Michelstaedter, and Martha Nussbaum, among others—as well as against the generic expectations of an academic first book, Carson turned to this same body of classical Greek literature, not in order to gain insight into the vexed political question of sexual identities and their regulation, but rather to gain purchase on the far more vexing human phenomenon of overwhelming desire—which is, she suggests with great eloquence and moral urgency, impossible to legislate, regulate or control. Carson's point seems to be that, if we turn to these texts for insight into the modern psychological concept of sexual identity, then we are almost certain to be disappointed. But if we turn to these same sources for insight into how one manages the invasion of self constituted by erotic desire, and the "loss of self" this invasion entails—the perception of a hole at the heart of our alleged wholeness which eros so often reveals, and in such maddening fashion—then the insights to be gleaned from these ancient texts may be dazzling. Certainly in terms of poetic and philosophical affect, *Eros the Bittersweet* dazzles.

Carson had this to say about Sapphic "sexuality" some years later, in 2002:

> Controversies about her personal ethics and way of life have taken up a lot of people's time throughout the history of Sapphic scholarship. It seems that she knew and loved women as deeply as she did music. Can we leave the matter there?[74]

This, I suggest, was Carson's studied approach already in 1986. To reduce eros to "sexuality" is to fail to take desire with full seriousness, to fail to take the bitter with the sweet, and to so confuse reaching out with taking in. It also threatens to reduce Greek poetry and philosophy to our way of thinking, anachronistically, and so to close ourselves off from any novelty of insight the Greek tradition may possess in its own right. The sexual self is modern; the desiring self is perennial.[75] Failure to make this distinction is to grasp a recognizably modern top, rather than to reach after a more elusive ancient one . . . and so to take delight in something other than understanding.

In the next three chapters, I will trace Carson's further development of her arch-metaphor of reaching without grasping—as an evocative translator, as an erotic and lyric poet, and as a virtuoso religious performer in words. Such a tracing will also require attending to Carson's subsequent and evermore subtle interweaving of the genres with which she plays most consistently and with which she dances most artfully. The result, as I have tried to suggest, is an oeuvre of unique poetic power and dazzling insight. That Carson's erotic reach exceeds her grasp accounts for the sheer power of her poetics. There is always a remainder, something that eludes our grasp. Carson's erotic poetics would have it no other way.

NOTES

1. Anne Carson, *Eros the Bittersweet: An Essay* (Princeton, NJ: Princeton University Press, 1986).

2. Friedrich Nietzsche, *Die Geburt der Tragödie*, in Giorgio Colli und Mazzino Montinari, eds., *Friedrich Nietzsche: Sämtliche Werke, Kritische Studienausgabe in 15 Bänden* (Berlin; Walter de Gruyter, 1967-1977), I:11–156 [hereafter KSA]. Nietzsche published a second edition of the work in 1886 with a new preface ("Attempt at a Self-Criticism") and a new subtitle ("Hellenism and Pessimism").

A good English edition is *The Birth of Tragedy and The Case of Wagner*, Walter Kaufmann, trans. (New York, NY: Vintage Books, 1967), 19–144.

3. That claim, and its mocking title, came from Ulrich von Wilamowitz-Möllendorf (1848–1931), a younger contemporary who was to become the very kind of classicist Nietzsche ultimately decried.

The German text of his review may be found in Karlfried Gründer, ed., *Der Streit um Nietzsches "Geburt der Tragödie"* (Hildesheim: Georg Olms Verlag, 1989), 27–55 (Wilamowitz published a second pamphlet with the same title in 1873, addressing himself to Nietzsche's chief defenders, at 113–135). An English version of the first pamphlet may be found as Ulrich von Wilamowitz-Möllendorff, "Future Philology!" translated by Gertrude Postl and edited by Babette Babich in *New Nietzsche Studies* 4.1/2 (2000): 1–32.

For more on the controversy, see my "Wilamowitz versus Winckelmann: On the Romantic Roots of Nietzsche's *Birth of Tragedy*," *New Nietzsche Studies* 10.3/4 (2017, 2018): 169–186.

4. Walter Benjamin, *Ursprung des deutschen Trauerspiels* (Frankfurt am Main: Suhrkamp Verlag, 1963).

The English version is Walter Benjamin, *The Origin of German Tragic Drama*, John Osborne, trans. (New York, NY: Verso, 1977).

5. Walter Benjamin, *The Origin of German Tragic Drama*, 7.

6. Walter Benjamin, *The Origin of German Tragic Drama*, 11.

7. Carlo Michelstaedter, *Persuasione e la rettorica* (Milano: Adelphi Edizione, 1982).

The English version is Carlo Michelstaedter, *Persuasion and Rhetoric*, Russell Scott Valentino, Cinzia Sartini Blum, and David J. Depew, trans. (New Haven, CT: Yale University Press, 2004).

I am grateful to Massi Massimiliano for introducing Michelstaedter's work to me, in the context of preparing an important Master's thesis on the book under my direction at Georgia State University in 2007.

8. Martha C. Nussbaum, *The Fragility of Goodness: Luck and Ethics in Greek Tragedy and Philosophy* (New York, NY: Cambridge University Press, 1986).

9. Martha C. Nussbaum, *Aristotle's De motu animalium* (Princeton, NJ: Princeton University Press, 1978).

10. Whether Carson's academic career suffered for this daring is not an easy question to answer. Certainly she has moved around a great deal. Whether this was by necessity or by literary design is unclear, and in any case, after 2000, the award of the Macarthur Fellowship gave her some financial independence and the greater mobility that comes with such notoriety.

Given the jealous guarding of her privacy, it is impossible to reconstruct Carson's *Curriculum Vitae* fully, but the evidence from various occasional interviews, articles and university resources suggests something like the following trajectory. After receiving her PhD from the University of Toronto in 1981 (and having already taught at the University of Calgary, 1979–1981), Carson taught at Princeton University (Classics, 1981–1987), Emory University (Classics, 1987–1988), and McGill University (mainly Classics, 1988–2002). When the Classics program at McGill was reorganized and folded into the Department of History in the late 1990s (Carson had long served the Classics program as Graduate Director), then Carson began dividing the academic year between McGill and various visiting appointments in the United States, including at the University of Michigan (fall 1999), the University of California at Berkeley (spring 2000), and the California College of Arts and Crafts in Oakland (2001–2002). Carson then joined the faculty in Classical Studies, Comparative Literature, and English Language and Literature at the University of Michigan (2003–2009). She has also served as A. D. White Professor-at-Large at Cornell University (2010–2013), and Visiting Distinguished Writer-in-Residence at Bard College (2014–2015). Carson then moved to the faculty at New York University in 2015, first as Professor of Creative Writing and now as Artist-in-Residence, where she offers a yearly course on collaboration ("Egocircus") with her husband, Robert Currie.

It is noteworthy that *Eros the Bittersweet* was recently named as "one of the best 100 nonfiction works of all time" by The Modern Library.

11. Anne Carson, *Eros the Bittersweet*, xi–xii.

12. See "The Top" (*Der Kreisel*, translated by Tania and James Stern) in Nahum N. Glatzer, ed., *Franz Kafka: The Complete Stories* (New York, NY: Shocken Books, 1971), 491. It is striking that Carson's preliminary riff on the story is every bit as long as the story itself.

13. She continues:

> Each time it reaches out, there is a shift of distance in mid-reasoning that prevents the answer from being grasped. Consider Zeno's well-known paradoxes. They are arguments against the reality of reaching an end. Zeno's runner never gets to the finish line of the stadium, Zeno's Achilles never overtakes the tortoise, Zeno's arrow never hits the target. These are paradoxes about paradox. Each one contains a point where the reasoning seems to fold into itself and disappear, or at least that is how it feels. Each time it disappears, it can begin again, and so the reach continues. If you happen to enjoy reasoning, you are delighted to begin again. On the other hand, your enjoyment of reasoning must entail some wish to arrive at a conclusion, so your delight has an edge of chagrin.
>
> In the bittersweetness of the exercise we see the outline of eros. You love Zeno and you hate him. You know there is a ruse operating in his paradoxes, yet you keep going back over them. And you keep going back to the paradoxes not because you would like to see Achilles overtake the tortoise but because you like trying to understand what kind of thing a paradox is. (Anne Carson, *Eros the Bittersweet*, 81)

14. Carson, *Eros the Bittersweet*, 3.

The reference is to Sappho's Fragment #130, according to the Loeb Classical Library edition, *Greek Lyric I: Sappho and Alcaeus*, D. A. Campbell, ed. and trans. (Cambridge, MA: Loeb Classical Library of Harvard University Press, 1982),

146–147. It was quoted by Hephaestion in his *Handbook on Meters*. Sixteen years later, Carson emended her translation to this:

> Eros the melter of limbs (now again) stirs me—
> sweetbitter unmanageable creature who steals in.

See *If Not, Winter: Fragments of Sappho* (Princeton, NJ: Princeton University Press, 2002), 264–265.

15. Carson, *Eros the Bittersweet*, 4.

16. Ibid.

That Carson refers to this two-line fragment as a "poem" is suggestive. Later, she will coyly observe that another one of Sappho's fragments (#105A) "is incomplete, perfectly" (*Eros the Bittersweet*, 27).

17. Carson, *Eros the Bittersweet*, 4-6. The phrase formed the title of Carson's dissertation on Sappho.

18. Carson, *Eros the Bittersweet*, "Now Then," 117–122.

Carson had already identified the essential role of temporality in the erotic pendulum swings between pursuer and pursued in her reading of the one complete Sapphic poem, her Ode to Aphrodite:

> In other words, the ellipse of an answer to Aphrodite's question [who wrongs you?] is deliberate: a deliberate dramatization of the universal law of justice on which lovers can rely just as surely as they can rely on the passage of time. Aphrodite's words imply that from the point of view of justice, it does not matter who the unjust girl is: in time everybody grows too old too be pursued. . . . [Sappho's] language emphasizes, especially by the repetition of the adverbs δηὖτε (15, 16, 18) and ταχέως (21, 23), the rhythm of time which orders erotic experience, creating and recreating the same impasse (δηὖτε) and ever proposing the same consolation (ταχέως). (231)

("The Justice of Aphrodite in Sappho I," in Ellen Greene, ed., *Reading Sappho: Contemporary Approaches* (Berkeley, CA: University of California Press, 1996), 226–232, which is an expanded version of an article Carson first published in 1980. As we will see in the next chapter, her reading of this Ode had evolved more than twenty years later, as evidenced in the publication of her groundbreaking edition of Sappho's fragments in 2002, but not on this point: "Sappho is stuck in the pain of the 'now,' Aphrodite calmly surveys a larger pattern of 'agains,'" (*If Not, Winter*, 358).

19. The noted Stephanus publishing house in Paris, perhaps best known for its canonical Plato volumes in Greek and Latin, also produced an early volume of Greek Lyric Poets which contained the representative Sapphic fragments in its second part: *PINDARI Olympia, Pythia, Nemea, Isthmia. Caeterorum Octo Lyricorum carmina, Alcaei, Sapphus, Stesichori, Ibyci, Anacreontis, Bacchylidis, Simonidis, Alcmanis, Nonnulla etiam aliorum. Omnia Graecè & Latinè* (Excudebat Henr. Stephanus, illustris uiri Huldrichi Fuggeri typographus, 1560), II: 33–71. This is a fairly small (6.5 X 13cm) octavo edition, which I have consulted in three consecutive editions, dated to 1560, 1566, and 1586 (the later editions added supplemental material to the end of each volume). Like the Plato volumes, this is also a bilingual Greek-Latin

edition containing (in order): a brief *Vita* of Sappho strictly in Latin; the Ode to Aphrodite; the Love Triangle Fragment; a number of commentaries from later writers [Plutarch, Stobaeus, various scholia (on Pindar, Apollonius of Rhodes, Euripides, and Sophocles), Eustathius, Hermogenes, Demetrius of Phaleron, Macrobius, Aristotle, Aristides, Polydeucus, the Etymologies, and Athenaeus; thirteen Sapphic quotations from Hephaestion's *Handbook on Meters* and *On Poems*; a citation from Achilles Tatius; and finally two epigrams ascribed to Sappho in the Greek Anthology.

I have been unable to locate the earlier and allegedly larger quarto Stephanus editions of 1554 (Ἀνακρέοντος Τηΐου μέλη / *Anacreontus Teii Odae*) and 1556 (*Anacreontus et eliorum lyricorum aliquot poetarum odae*, edited by G. Morelius and R. Stephanus), so I cannot speak to their contents, but that is beside the present point.

The decisive Renaissance shift to a larger corpus of Sapphic fragments may be attributed to the work of Fulvio Orsini (1529–1600), in his remarkable volume, *Carmina Novem Illustrivm Feminarvm, . . . et Lyricorvm . . . Elegiae . . . Bvcolica* [*Poems of Nine Illustrious Women, . . . and Lyric . . . Elegiac . . . Bucolic*] (Antwerp: Ex officina Christophori Plantini, 1568), 2–36. Three things are notable about this remarkable volume. First, like Stephanus, Orsini also selects the texts of nine lyric Greek poets, but he eliminates Pindar and adds eight more women (by contrast, in the Stephanus volume, Sappho's was the sole female voice). Second, Orsini arranges the fragments thematically, including seven under the heading "to a female beloved" [πρὸς Γυναῖκα ἐρωμένην], in which he places the Love Triangle, Pleiades, and Bittersweet Fragments. Third, Orsini provides sixty-five Sapphic fragments in all, including some which do not appear in modern editions. The book is larger (12 X 18 cm), beautifully produced, and legible in a way that the Stephanus volumes are not. (Interestingly, this same Plantini publishing house in Antwerp also produced its own version of Stephanus's Greek Lyric Poets, in a slightly more legible format [9 X 12 cm] in 1567.)

The reach of Orsini's scholarship was exceptionally long; it still served as the model for the far more expansive (20 X 25 cm) scholarly edition by J. Christian Wolf, *Sapphus, Poetriae Lesbiae, Fragmenta et Elogia* (Hamburgi: Apud Abrahamum Vandenhoeck, 1733), to which was added a second volume with Orsini's eight other Illustrious Female Poets, *Poetriarum Octo, Fragmenta et Elogia* (Hamburgi: Apud Abrahamum Vandenhoeck, 1734).

A final point of interest concerns the other eight women in Orsini's compendium: Erinna of Lesbos (37–40), Myro of Byzantium (41–44), Myrto of Anthidonia (44), Corinna of Tanagra (45–48), Telesilla of Argos (49–52), Praxilla of Sicyon (53–54), Nossidis the Poetess (55), and Anyte of Epidauros (56–60). How Orsini selected these elusive figures is uncertain, but a recent article [W. Robert Conner, "Women Poets and the Origin of the Greek Hexameter," *Arion, Third Series* 27.2 (2019): 85–110] suggests that Pausanias's *Guide to Greece* may have been the source, given Pausanias's distinctive and really quite extensive interest in women who were the poetic equals of men. Pausanias discusses Sappho (I.25.1 and 29.2; VIII.18.5; IX.27.3 and 29.8), Myro (IX.5.8), Myrto (VIII.14.12), Corinna (IX.22.3ff), Telesilla (II.20.8 and II.35.2), Praxilla (III.13.5), and Anyte (X.38.12, with whose story the entire *Guide* ends); only Erinna and Nossidis are absent.

20. Two important new poems were discovered and published in 2004; then a new set of five papyri, containing portions of nine poems, came to light and were published in 2014. For the first two poems, see: Michael Gronewald and Robert W. Daniel, "Ein neuer Sappho-Papyrus," *Zeitschrift für Papyrologie und Epigraphik* 147 (2004): 1–8, and "Nachtrag zum neuen Sappho-Papyrus," *Zeitschrift für Papyrologie und Epigraphik* 149 (2004): 1–4; Stefano Buzzi and Antonio Alioni, eds., *Nuove acquisizione di Saffo e delle lirica greca: per il testo di P. Köln inv. 21351* (Alexandria: 2008); Emily Greene and Marilyn B. Skinner, eds., *The New Sappho on Old Age: Textual and Philosophical Issues* (Washington, DC: Hellenic Foundation Publications, 2009); and Dirk Obbink, "Two New Poems by Sappho," *Zeitschrift für Papyrologie und Epigraphik* 189 (2014): 32–49, as well as "Interim Notes on 'Two New Poems of Sappho,'" *Zeitschrift für Papyrologie und Epigraphik* 194 (2015): 1–8.

For the more recent papyri, see: Simon Burris, Jeffrey Fish, and Dirk Obbink, "New Fragments of Book 1 of Sappho," *Zeitschrift für Papyrologie und Epigraphik* 189 (2014): 1–28; Anton Bierl and André Lardinois, *The Newest Sappho (P. Sapph. Obbink and P. GC inv. 105, frs. 104): Studies in Archaic and Classical Greek Song*, Volume 2 (Leiden and Boston: E. J. Brill, 2016); and Thea S. Thorsen, "The Newest Sappho (2016) and Ovid's *Heroides* 15," in Thea S. Thorsen and Stephen Harrison, eds., *Roman Receptions of Sappho* (New York, NY: Oxford University Press, 2019), 249–264.

Professor Obbink, for whom one of the new papyri is named, is now on administrative leave from Christ Church College, Oxford, having been embroiled in a very strange papyrological controversy. He is accused of having stolen several Oxyrhynchus fragments from the University collection, including what is alleged to be the oldest extant gospel fragment (a first-century fragment from Mark's gospel), and of selling them to the Museum of the Bible in Washington, DC. The papyri have been returned to Oxford, but the final disposition of Professor Obbink's case is not known as of this writing. The echoes of the intrigue in Eco's *The Name of the Rose* are striking.

Brent Nongbri concluded his superb study with news of this discovery, once again a gospel fragment taken from mummy cartonnage, and he demonstrated his customary agnosticism about it (Brent Nongbri, *God's Library*, 269–271).

21. Carson, *Eros the Bittersweet*, 12.

22. Carson, *Eros the Bittersweet*, 12–13. By 2002, her rendering of this fragment had evolved slightly, as we will see in the next chapter.

23. One of the most insightful reception histories of this poetic fragment may be found in Glenn W. Most, "Reflecting Sappho," *Bulletin of the Institute of Classical Studies* 40 (1995): 15–38. Confronted with a wealth of later testimonia about Sappho, Most identifies three primary strategies for making sense of them: a) duplication, (17–19), suggesting that there were two Sapphos rather than one, and dividing the traditions accordingly; b) narrativization (19–21), which sets all of the conflicting details in a chronology of personal development, identifying when and how Sappho changed; and c) condensation (21–26), the Romantic claim that the paradoxes were in fact Sappho's own, making her a premonition of the nineteenth-century Romantic poet. It bears noting that this same century witnessed the rise of scientific philology

and psychology, such that the quest for Sappho's sexual identity in the fragments suddenly took center stage. The Love Triangle Fragment, Most demonstrates, defies this modern interpretive gambit, given the utter ambiguity of gender references throughout, and the poetic interest in the persistence of desire.

24. Carson, *Eros the Bittersweet*, 13.
25. Carson, *Eros the Bittersweet*, 16.
26. Carson, *Eros the Bittersweet*, 17.
27. Carson, *Eros the Bittersweet*, 30.
28. Carson, *Eros the Bittersweet*, 33.
29. Carson, *Eros the Bittersweet*, 39.
30. Carson, *Eros the Bittersweet*, 42.
31. Carson, *Eros the Bittersweet*, "Alphabetic Edge," 53–61.

For more on this essential idea, see the classic study by Walter Ong, *Orality and Literacy: The Technologizing of the Word* (New York: Methuen, 1982, Routledge, 1988), 84–91.

32. Crucially, "voiceless letters" (*aphôna grammata*) is the term that Plato uses to describe vowels (*Philebus* 18b–d).
33. Carson, *Eros the Bittersweet*, 77–90.
34. Carson, *Eros the Bittersweet*, 91–101.

Given the common association of courtesans (*hetairai*) with riddles, since their complex social roles are essentially social riddles, a fragment from Aristophanes (#194) is relevant here.

Sappho is depicted there as a riddler, asking what it is that possesses a feminine nature (*physis thêleia*), yet bears unborn children who have no voice. Her male interlocutor guesses that she is referring to a city (*polis*), since the Greek noun is feminine, and that the children will become orators and rhetoricians. No, Sappho replies, the female nature in question is a letter (*epistolê*), also a feminine Greek noun, who carries voiceless (*aphôna*) children within her—namely, the letters (*grammata*). The idea here is that written letters do not speak, but they can nonetheless communicate far and wide.

This material is beautifully discussed in Kate Gilhuly, "Lesbians Are Not from Lesbos," in Ruby Blondell and Kirk Ormand, eds., *Ancient Sex: New Essays* (Columbus, OH: The Ohio State University Press, 2015), 143–176, esp. 163–165.

35. Carson, *Eros the Bittersweet*, 70.
36. Carson, *Eros the Bittersweet*, 111.
37. Ibid.
38. Carson, *Eros the Bittersweet*, 117–122.
39. Carson, *Eros the Bittersweet*, 118.

For a review of this literature, see Sarah T. Mace, "Amour, Encore! The Development of δηὖτε in Archaic Lyric," *Greek, Roman and Byzantine Studies* 34 (1993): 335–364. Mace highlights the essential erotic trope being one that links eros (as a noun) to me (as an object) through this strange repetitive tense (336), "Eros . . . me, again," and she admits that Sappho's Ode to Aphrodite is doing something altogether more subtle and "literary" with the trope (355–361). That makes it all the more strange that Carson's discussion is never mentioned in the essay.

40. Carson, *Eros the Bittersweet*, 119.
41. Anne Carson, *If Not, Winter: Fragments of Sappho*, 2–5.
42. And there is more. In the lover's imagination, Carson suggests, we desire "*now*" to become "*then*" . . . and yet if and when it does so, when we act very much like Kafka's failed philosopher, then we will have what we desire . . . and so stop desiring.

"You cannot want that, and yet you do. Let us see what this feels like" (Carson, *Eros the Bittersweet*, 111). The line is so striking that I think it warrants repeating here.

43. Carson, *Eros the Bittersweet*, 117.
44. Carson, *Eros the Bittersweet*, 123.
45. In the words of Guy Davenport:

When Sokrates took Sappho's desire for the young and fused it with the process of learning, sublimating it and disciplining it with stoic restraint, he gave the genius of the West a philosophical idea that lasted almost two thousand years.

See his "Introduction," to Anne Carson, *Glass, Irony and God* (New York, NY: New Directions, 1995), x.

All I wish to add to this provocative description is the suggestive possibility which Plato clearly offers us here, namely, that Socrates was less "stoically restrained" than all that.

46. This is a recurrent trope in various dialogues of Plato's so-called Middle Period. Recalling the day of Socrates's execution, Phaedo recounts something very odd: "a very strange feeling came over me, truly a mixture of pleasure and pain . . . and all of us were in the same condition, sometimes laughing, sometimes weeping" (*Phaedo* 59a). Plato considered such strangely mixed emotional territory closely, such that eros becomes a grand, overarching metaphor for the philosophical life. In the *Phaedrus*, we learn that certain forms of madness are not irrational; they are gifts from the gods—poetry and erotic love, especially. In the *Republic*, Socrates suggests that poetry is like a lover we know is wrong for us; he suggests a "break-up" between philosophy and poetry . . . unless someone can speak in poetry's defense. (It is my view that the *Phaedrus* is intended to be that defense.) In the *Symposium*, Socrates insists that the poet who writes comedy must write tragedy, too, and vice versa. Aristophanes (the comedian) and Agathon (the tragedian) drunkenly agree, before nodding off. Even as late as the *Philebus*, Plato will return to this fascination with distinguishing various types of pleasure, and linking them to pain: "a man, or any other animal, experiences both pain and pleasure at once" (*Philebus* 36b). We are thus invited to think about that strange hybrid genre, *tragicomedy*, and the mixing of conflicting elements: tears and laughter, pleasure and pain. The *Phaedo* is one such tragicomedy; the *Phaedrus* may be another.

For more on this erotic trope, see Louis A. Ruprecht Jr., *Symposia: Plato, the Erotic and Moral Value* (Albany, NY: State University of New York Press, 1996), 28–32.

47. Carson puts the problem this way:

The *Phaedrus* is a written dialogue that ends by discrediting written dialogues. This fact does not cease to charm its readers. Indeed, it is the fundamental erotic feature of this *erôtikos logos*. Each time you read it, you are conducted to a place where something paradoxical happens: the knowledge of Eros that Sokrates and Phaedrus have been unfolding word by word through the written text simply steps into a blind point and vanishes, pulling the *logos* in after it. Their conversation about love (227a–57c) turns into a conversation about writing (257c–79c) and Eros is not seen or heard again. This act of dialectical interception has, since antiquity, perplexed those who wish to say concisely what the dialogue is about. But there is nothing inappropriate here. If you reach for the *Phaedrus* to get hold of Eros, you will be eluded, necessarily. He never looks at you from the place from which you see him. Something moves in the space between. That is the most erotic thing about Eros. (Carson, *Eros the Bittersweet*, 166–167)

Eros, that is to say, is a spinning top that eludes writing's desirous grasp. For more on the "non-controlling art of writing" this insight would seem to demand, see Martha C. Nussbaum, "Love and the Individual," in *Love's Knowledge* (New York, NY: Oxford University Press, 1990), 314–334, where the complex structure of the *Phaedrus* provides an equally complex structure to her arguments.

48. Carson, *Eros the Bittersweet*, 123.
49. Carson, *Eros the Bittersweet*, 130.
50. Carson, *Eros the Bittersweet*, 124.
51. Carson, *Eros the Bittersweet*, 133.
52. Carson, *Eros the Bittersweet*, 131–132.
53. Plato, *Phaedrus* 246a: "as to its form (*ideas*) . . . saying what it is like (*eoiken*) is both humanly possible and easier."
54. Carson, *Eros the Bittersweet*, 137.
55. Carson, *Eros the Bittersweet*, 136.
56. Ibid.
57. Carson, *Eros the Bittersweet*, 144.
58. Carson, *Eros the Bittersweet*, 149.
59. Carson, *Eros the Bittersweet*, 152–153. She continues:

The point of time that Lysias deletes from his logos, the moment of mania when Eros enters the lover, is for Sokrates the single most important moment to confront and grasp. 'Now' is a gift of the gods and an access onto reality. . . .

Sokrates' answer to the erotic dilemma of time, then, is the antithesis of Lysias' answer. Lysias chose to edit out 'now' and narrate entirely from the vantage point of 'then'. In Sokrates' view, to cross out 'now' is, in the first place, impossible; it would mean losing a moment of unique and indispensable value. Sokrates proposes instead to assimilate 'now' in such a way that it prolongs itself over the whole of life, and beyond. Sokrates would inscribe his novel within the instant of desire.

60. Carson, *Eros the Bittersweet*, 154–164.
61. Carson, *Eros the Bittersweet*, 66.
62. Maximus of Tyre, *Orations* 18.9, as found in David A. Campbell, ed., *Greek Lyric I: Sappho and Alcaeus* (Cambridge, MA: Loeb Classical Library of Harvard University Press, 1982), 92–93.

For more commentary on this comparative remark, see Anne Carson, *If Not, Winter: Fragments of Sappho*, 383:

Mythweaver might also be rendered 'teller of tales' or 'creator of fictions' or 'poetic inventor.' Why does Eros weave myths? Perhaps because desire acts in lovers as a lure for the whole life of the imagination—without which neither love nor philosophy could nourish itself very long.

63. Carson, *Eros the Bittersweet*, 169–170.
64. Carson, *Eros the Bittersweet*, 170.
65. Pauline Jaccon, of the Translation Studies and English Literature program at the Sorbonne Nouvelle in Paris, has suggested that the way *eros* acts on the mind of a lover, and knowing on the mind of a thinker, may be fruitfully related to the way faith acts in the mind of a believer. On the one hand, this idea brilliantly stages the Romantic linkage of art, religion, and philosophy (with art as a stand-in for the labor eros performs in Carson's work), as the three "works of spirit" inspiring new ways of seeing. More specific to Carson's oeuvre, the linkage brilliantly explains the religious connections Carson explored in her 2005 book, *Decreation*, which I will discuss in the fourth chapter.

Jaccon is completing a dissertation on Carson's poetics, with special attention to her translation and storytelling practices. I am deeply indebted to her for many enriching discussions.

66. Maximus of Tyre, *Orations* 18.9, in David A. Campbell, ed., *Greek Lyric I: Sappho and Alcaeus*, 20–21.
67. Homoerotic, *and hierarchical*, we should add, which is what explains the vital impermanence of Greek eros: the beloved, whether boy or girl, must outgrow the role of *erômenos* and take up the role of *erastês*, in time. Carson made that erotic law, which is the law of temporality itself, central to her first reading of Sappho's Ode to Aphrodite: "this is an eternal principle which can be relied on as confidently as can the fact that time passes and young people grow old and lovers love without return, δηῦτε ... δηῦτε ... δηῦτε" ("The Justice of Aphrodite in Sappho I," 232).
68. One of the most remarkable verbal ploys which Plato exploits in the Middle Period dialogues is to bandy about two forms of the same word which would have been indistinguishable in Attic Greek as written in the fifth to fourth centuries BCE: ΕΡΩΤΑ. Accented on the antepenult (ἔρωτα), it is the accusative noun form of the word eros; accented on the penult (ἐρώτα), it is the imperative verb form for asking a question ("ask!"). This is to say, we have here a profound Platonic pun designed to highlight the fact that there is nothing more alluring and attractive than a question, a questioner, and the wonder they can create when happily joined.

See Ruprecht, *Symposia*, 105–107.

69. Sir Kenneth Dover, *Greek Homosexuality* (Cambridge, MA: Harvard University Press, 1979). Carson spent a year studying Greek meter with Dover at St. Andrews while pursuing her Master's degree in Classics at the University of Toronto.
70. John Boswell, *Christianity, Homosexuality and Social Tolerance: Gay People in Western Europe from the Beginning from the Beginning of the Christian Era to the Fourteenth Century* (The University of Chicago Press, 1980).
71. Michel Foucault, *Histoire de la sexualité*; Vol. I, *La volonté de savoir* (Paris: Editions Gallimard, 1976) and Vol. II, *L'usage des plaisirs* (Paris: Editions Gallimard, 1984). English translations appeared in 1978 and 1985, respectively.

72. Sidney Abbott and Barbara Love, *Sappho Was a Right-On Woman: A Liberated View of Lesbianism* (New York, NY: Stein and Day, 1972).

A more recent exercise in this same vein is Jane McIntosh Snyder, *Lesbian Desire in the Lyrics of Sappho* (New York, NY: Columbia University Press, 1997), a text which dances between the scientific aspirations of philology and the current politics of sexual and gender identity in ways that are highly suggestive for their contrast to what Carson aspires to see in these same texts.

73. Specifically, in the case of ritualized homosexual rape on Crete (Carson, *Eros the Bittersweet*, 24).

74. Anne Carson, *If Not, Winter: Fragments of Sappho*, x.

75. For more on this idea, see Louis A. Ruprecht Jr., "Finding and Losing One's Way: Eros and the Other in Greek Tragedy and Philosophy," in Sarah LaChance Adams, Caroline Lundquist, and Christopher Davidson, eds., *New Philosophies of Sex and Love: Thinking Through Desire* (London: Rowman & Littlefield, 2017), 15–34.

In the fourth chapter, we will see Carson begin to trouble over the religious implications of our speech regarding such "selves."

Chapter 2

Translation as Modern Criticism, Creation and Conjuring, or, The Musing Scholar

I like the space between languages because it's a place of error or mistakenness, of saying things less well than you would like, or not being able to say them at all. And that's useful I think for writing because it's always good to put yourself off balance, to be dislodged from the complacency in which you normally go at perceiving the world and saying what you've perceived. And translation continually does that dislodging, so I respect the situation—although I don't think I like it. It's a useful edge to put yourself against.

—Anne Carson, interview with Kevin McNeilly (*Canadian Literature* 2003)

Looking at the gaps between the words as you move from one language to another, and the way meaning disappears into the gaps—that experience is what I value most about translation. We operate all the time with language as if it says what we mean. It never does, but you don't realize the flaccidity of that until you are actually trying to make one thing in one language into another language. It's like being on the surface with a lot of cracks in it and looking down through the cracks to something like another world down there that you can almost see, almost express, but not quite.

—Anne Carson, interview with Eleanor Wachtel (*Writers & Company* 2016)

* * * * *

There was a great deal of translating to be done in the preparation and rendering of *Eros the Bittersweet*. Translation represents both the place and the practice where Anne Carson's profound *scholarly* skills and interests arguably lie most lightly, and yet penetrate most deeply. She once quipped that she would not know what to say when teaching Sappho's poetry if she did not have the Greek language to talk about, as a sort of pedagogical fallback. Sappho herself is ineffable.

Translations and critical editions of ancient texts are the life's blood of most classical scholars. Anne Carson has contributed in significant and manifold ways to this classical sub-genre, but here too, she approaches the task from an oblique angle, what she once called "that puzzle mode of mind."[1] Translation's importance, for her, involves a spiritual practice, and intellectual puzzlement, rather than a scholarly production.[2] It might almost be likened to an act of spiritual conjuring, where conjuring involves the art of reaching, rather than grasping, aiming at the ever-elusive: "what you can almost see, almost express, but not quite."

As *Eros the Bittersweet* testifies, Anne Carson has been dwelling with Sappho's poetic fragments for more than thirty years. This conversation over three decades or more has produced what, in the end, we might best think of as *a love letter*. I intend this phrase in the multiple registers Carson explored first in *Eros the Bittersweet*. Letters may be symbol-strokes that mark a sound, or, in the case of vowels, that serve to mark an absence of sound. Letters are also epistolary gifts that attempt, and poignantly fail, to bridge the maddening gap that separates absent lovers in space and time. The image of translation as love letter may help us to highlight the erotic triangulation that Carson places at the very heart of her practice. "Most of us, given a choice between chaos and naming, between catastrophe and cliché, would choose naming. Most of us see this as a zero-sum game—as if there were no third place to be: . . . Translation is a practice . . . that does seem to give us a third place to be."[3] That third place, we now see, mirrors the space in between lover and beloved that animated Sappho's Love Triangle Fragment and inspired some of the richest reflection in *Eros the Bittersweet*. For Carson, then, translation is yet another *erôtikê technê*, an erotic art. There are three practices involved here: the writing, then the reading, then the translating There are also (at least) three separate bodies here: the classical author, Anne Carson as translator, and we who read what comes between them. Such is the reach that attempts to bridge bodily separation across space and time; such is her conjuring practice of the Classics.

What emerged out of Carson's long scholarly meditation and patient poetic conjuration was the publication in 2002 of her long-awaited critical edition of Sappho's fragments, *If Not, Winter*.[4] Perhaps the most striking difference in this latter presentation of Carson's Sappho is captured by the subtitle: "*fragments* of Sappho." Everything about this 2002 volume serves to remind us that we do not have Sappho whole; we are overwhelmed by the papyrological (and other) holes in the received record of Greek lyric poetry.[5] In other words, the chaos and the names are joined here. The cover image of Carson's translation boasts two disjointed pieces of a ragged papyrus with some writing and images barely visible upon the threaded surface. The presentation of the actual fragments, with fragmentary Greek originals and Carson's English renderings juxtaposed on facing pages, goes to great lengths to emphasize all that we do not know, or no longer know.

Here is one example of this new Sapphic view, taken virtually at random:

103Cʙ	103Cʙ
]α. [	]
ἔ]κλυον ε[	]they heard
]ρανν... δες δ[	]
πα]ρθενικαις. [	]maidens
].μ[	]
].[	]

We cannot help but notice all the brackets first, suggestive of the ragged edges of the papyrus fragment before us. To this point, Carson tells us:

> I emphasize the distinction between brackets and no brackets because it will affect your reading experience, if you allow it. Brackets are exciting. Even though you are approaching Sappho in translation, that is no reason you should miss the drama of trying to read a papyrus torn in half or riddled with holes or smaller than a postage stamp—brackets imply a free space of imaginal adventure.[6]

Letters appear singly or in small clusters. Some are semi-legible. Many lines contain too little for Carson even to venture a guess at their meaning.[7] So six lines of fragmentary Greek, ranging from a nearly complete word to a single punctuation mark, are rendered in two lines of English, containing three words in total. We have been placed on notice that making a whole out of these decidedly dispersed and damaged elements will not be easy.

If we consider the matter in light of the previous chapter, then this may seem like a repudiation of Carson's previous scholarly practices. After all, in 1986, Carson was so bold as to assemble an entire erotic theory out of Sappho's fragments (with Platonic supplements, to be sure). Consider her rendering of the Love Triangle Fragment in that earlier endeavor:

> He seems to me equal to gods that man
> who opposite you
> sits and listens close
> > to your sweet speaking
>
> and lovely laughing—oh it
> puts the heart in my chest on wings
> for when I look at you, a moment, then no speaking
> > is left in me
>
> no: tongue breaks, and thin
> fire is racing under skin
> and in eyes no sight and drumming
> > fills ears
>
> and cold sweat holds me and shaking
> grips me all, greener than grass
> I am and dead—or almost
> > I seem to me.[8]

Not much has changed if we turn to her rendering of the same fragment in 2002:

> He seems to me equal to gods that man
> *whoever he is* who opposite you
> sits and listens close
> > to your sweet speaking
>
> and lovely laughing—oh it
> puts the heart in my chest on wings
> for when I look at you, *even* a moment, no speaking
> > is left in me
>
> no: tongue breaks and thin
> fire is racing under skin
> and in eyes no sight and drumming
> > fills ears
>
> and cold sweat holds me and shaking
> grips me all, greener than grass

> I am and dead—or almost
> I seem to me.
>
> *But all is to be dared, because even a person of poverty*[9]

This is one of those rare Sapphic fragments that we possess because it was quoted in a rhetorical handbook, so there are no brackets to contend with. The most striking change in 2002 is Carson's inclusion of that last line, which confirms that this poem is indeed a fragment, a fragment that breaks off maddeningly after the first line of the abortive fifth Sapphic stanza. In 1986, Carson omitted that last line, thereby presenting the fragment as if it were complete, in order to develop the spatial idea she found so compelling within the image. She called Sappho's fragments "incomplete, perfectly," as we may recall. To play with her own punning in *Eros the Bittwersweet*, we might wonder if Carson has now become more interested in Sappho's holes, than in creating poetic wholes out of her fragments. Whatever the answer to that question, Carson certainly seems more inclined to view Sappho's verse as holy, which would become a matter of great importance to her just a few years later, when she published *Decreation* in 2005, as I will show in greater detail in the fourth chapter.

A slightly different, infinitely more subtle, and startling suggestion of what Carson is up to appears in the very first line of the very first fragment (in reality, a complete text of sacred song) in the corpus, Sappho's justly famous Ode (or Hymn) to Aphrodite:

> Πο⸤ικίλοφρο⸥ν ἀθανάτ᾽Ἀφρόδιτα
> ---
> Deathless Aphrodite of the spangled mind,[10]

This time, three Greek words (only one with half-brackets) are doubled to six in English. But there is much more to this translation than meets the eye of the lexical accountant. It concerns the very first word in the very first line of the very first Sapphic fragment to be included in all modern editions of Sappho's poetry.

1.1 "of the spangled mind": two different readings of the first word of Sappho's first fragment have descended to us from antiquity: *poikilothron* (printed by Lobel, Page, Campbell, and Voigt) and *poikilophron* (printed here). The word is a compound adjective, used as an epithet of Aphrodite to identify either her "chair" (*thron-*) or her "mind" (*phron-*) as *poikilos*: "many colored, spotted, dappled, variegated, intricate, embroidered, inlaid, highly wrought, complicated, changeful, diverse, abstruse, ambiguous, subtle." Now certainly the annals of ancient furniture include some fancy chairs, especially when gods sit on them; and initial mention of her throne provides an elegant point of departure for the downrush of Aphrodite's next motion. On the other hand, it is Aphrodite's agile mind that seems to be at play in the rest of the poem and, since compounds of *thron-* are common enough in Greek poetry to make this word predictable, perhaps Sappho relied on our ear to supply the chair while she went on to spangle the mind.

Other examples of the adjective *poikilos* or its compounds occur in Sappho frr. 39.2, 44.9, 98a11, 98b1, 98b6; cf. also Alkaios fr. 345.2 (of a bird's throat) and fr. 69.7 (of a man with a mind like a fox).[11]

Something altogether remarkable has been suggested here—a whole series of somethings, in fact. First and foremost, Carson has differed from the scholarly establishment in her own determined judgment about what the first word of the first line of Sappho's Hymn actually was: "spangled mind" rather than "glittering throne." It makes for a notable poetic (and noetic) difference and, by her own reckoning, it sets Carson at odds with all four of the major recent editors of Sappho's Greek fragments. Carson's mind is ever her own, suggestively "spangled" in its own lyrical way. Next comes the translator's piling on of synonyms for that single Greek word, *poikilos*,[12] as a way to emphasize that words possess semantic ranges, such that one-to-one translational correspondences rarely, if ever, render faithfully. This rich word-list is then followed by Carson's reasoned judgment that it makes far more sense of the poem's eventual thrust to emphasize the many-splendored mental gymnastics of which the love goddess is capable at the outset, rather than the fanciness of her seating arrangement. Finally, Carson draws our attention to the repeated use of this term in the Lesbian dialect. It is, in short, an impressive critical apparatus, such as one finds in critical editions of almost all classical ancient poets.

But the note is also naughty, vaguely Nietzschean,[13] and wickedly funny. Halfway through the note, when we are informed that—"certainly the annals of ancient furniture include some fancy chairs, especially when gods sit on them"—the tone shifts and Carson justifies her emendation, in part, by slyly accusing her colleagues of having more scholarly sophistication than poetic and performative sense. Poetic sensibility here trumps philological acuity; the question is how poets, not scholars, make the things they make with words. Sappho was a poet, not a philologist or a pedant.

In this same light, consider another note, designed to supplement Carson's interpretation of Fragment 104a ("Evening/ you gather back/ all that dazzling dawn has put asunder:/ you gather a lamb/ gather a kid/ gather a child to its mother"):

104a Cited by the literary critic Demetrios, who comments: "Here the charm of the expression lies in its repetition of 'gather'" (*On Style* 141). Catullus imitates these verses in a poem that is a wedding song (see his poem 62, especially vv. 20–37); maybe Sappho's poem is nuptial too—telling of the pathos of the bride one fine evening when the repetitions of childhood end. I read somewhere once that ancient marriage rites may have included a burning of the axle of the chariot that brought the bride to her bridegroom's house—no going back.[14]

Here again, we meet the same impressive font of relatively obscure classical sources on rhetoric (Demetrius's *On Style*), and the same array of Latin poetic parallels (from Catullus, notably enough). But I know of very few other classical scholars who could or would shift gears in this way, and say, with either a straight face or a delighted smirk, "I read somewhere once that"[15]. . . and then develop that vague, unfounded memory in a way that is as shatteringly poignant as is this note.[16] The effect is uncanny—if you like that sort of thing. I do like it, very much. But it can rankle a certain kind of classicist, the kind who prefer a latter-day Wilamowitz, let's say, to a Neoclassical aesthetic pamphleteer like Winckelmann or a Neoclassical lyricist like Nietzsche.

Carson introduces her labor of love by distinguishing between three different kinds of Sapphic fragments. Those preserved on papyrus are the ones with all the brackets: they are fragmentary, hole-y, and difficult to render, as we have already seen. But another class of Sapphic fragments come from quotations by later rhetorical and grammatical writers. These tend to be complete lines or stanzas, but never actually entire poems, except in the case of the Ode to Aphrodite. Third, there are citations without larger context, in which Sappho is credited with coining a term (like "bittersweet"), making an unprecedented connection (like calling the moon "silver"), expressing a unique insight (like the symptomatology of unfulfilled longing in the Love Triangle Fragment), or what have you.

Carson next explores three strategies of translation for the challenges raised by these three rather different types of Sapphic fragment. As to the last of the three, the indirect citations from other classical authors, she opts for omission, pure and simple.

> As acts of deterrence, these stories carry their own kind of thrill—at the inside edge where her words go missing, a sort of antipoem that condenses everything you ever wanted her to write—but they cannot be called texts of Sappho's and so they are not included in this translation.[17]

For the longer quotations and one complete poem, Carson opts for a strategy we might simply call "transparency" (though as we will see, no concept could be less simple than such a word for such a kind of literary or translational clarity).

> In translating I tried to put down all that can be read of each poem in the plainest language I could find, using where possible the same order of words and thoughts as Sappho did. I like to think that, the more I stand out of the way, the more Sappho shines through. This is an amiable fantasy (transparency of self) within which most translators labor.[18]

Naturally (coyly, and playfully, perhaps bittersweetly as well), Anne Carson knows that she is not being—cannot be—"transparent."[19] That issue, of the non-transparency and elusiveness of the writing self, will prove to be a dominant theme (and a religious one, at that) in *Decreation*, a point I will take up in more detail in the fourth chapter.

I have already noted the considerable interventions lying behind the scenes (and buried in the notes) of the very first line of the very first poem that Carson takes up as a translator of Sappho. "Transparency" does not describe this practice; here, Carson confesses to being even more intrusive when and where she feels that this is warranted by the fragment in question. We might think of this translational practice as one of frank authorial imposition.

> In translating [the] stranded verse I have sometimes manipulated its spacing on the page, to restore a hint of musicality or suggest syntactic motion. For example the sentence cited by Chrysippos becomes:
>
> > Not one girl I think
> > who looks on the light of the sun
> > will ever
> > have wisdom
> > like this[20]

Carson justifies this more intrusive practice by citing none other than Walter Benjamin's seminal 1923 essay, "The Task of the Translator" [*Die Aufgabe der Übersetzers*], in her own defense, noting his justly famous aspiration to "aim[] at that single spot where the echo is able to give, in its own language, the reverberation of the work in the alien one."[21] We witness three terms, yet again here: two languages and the translational space between them; hence the eroticism in Carson's view of translation as a loving, as well as scholarly, practice.

We have now been introduced to three translational strategies: transparency, imposition, and omission. Let us see how they factor in Carson's work on several exemplary lyric occasions. We have already looked at three of the "canonical" Sapphic fragments: the Ode to Aphrodite, the Love Triangle Fragment, and the Bittersweet Fragment. Here, then, is the fourth, the Pleiades Fragment:

> Moon has set
> and Pleiades: middle
> night, the hour goes by,
> alone I lie[22]

Carson confesses to a lingering uncertainty about the fragment's genuineness. "Cited by Hephaistion in his metrical *Handbook* (11.5) as two tetrameter verses without authorial ascription; cited by Apostolius and his son Arsenius, compilers of proverbs in the fifteenth century, as Sappho's; not included among Sappho's fragments by most modern editors."[23] But include it Carson does, for reasons she wishes us to contemplate. I will take up the reasoning implicit here again in the conclusion, after we have had the occasion to examine more of Carson's poetic and spiritual reasoning in subsequent chapters. For this fragment is a uniquely poetical conjuring by night-light.

Let me shift our gaze outside of the narrow Renaissance "canon" now, in order to examine several more poignant examples of Sappho's artistry, and of Carson's. The next fragment I would like to explore (#16) is popular and very well-known now, since it was discovered at the Egyptian site of Oxyrhynchus in the twentieth century. It beautifully displays Sappho's versatility (and irony) when treating heroic (mainly Homeric) themes:

> Some men say an army of horse and some men say an army on foot
> and some men say an army of ships is the most beautiful thing
> on the black earth. But I say it is
>   what you love.
>
> Easy to make this understood by all.
> For she who overcame everyone
> in beauty (Helen)
>   left her fine husband
>
> behind and went sailing to Troy.
> Not for her children nor her dear parents
> had she a thought, no—
>   ]led her astray
>
>   ]for
>   ]lightly
>   ]reminded me now of Anaktoria
>   who is gone.
>
> I would rather see her lovely step
> and the motion of light on her face
> than chariots of Lydians or ranks

>   of footsoldiers in arms.
>
>   ]not possible to happen
>   ]to pray for a share
>   ]
>   ]
>   ]
>   ]
>   ]
>   toward[
>
>   ]
>   ]
>   ]
>   out of the unexpected.[24]

Carson's notes to this fragment, whose uncertain lost lines and uneven pacing she is at pains to underscore, brilliantly capture most of the important discussion surrounding it. The first centers on Sappho's ironic Homeric turnabout, where the beauty of an infantry, a cavalry, or navy in battle array is exceeded by the beauty of the lover. Carson sees the poetics at play this way:

> Sappho begins with a rhetorical device called a priamel, whose function is to focus attention and to praise. The priamel's typical structure is a list of three items followed by a fourth that is different and better. Sappho's list marshals three stately masculine opinions, then curves into dissent. Her dissent will solidify as Helen in the next stanza.[25]

The dissent, of course, suggests that the superior beauty of the lover is proven by the lengths to which such beauty may drive us. It drove ten thousand ships to Troy, after all. But who drove Helen? This question raises a dense set of philosophical concerns regarding agency, free will, and moral culpability, that were to be central to most post-classical reflections on Helen. Does beauty drive us, or do we naturally incline toward beauty? Did Helen leave her husband, or was she led away?[26]

> Because of the corruption of these central verses it is impossible to say who led Helen astray (could be Aphrodite, Eros, or some principle of delusion like Atê) or how Sappho managed the transition from Helen to Anaktoria "who is gone." It is a restless and strangely baited poem that seems to gather its logic into itself rather than pay it out. Rather like Helen. Beauty comes out of unexpectedness, and stares at us, "as though we were the ones who'd made a mistake," as Yannis Ritsos says in a poem "Expected and Unexpected," in *Ritsos in Parentheses*, translated by E. Keeley (Princeton, 1979), 160–161.[27]

With brilliant sensitivity to the poem's divided rhetorical structure and its strangely elusive erotic flow, supplemented with a catching line from an important Modern Greek poet, Carson plumbs the full depths of Sappho's irony and poignancy in this fragment. If she has not quite managed to make it whole (whole beauty is the perennial fiction of romantic poetry and remembrances of Helen, alike), she has made sense of it, by enabling it to possess a rich sensibility and fulsome fleshiness.

We would do well to notice how this ambivalence concerning Helen's agency mirrors the dissonance in Carson's approach to the art of translation. Tempted by the image of being a transparent cipher, a passive vehicle with which to embody her passionate desire for these Sapphic texts—themselves so textually and materially elusive—Carson nonetheless asserts her own creativity in responding to this desire, to the beauty of what she sees so artfully. Leading? Or being led? This is not a question Carson is inclined to answer in one way only.

Next I turn to some of the shorter surviving Sapphic fragments, some very short indeed, in which Carson nonetheless finds occasion to exercise her poetic and scholarly creativity both in the text and in her notes. The next fragment I would like to consider consists of just two words in Greek, three in English:

> *optais amme*
> \---
> you burn me[28]

This tantalizingly brief fragment prompts a very long note, where Carson muses once again on the topic of translation and its perennial challenges.

> Translation of this fragment raises the problem of pronouns in Sappho. Her Greek text actually says "us" not "me." Slippage between singular and plural in pronouns of the first-person is not uncommon in ancient poetry; the traditional explanation is that much of this poetry was choral in origin, that is, performed by a chorus of voices who collectively impersonate the voice that speaks in the poem. A glance at Sappho's fragments 5, 21, 24a, 94, 96, 147, 150, all of which employ a first-person-plural pronoun where the modern ear expects singular, will show the extent of the phenomenon. I translate "us" as "us" in all those other examples. But the fragile heat of fr.38 seems to me to evaporate entirely without a bit of intervention.
>
> On the other hand, I may be reading this sentence all wrong. Erotic fire has a history, not only in Sappho (see fr.48) but also in later lyric poets (e.g. Anakreon fr.413 *PMG* and Pindar *Pythians* 4.219). The verb I have rendered as "burn" can also be translated as "bake, roast, broil, boil" and so suggest a concrete figure for the "cooking" of passion that is to be found in Hellenistic

literature, e.g., in an epigram of Meleager who pictures Eros as "cook of the soul" (*Palatine Anthology* 12.92.7–8; cf. Also Theokritos *Idylls* 7.55 and Kallimachos *Epigrams* 43.5). If burning means cooking and "you" is Eros, this becomes a very different poem—a cry to the god who plays with fire from the community of souls subjected to its heat.[29]

In addition to the remarkable range of classical and post-classical learning Carson displays so deftly in her notes, we see (now, again) the close attention she pays to the semantic range and poetic value of single words, as well as some subtle poetic reflection on how words of such density may work in combination. Thus, two simple Greek words each warrant a full paragraph, and the semantic range of each one, their evocative poetic history in later Greek, suggest radically divergent interpretive possibilities. The translator, in many cases, must simply choose among them. But in these notes, Carson provides us with a compelling glimpse of the translator in her workshop, and a deeper sense of alternative poetic understandings. There is more than "a bit of intervention" in this endeavor. But this example well illustrates Carson's work as a translator to be entirely continuous with the dance she first choreographed in *Eros the Bittersweet*. She is building something, but it is much more than a theory.

This is perhaps even more clearly evident in Fragment #146, one of Sappho's most evocative:

> *mête moi meli mête melissa*
> ---
> neither for me honey nor the honey bee[30]

The onomatopoetic quality of Sappho's five m-words in a row, imitating the subtle humming of the honeybee, are relatively self-evident.[31] Carson captures something of that lyrical playfulness with her cadence and the subtly intuitive inner rhyme. But here once again the notes reveal how much more is going on in her laboratory, and, uniquely in this case, show us a translator incapable of making up her mind, unable to rest content with a single pass at the line in question.

> **146** In a rhetorical treatise *On Figures of Speech* (25) the first-century-B.C. grammarian Tryphon preserves this phrase as an example of a proverb; its proverbial sense is interpreted by the second-century-A.D. lexicographer Diogenian: "used of those unwilling to take the good with the bad" (*Proverbs* 6.58). Since bees and honey are frequently associated with Aphrodite in ancient cult and religious symbology, the proverb may also imply a renunciation of things aphrodisiac.
>
> Other translations occur to me, e.g.:

> mellowsmelling honey
> yellowstinging bee
> honey, Honey?
> no not me[32]

To be sure, the floral and fertilizing imagery possesses a strong whiff of sensual and sexual delight, whether the poet is rejecting their temptation or not. Carson has had a great deal to say about flowers and sex in some of her most recent poetry, as we will see in subsequent chapters. But she discovered this same subtle connection between beauty, delicacy, phermone and fertility in many of the Sapphic fragments that have so long preoccupied her.

Undoubtedly the most creative and elusive of all our surviving Sapphic examples to explore this theme are two fragments which are often read reciprocally, Fragments ##105A–B:

105A

> as the sweetapple reddens on a high branch
> high on the highest branch and the applepickers forgot—
> no, not forgot: were unable to reach

105B

> like the hyacinth in the mountains that shepherd men
> with their feet trample down and on the ground the purple
> flower[33]

For those who read these enticing fragments together, as I agree that we should, it is hard to miss the dramatically opposed ways in which the color spectrum of red-to-purple (Sappho's evident favorite, or at least the most common color on her poetic palette) is produced from a flower. In the first, a flower's fruit is left alone and ripens to redness, undisturbed. In the second, a hyacinth flower is trampled underfoot by men and bleeds its color into the ground. Given the sensual swirl we have already encountered here—of flowers, bees, pollenation, and fertility—we might be permitted to perceive in these images Sappho's poetic meditations on "deflowering" as well. Carson, in one of four separate notes that she appends to these two short fragments, is less certain: "**105b** Comparison with an epithalamium of Catullus (62.39–47) has suggested to some editors that this fragment intends an image of defloration."[34]

Unconvinced, Carson expresses her own evident delight in the translational and conceptual challenges presented by the first of these two fragments. She is especially challenged by the question of how to represent an incomplete simile, and how to justify repetitive word choices not paralleled in the Greek. The notes are, once again, poetry in intellective motion:

> **105a.1 "as":** the poem begins in a simile which has no *comparandum* and a relative clause which never reaches completion in a main verb. It may be an epithalamium; Himerios refers to these verses in a discussion of wedding songs ("Sappho likens a girl to an apple" *Orations* 9.16) and George Eliot mentioned them in connection with Mrs. Cadwallader's marriage plans for Celia and Sir James ("for he was not one of those gentlemen who languish after the unattainable Sappho's apple laughing from the topmost bough": *Middlemarch,* chapter 6). If there is a bride here she remains inaccessible; it is her inaccessibility that is present, grammatically and erotically. Desiring hands close upon empty air in the final infinitive.
>
> **105a1–2 "high . . . high . . . highest":** I have stretched out the line to imitate a trajectory of reaching that is present in the sound of the Greek (akro . . . akron . . . *akrotato*) and in the rhythm (dactyls slow to spondees) as the apple begins to look farther and farther away.
>
> **105a.2–3 "forgot—no, not forgot":** self-correction emphasizes desire's infinite deferral. Self-correction is also apparent in the Greek prosody of the poem, which includes seven instances of correption or elision, metrical tactics designed to restrain a unit of sound from reaching beyond its own position in the rhythm. (Elision is the cutting away of a vowel at the end of a word when it is contiguous with a vowel at the start of the next word. Correption is the shortening of a long vowel or diphthong, from two beats to one, before a following vowel). Three of these instances affect the ardent preposition *epi* which can express location or motion: "on, upon, to, toward, aiming at, reaching after." The final infinitive is a compound of this preposition: *epikesthai*.[35]

There is a lot going on in these six short lines of compressed poetry, to say the least. There is a lot going on in the mind of the poet-translator who is attempting to provide some sense of that vast mental and modal activity in English. Carson's hands, too, "close upon empty air" at times, much to her puzzlement and delight. I have been tracing how notes of this kind provide evidence for the intense intellectual engagement that characterizes Carson's approach to the translation of Greek poetry and prose. The poetic renderings of the lines, and the long excurses in the notes are designed to work toward a common purpose: sheer delight. Anne Carson the translator is first and foremost a poet, understanding, as she does, how words are designed to do the work they do, as well as the strident demands of lyricism for poetry and for poetic effect. Recall the quip: She would not know what to say without the Greek language to talk about.

But Anne Carson is also a philosopher, one who delights in multiple forms of understanding. In this, her conclusive presentation of Sappho's fragments, we are given to understand that what she is grappling with here—in these two fragments, which become a paradigm for all the rest—is what she already alerted us to more than fifteen years previously: the dynamic dance and indissoluble tension which link-and-yet-forever-separate reaching and grasping. Carson, as a translator, may reach for the apple of poetic meaning, yet she remains finely aware of all that necessarily eludes her grasp. To grasp more tightly to these fragments would not result in better translations; it would simply bleed their meaning out.

* * * * *

I have devoted considered and close attention to Carson's seminal 2002 translation of Sappho's fragments because it is so perfectly illustrative of the versatility, the scholarly luxuriousness, and the lyrical economy combined with intellectual generosity that place such a unique stamp on her translations. This is continuous with what we met in *Eros the Bittersweet*: uniquely creative exercises in classically inspired reflection, all of them aiming at spirited delight. Carson marries scholarly and poetic insights with unparalleled subtlety, and her lyrical grace makes it seem deceptively simple. It is decidedly not simple.

It is important to add at this point that Carson has devoted far more of her time and energy to the translation of Greek drama, Athenian tragedy specifically, and that in the past decade in particular, she has dedicated these energies almost entirely with an eye to staged performance.[36] Here we see Carson's interest in embodied and bodily aesthetics take on new breadth and depth. Live theater relies entirely on the commitment of embodied dramatic artists to be in the same space and time for long periods—both in practice, and in performance. In the live staged performances, the bodily presence of the audience-goers adds a powerful additional dimension and effect. Dramatic-erotic energies carom off the various players, multiplying the effects of triangulations with which Carson has been preoccupied for so long. In Sappho's case, a song ought not be reduced to a lyric. In Greek drama, a script is not comparable to a book, nor a play to a movie. In comparison to the pregnant hole that erotic triangulation reveals, the spaces with which theatrical books and filmic screenplays deal seem simply empty. Carson has become interested in envisioning, and empowering, a fuller notion of emptiness in ways that link her earliest erotic philosophizing to her more recent work on religious mysticism. I will return to these matters in the fourth chapter.

As with her prior work on Sappho and Greek lyric, so too with classical Greek drama, Carson combines several varying techniques in her renderings of Greek form: the reach for transparency and simplicity; the grasp of artistic imposition and creative adaptation; both of these mingled with an elusive kind of sly elision.

First, then, let me turn to the role of her most creative adaptations. Carson has published two collections of Greek tragedies in her own translations, as well as four independent plays. In the case of both collections, she creates the illusion that plays which were neither written nor produced together nevertheless may constitute a kind of thematic and performative unity. Acknowledging that Greek tragedy was originally produced in series—three tragedies followed by a semi-serious satyr-play—Carson has created one tetralogy and one trilogy out of the building blocks of the individual Greek dramas that have survived into our own times . . . another classically inflected desire of creating wholes out of fragments. The first such collection is entitled *Grief Lessons*,[37] and in it, Carson juxtaposes four plays by Euripides: *Herakles*, *Hekabe*, *Hippolytos*, and *Alkestis*, the last of these possessing the semi-seriousness of what we take the *satyr play* to have communicated.

Four years later, and in collaboration with New York director, Brian Kulick, Carson returned to the idea of the tragic trilogy and, building upon the only surviving example of such a trilogy (Aeschylus's Oresteiian Trilogy), Carson created a new, non-Aeschylean trilogy by incorporating one play from each of the three major Athenian tragedians whose work has survived that dealt with that trilogy's main myth: Aeschylus's *Agamemnon*; Sophokles's *Elektra*; and Euripides's *Orestes*. Entitled *An Oresteia*,[38] the production maps the dramatic arc first envisioned by Aeschylus but in decidedly more modern terms, by tracing the lineage of the doomed family of the Atreides—from the father, to the daughter, to the son. The dramatic effect—that is to say, the overall sense of a looming fate, or doom—can be shattering.[39]

In the past decade, during which her earlier role as a Professor of Classics and Comparative Literature has been supplanted by that of Writer/Artist-in-Residence, Carson has concentrated her activities on translating ancient plays for modern, live performance. She has also taken to collaboration, unusual for her—and not just with theater directors, but with visual artists, too. This may be viewed as another kind of Nietzschean intervention, designed to remind her Classics colleagues and the general public that plays are embodied performances, not just books to be read (or translated) in isolation. This public activity has intensified since Carson joined the faculty at the New York University in 2015. Her pace of publication has slowed as a result. Or rather,

her choreography and curation of the Classics is now a more central part of her scholarly practice.

Carson has recently published four new translations of Greek tragedy (she also published a cartoon version of Euripides's *Trojan Women*, with illustrations by Rosanna Bruno, as this book went to press): three by Euripides, including *Iphigeneia Among the Taurians*,[40] the *Bakkhai*,[41] and *Helen*.[42] She has also devoted a great deal of thought to Sophocles's *Antigone*, as we shall see.[43] Each of these four plays has enjoyed a very long history of theatrical and translational production, much like Sappho's fragments, so Carson has once again elected to traverse some very well-trodden classical ground. And along the way, something in her translational practices has changed—significantly, if subtly, as I will illustrate at the close of this chapter.

I have already adopted the interpretive approach of using Carson's lyrical writing *about* her translations to open up a window onto her workshop, so as to see more closely the way she approaches her linguistic and stylistic choices. The beauty and rich insights proffered in her expanded notes for the 2002 Sappho volume can seem far more lyrical in their way than the bracketed and stop-start presentation of the fragments themselves. I note something similar in the translator's prefaces that Carson has composed for her more recent translations of Greek drama. The Translator's Preface too is a set piece, of course, very nearly a genre in its own right for most classical translators. A number of proverbial notes tend normally to be sounded there: Classical Greek is notoriously difficult to render into English, especially its rhythm and tonality; every translation is an approximation and none is ever finished; important historical details about events in Athens may contribute to our understanding, if and when secure dating of the plays can be established; and yet secure dating is often very hard to secure. These are scholarly commonplaces; there is little commonplace in Carson's prefatory meditations on the plays entrusted to her care.

Rather, Carson's prefaces once again (now, again) illustrate her powerful sensitivity to the cadence and raw power of the Classical Greek language, as well as her theatrical and performative sense of what actions and images this ancient language managed to put on view for its audience. What is clear, as was clear in her first book, and in the Sappho volume as well, is that these are all insights borne from long years of meditating upon these texts as performative poetry, much as Sappho's songs presumably were.

First, then, I will turn to her hybrid Oresteiia. Of Aeschylus's *Agamemnon*, she observes the following:

> It is like watching a forest fire. Big, violent, changing every minute and the sound not like anything else. Every character in *Agamemnon* [except Kassandra] sets fire to language in a different way. . . .

> As a translator, I have spent years trying to grasp Kassandra in words. . . . Eventually I accepted that what is ungraspable about Kassandra has to stay that way. Aiskhylos has distilled into her in extreme form his own method of work, his way of using his mind, his way of using the theater as a mind. . . .
>
> Violence in *Agamemnon* emanates spectacularly from one particular word: justice. Notice how often this word recurs and how many different angles it has. Almost everyone in the play claims to know what justice is and to have it on their side. . . . The play shows that the word makes different sense to different people and how blinding or destructive it can be to believe your justice is the true one. This is not a problem with which we are unfamiliar nowadays. As Kassandra says, "I know that smell" (886, 983).[44]

There is a great deal packed into these observations, above and beyond their scholarly punch. Aeschylus's *Agamemnon* famously begins with a night watchman complaining of the cold and isolation of his evening perch; then, quite suddenly, he sees the torches and bonfires on the horizon announcing Troy's dramatic demise. This play, the first of Aeschylus's trilogy, would presumably have begun at sunrise, so the glow of the horizon would have been there for the audience to see with him. Carson's analogizing of this opening scene to fire watches captures the dramatic atmosphere perfectly. Her fascination with the figure of Cassandra, whose prescience exists outside of normal language, raises translational and religious questions to which Carson has returned repeatedly ever since working closely on this play. And as for the polyvalent appeals to justice in the context of vengeance and vendetta, yes, we do still know that smell.

Of Sophocles's *Elektra*, she observes this, based once again on her decades-long attention to the grievous poetic soundings of Greek lyric and language:

> Her name sounds like a negative adjective: "alektra" in Greek means "bedless, unwed, unmarriageable." Her life is a stopped and stranded thing, just a glitch in other people's plans. Her function and meaning as a human have been reduced to one activity—saying no to everything around her. No to her father's murder . . . no to her mother's adultery . . . no to going on with her life . . . no to breaking off her lament.
>
> People sometimes say of Elektra that her mourning is excessive. She would not disagree. . . . [Her] horrific command to Orestes
>
> *Hit her a second time, if you have the strength!*
>
> Is a direct quotation of her father's pitiful
>
> *Again! I am hit a second time!*

> It's as if the whole family were there, knee-deep in blood, and Elektra is killing her mother with her father's words. Why would Sophokles do this? To emphasize Elektra's awful command of language as a weapon? To remind us of Klytaimnestra's crime and close the cycle of vengeance in this house? To reopen Agamemnon's wounds and suggest that vengeance here will never end? To trump Aiskhylos? To pay homage to Aiskhylos? Perhaps all these at once. Sophokles is a complex poet working in a complex tradition. His audience enjoys all kinds of play with masks. All kinds of uses of urns. They do not come to the theater for comfort.[45]

Here Carson looks with laser-like precision on the way a complex poet working in a complex and competitive tradition will necessarily have many sides, generate many effects. Yet one of the effects that Sophocles, perhaps the most ventriloquist of the great Attic tragedians, manages here is to create a single-minded character who speaks in a rigid and unwavering voice that sounds a single note, endlessly repeated. Elektra is utterly and entirely defined by the original crime of her father's murder: it is all she can think of; it is all she wishes to think of. The originary crime defines her, more than any other member of the clan. Vengeance has become her sole (pre)occupation. And in that singleness-of-mind, she finds a way to gore a second person with the selfsame word-weapons.

Turning to her brother, as depicted by Euripides, Carson notices something quite different.

> When we first meet Orestes in *Orestes*, he is asleep. This sets up a relationship between us and him that will continue through the play. To see Orestes flounder about in decisions and actions as the story proceeds is like watching someone twitch in their sleep and let out the occasional scream. He is present but opaque to us . . . All in all, Orestes is a peculiar customer—not exactly insane but strange and unknowable. His consciousness is entirely his own. And in this respect he is a typical Euripidean creation. Euripides introduced to the Greek tragic stage a concern for the solitary, inward self, for consciousness as a private content. . . .
>
> Euripides produced *Orestes* in 408 B.C. Later that same year, he left Athens and went to Macedonia, where he died in less than two years. There is no historic evidence to explain why a highly successful playwright would go into voluntary exile at the age of seventy-three. But it makes *Orestes* his last statement to the Athenians—and a wild, heartless, unconstruable statement it is. If I take it as a story of real people, I can find no character to like in the play. . . .[46]

We should notice how craftily Carson weaves her insights about the three plays together here. Orestes, unlike Elektra, wavers. Everything of importance is happening in the depths of his mind, whereas Elektra exists all on the surface, her lust for vengeance in plain view. Orestes is opaque, strange, and unknowable—like Cassandra. We cannot like him because we cannot know him, and in Euripides, we cannot really like anyone for much the same reason. He is the poet in whom psychological depth appears with full force, which is why many view him as the most modern of the three ancient tragedians. So a meditation on the psychology of Orestes subtly morphs into a psychological analysis of Euripides, who is equally unknowable (it is an open question whether Carson is implying that he is therefore also unlikeable—her own affections for him are evident). He is, in short, a dark clown, the fulcrum point around which both ancient tragedy and comedy pivoted, just prior to Athens's downfall. Did Euripides leave Athens, or did Athens abandon the poet? This is a burning political question. And, by cruel implication, Carson is warning her American audience, at war for close to a decade at that point, that they too "know that smell."

I noted at the outset of this chapter how much translating lay behind the creation of *Eros the Bittersweet*. Carson needed to translate Sappho and Plato closely, over a long period of years, in order to be able to come to some sense—never fully settled, yet always mesmerizing—of their complex meanings, and the implications of those meanings for contemporary readers. So, too, here. We can sense how Carson's unerring sensitivity to the nuances of the Greek tongue, coupled with her more recent experiences of the necessities of staged performance, result in brilliant insights about central characters in the plays, as well as the poets who created them. The results are altogether remarkable. Comparing all of this to her earlier practice in the 2002 Sappho volume, it is as if Carson has now elected to put the critical apparatus up front, as vaguely preparatory for the translations that follow. Now we get the scholarly reflection first; that done, we may settle into our seats and enjoy the show.

The artifice of creating "*An* Oresteia" in this way has also provided Carson with an occasion to reflect on the distinctness of each of these three Athenian poets. The somber Aeschylean concern with justice and outward doom turns toward inwardness and an interest in individual character first in Sophocles, and then morphs into the preoccupations of the Euripidean soul in collusion, and collision, with itself. From the city (*polis*) to the self (*psychê*):[47] the trilogy thus becomes a creative history lesson on the single century of the most creative (and explosive) Greek drama that was ever created in Athens or anywhere else in Greece.

Carson's task in *Grief Lessons* is somewhat different. Here, she is more concerned with the soul than with the city, attempting to elucidate the unique qualities that make Euripides seem so very modern, on the one hand, and so maddeningly elusive on the other. The title also coyly poses the question of whether "grief lessens" with time, as Kazim Ali has pointed out so elegantly.[48] Of tragedy as a genre, Carson offers the following observation:

"Why does tragedy exist? Because you are full of rage. Why are you full of rage? Because you are full of grief."[49] Grief, which makes you mad, can lead to madness. Hence Carson's desire to derive "grief lessons" from the emotional inwardness and the soulful self-divisions provided by Euripidean tragedy. "Grief and rage—you need to contain that, to put a frame around it, where it can play itself out without you or your kin having to die. There is a theory that watching unbearable stories about other people lost in grief or rage is good for you—may cleanse you of your darkness."[50] But how can Euripides—that dark clown of the Athenian tragic poets, the one most obsessed with the damage done by all-encompassing wars and never-ending family intrigues—ever hope to cleanse? We will need to think again about what Aristotle says about tragic *katharsis*. Whatever it is, it is not a cleansing. A burnishing, perhaps; a transformation, absolutely. But it operates through the medium of sacrificial fire.

> Curious art form, curious artist. Who was Euripides? The best short answer I've found to this is an essay by B. M. W. Knox, who says of Euripides what the Corinthians (in Thucydides) said of the Athenians, "that he was born never to live in peace with himself and to prevent the rest of mankind from doing so." Knox's essay is called "Euripides: The Poet as Prophet." To be a prophet, Knox emphasizes, requires living in and looking at the present, at what is really going on around you. Out of the present the future is formed. The prophet needs a clear, dry, unshy eye that can stand aloof from explanation and comfort. . . . There is in Euripides some kind of learning that is always at the boiling point.[51]

After examining Euripides the playwright, Carson turns to three of Euripides's most unambiguously boiling-point thrillers, and then to one of his most ambiguous. Her insights have by now been honed to a very fine point, given her decades-long immersion in staged Greek drama.

She begins with the *Herakles,* a terrifying play in which we witness the greatest of all Greek heroes, the man who has just harrowed Hades, reduced to suicidal grief; maddened by the gods, he slays his family immediately after saving them. The question is how to go on living within this grief and guilt, and it is the sudden, surprising offer of friendship by Theseus that will enable him to do so. Herakles is thus the half-man (son of Amphitryon), half-god (son of Zeus) who has been reduced by the gods to the most fragile point of his humanity. This is the precise point that Euripides will almost magically find a way to elevate. Here is how Carson sees that alchemical work, dramatically:

> Herakles is a two-part man. Euripides wrote him a two-part play. It breaks down in the middle and starts over again as does he. Wrecks and recharges its own form as he wrecks and recharges his own legend. . . . Herakles' flesh is a

cliché. . . . How do you overturn a cliché? From inside. The first eight hundred lines of the play will bore you, they're supposed to. . . . Herakles has reached the boundary of his own myth, he has come to the end of his interestingness. . . . Then from inside his *berserker furor* he has to build something absolutely new. New self, new name for the father, new definition of God. The old ones have stopped. It is as if the world broke off. Why did it break off? Because the myth ended.[52]

Euripides is here shown to be the heterodox poet of broken worlds and broken myths, and Herakles as a broken man: this deep and disturbing ambiguity has rarely been captured better. And it is an insight only comprehensible as what Carson here characterizes as a "grief lesson." There is nothing cleansing about this lesson: we felt pity and fear before, and we feel it now. The trick, the best that we may hope for, is to feel them differently.

From this acme of heroic male despair, Carson shifts her focus to gender in Greek tragedy, turning to two tragic heroines: Hekabe, the surviving queen of fallen Troy; and Phaedra, the eros-maddened suicide. The *Hekabe* is positively Lear-like in its continual exposure of the audience to war-induced horror. "The worst is not,/ So long as we can say, 'This is the worst.'"[53] Shakespeare said that, but Euripides *showed* it. Here is how Carson frames the singular horror of a doomed city whose cruel destruction at Greek hands we have been forced to witness on stage, virtually in slow-motion, without being permitted, or able, to turn away:

[Hekabe's] story is a war-story and Euripides develops it around two of the ugliest principles that govern war stories—necessity and revenge. Necessity takes the form of a demand by the Greek warrior Achilles—who by this time is dead so the demand issues from a ghost—that a female human being should be slaughtered on his tomb as a sacrifice to himself. Revenge is embodied in Hekabe, the ancient queen of Troy whom we see transformed by the atrocities of war into a vengeance maniac. She is on stage throughout the play. At first she acts ancient, broken, hysterical. She watches her daughter Polyxena led away to be sacrificed to Achilles and falls flat on the ground in despair. Then something changes. News comes to her of the treacherous murder of her son Polydoros— the only son she had left—and suddenly she rises up, assembles herself one last time to action. She is jubilant, she is vicious, she is a shocking thing to see. Euripides pushes her to the very limit of human being and then, on the last page of the play, pushes her beyond. In the final scene Hekabe receives a prophecy that at her death she will suffer metamorphosis into a dog. . . . Really there is nowhere else for her to go but out of the species.[54]

Hekabe had witnessed forty-nine of her fifty sons killed during the decade of war over which she had presided with her husband. Losing the last son, together with her husband and daughter, is in this instance a literal ending, closing the book on an entire family, a city, and an empire. There is nothing, absolutely nothing, left for her to lose, save her humanity. That human beings can reduce themselves and one another to animal frenzy and animal cruelty offers another kind of grief lesson. Clearly, if Euripides intends *katharsis* in this play, then there is nothing clean about it.

In Phaedra, we meet a very different kind of heroine, and a very different type of tragedy. We have moved from war to love, flip sides perhaps of a single overwhelming passion in which anger and grief are joined in full measure. We saw Sappho adapt Homeric war music to erotic lyrics of her own design; something similar is at work here. The *Hippolytos* is perhaps Euripides's most finely crafted play. In it, he takes the logic of polytheism to its mythic limit—with the poetic implication being (now, again) that myths can simply come to an end. They may run out of energy, run out of room, box us into their falsifying logics of vengeance. And here once again Euripides's lesson seems Lear-like: "As flies to wanton boys, are we to th' gods:/ they kill us for their sport."[55] The play is framed by two goddesses: Aphrodite at the beginning; and Artemis at the end. Inside of this frame, human beings act as if they are really deliberating and deciding, really in control of their own affairs. They are animated by emotions, by love and shame, primarily, but hatred, too. But in the play's preface, we learn that the two goddesses are embattled, and the tools they have at their disposal are people. Aphrodite is exercised at Hippolytos's refusal to grant her due honor; he is exclusive in his affection for the virginal and asexual Artemis. Aphrodite opts to punish him and at the same time to check Artemis's pride. Her weapon is eros, naturally enough. And here, as elsewhere, it is more bitter than sweet. She causes Phaedra to fall in love with her stepson, a young man who is depicted in this play as very like her husband, Theseus, a sort of younger second-self. Near death, she confesses the heartfelt cause to her Nurse. The Nurse tells Hippolytos, who explodes in a torrent of misogynistic rage. Phaedra, already on the edge, tips over. She suicides, but she leaves a lying death-note accusing Hippolytos of attempted rape. At this awful moment, Theseus returns (he had just been saved by Herakles, as we will recall, who would return next to his own home and perform a similar act of self-destruction). Theseus exiles his son, then asks Poseidon to kill him. The god consents. Only after the son has been ripped to pieces by his own horses does Theseus learn the truth. Artemis informs Hippolytos that it is not permitted for the gods to be present at a human being's death, but she promises to kill whatever mortal man next finds Aphrodite's favor. Small comfort, this, to a dying mortal. If there is a grief lesson here, it is perhaps only the reminder that grief and rage go together, and that gods who feel such things are of little use to us.

Carson captures the essence of this awful play brilliantly, in a single, captivating image: "The *Hippolytos* is like Venice. A system of reflections, distorted reflections, reflections that go awry. A system of corridors where people follow one another but never meet, never find the way out. There is no way out, all corridors lead back into the system."[56] But she is also fascinated by another elusive element of this tragedy. There is ancient testimonial evidence to suggest that the play we have is a revision Euripides performed, perhaps to overcome the negative reaction to his first staged version of the play. A Byzantine scholiast suggests that this second play "corrects what was unseemly and worthy of rebuke"[57] in the first version. The trouble is that we no longer know what the objectionable matter was. Perhaps Phaedra was not depicted nobly enough. It would make a vast dramatic difference if she revealed her passion directly to Hippolytos, rather than being betrayed to him by her Nurse.

Carson appends an imaginary letter by Euripides to this book, entitled "Why I Wrote Two Plays about Phaidra," in which s/he imaginatively addresses the question. We will see this fascinating hybrid practice many times in the next two chapters: the startling combination of deep classical learning, a fragmentary lyric tradition, filtered now through Carson's modernist poetic temperament, and the sheer luxuriousness of her prose. As with Sappho in 1986, she is rendering a fragmentary classical past in a compelling present tense. That, I am suggesting, is a fitting description of the entirety of her translational practices since we first met them in *Eros the Bittersweet*. Ever conversant with oblique classical material, Carson uses "nineteen short fragments and two line-paraphrases"[58] to try to get to the heart of an elusive Euripidean mystery. Unsurprisingly, mystery is what she finds there, The Big One, whose outlines she has been tracing throughout her career:

> I don't understand, I could never have predicted, your hatred of this woman. It's true she fell in love with someone wrong for her but half the heroines of your literature do that, Helen, Echo, Io, Agave, all of them. Phaidra's love was for her step-son, and it excited you badly, maybe not the incest so much as the question of property rights—ditch the old man, marry the son, keep the estate. Truth is often, in some degree, economic. Which isn't to say her passion for Hippolytos was fake. Women learn to veil things. Who likes to look straight at real passions? Looks can kill. I would call "feminine" this talent for veiling a truth in a truth. . . .
>
> *Hippolytos Veiled* was what I called the first attempt to write a play about Phaidra. This play did not succeed. It disappointed you. You thought the title meant Hippolytos would be shown in scenes of deep revulsion. . . . You thought the shame was his, the veil was his, the love was wrong in some simple way that you could grasp before the first choral song. But we all burned our hands on that Phaidra, didn't we? It was her shame that ate the play. And her shame wasn't simple. It pullulated and turned on itself and stank at the bottom of the pit of

the question of desire—what is the question of desire? I don't know. Something about its presumption to exist in human forms. Human forms are puny. Desire is vast.[59]

Carson has made Phaedra a shocking stand-in for Euripides himself, and a spokesperson for her own erotic philosophy. Phaidra, like Euripides, knows that desire is vast. Grief's components, alternating between shame and rage, ricochet from lover, to beloved, to spectator, and back again. We have returned to the sometimes-playful, sometimes terrifying, lesson already presented in *Eros the Bittersweet*. It is as if we never left.[60]

* * * * *

Carson returned, as I have noted, to translating Greek drama in the new decade inaugurated in 2010, but her interests now appeared to be almost entirely aimed at the unique embodied challenges of staged performance, rather than simply "that puzzle mode of mind" that inspires the general translation of Greek into English. It is somewhat surprising that she has dedicated her attention more recently to several of the most frequently translated plays in the entire Greek dramatic repertoire. In 2013, she published a translation of Euripides's "Iphigenia Among the Taurians," the last of her translations to include line numbers which would enable the reader to consult the Greek original . . . or any other English translations. From now on, it would seem, Carson's translations must stand (and be spoken) on their own. They are conceived as scripts now, not scholarly editions. Carson is coyly reminding her classical colleagues that this is what the great Athenian tragedies originally were: not books, but scripts. The committed translator should aim to reflect that fact.

Her *Iphigenia* is also the last translation to receive a traditional Translator's Preface. In it, Carson confesses to her continued fascination (along with Euripides, it would seem) with "the tragic vicissitudes of the house of Atreus." The play, she feels, also shows Euripides at the height of his creative power, possessing an unprecedented daring in the rewriting of classical myths: when they "come to an end," they presumably need a revision. We will recall that Iphigenia was the eldest daughter of Agamemnon and Clytemnestra; through an astonishingly un-erotic ruse, her father had her delivered to the port of Aulis on the false pretense of a marriage proposal from Achilles. In actual fact, the girl was to be sacrificed to Artemis in order to bring an end to the doldrums that shackled the Greek fleet to the port, unable to embark for Troy. It was her murder that was the first crime to set Agamemnon's wife against him and eventually to decide her upon murder.

But in this Euripidean version, Iphigenia escaped her fate, thanks to the strange intervention of Artemis, who replaced her with a sacrificial animal, then spirited the girl away to an isolated sanctuary in the land of the Taurians. Ironically, Iphigenia presides there over a temple to Artemis, and sacrifices any stranded Greeks who stray this far from "civilization." She has been at this grisly work for many years.

Her brother, Orestes, was a sibling too young at the time of her departure to remember her. He killed his mother to avenge his father, then was pursued by the chthonian forces of the Furies for the crime of shedding kindred blood. Tried at the sacred court in Athens and acquitted, Euripides imagines that Orestes is still hounded by the Furies. Apollo informs him that he can be free of this curse once and for all only if he steals the ancient statue of Artemis from her sanctuary in the land of the Taurians. He travels there with his loyal comrade, Pylades, committed to the theft. Both Greeks are eventually captured and, on the verge of their execution by his unwitting sister, the siblings' identities are revealed at the last moment. They then arrange to steal the statue together and flee the land of the Taurians. It is a reunion founded on criminality, which seems ominously fitting for this tortured household.

Carson reflects briefly on the curious permutations of Greek mythology at which Euripides excels, demonstrating as well a new(er) interest in the long history of classical re-reading.[61] Not among Euripides's most popular plays in antiquity, this *Iphigenia* enjoyed far-flung notoriety in Renaissance and Early Modern Europe. Other playwrights adapted the play, among them Giovanni Rucellai (*L'Oreste*, 1525), Jean Racine (*Iphigénie en Tauride*, which he worked on for three years, 1673–1676, but never finished), and Anslem Feuerbach (1862). It was in the eighteenth century that the Taurian wave truly crested: in painting (with Giovanni Battista Tiepolo, Benjamin West, and Winckelmann's antagonist, Henry Fuseli[62]), on the stage (with John Dennis, Johann Elias Schlegel, Claude Guimond de La Touche, and Wolfgang von Goethe), and in opera (with Domenico Scarlatti and Christoph Willibald Gluck). Carson grants equal stature to twentieth-century dance adaptations by Isadora Duncan (in 1916) and Pina Bausch (in 1974). Clearly, the modern *performative* afterlife of this play has been an exceptionally long one.

Carson now appears to be placing herself more explicitly in that long tradition of performative re-reading.

We might compare this to the dramatic afterlives of two dramatic masterpieces already preeminent in antiquity: Sophocles's *Antigone* and Euripides's *The Bacchae*. The *Antigone*, in particular, has been perennial. As George Steiner famously put the matter:

> It has, I believe, been given to only one literary text to express all the principal constants of conflict in the condition of man. These constants are five-fold: the

confrontation of men and of women; of age and of youth; of society and of the individual; of the living and the dead; of men and of god(s). The conflicts which come of these five orders of confrontation are not negotiable. Men and women, young and old, the individual and the community or state, the quick and the dead, mortals and immortals, define themselves in the conflictual process of defining each other. Self-definition and the agonistic recognition of "otherness" (of *l'autre*) across the threatened boundaries of self are indissociable. . . . To arrive at oneself—the primordial journey—is to come up, polemically, against "the other." The boundary conditions of the human person are those set by gender, by age, by community, by the cut between life and death, and by the potentials of accepted or denied encounter between the existential and the transcendent.[63]

It may well be that Carson perceives *The Bacchae* to be equally perennial in the way it embodies many of these same thematic conflicts. She certainly goes to great lengths, unlike Nietzsche, to establish Euripides as Sophocles's worthy dramatic successor. Carson published translations of both the *Antigone* and the *Bacchae* in 2015, without line numbering and absent the anticipated Translator's Prefaces. Here once again, we are witnessing her translations designed as scripted, not scholarly, performance.

In the case of the *Antigone*, Carson was asked to produce the translation by Dutch director Ivo van Hove, who did not find her previous version, *Antigonick*,[64] either palatable or playable. Originally offended by the suggestion that she had not really "translated"[65] the play in her previous pass, Carson eventually relented and produced this version, thoroughly enjoying herself in the process.[66] The play premiered in Luxembourg on February 25, 2015, with Juliette Binoche in the title role, then toured internationally for eight months, with a final performance in Ann Arbor, Michigan, on October 14, 2015.

Carson's "introduction" to the *Antigone* contents itself with a discussion of two cases of "untranslatability."[67] The first concerns a single line (line 943): "I was caught in an act of perfect piety." The problem, Carson feels, is how to suss out the concept lying behind that apparently simple word, "piety."

> Now consider the English word "piety." Can we hear in it any flicker of the original sacral force of *eusebeia*? Derived from the Old French word for "pity," the word "piety" came over into English c.1540 as a term for religious devotion or "moral vertue" (OED). In modern usage it seems to me to lack the depth and dread of the Greek word—perhaps English has lost touch with true religiosity. Our pieties are more a matter of protocol than dread. And where *eusebeia* always implies ritual action, "piety" represents a mood rather than a pressure to act. Nonetheless, there we are. I could not find, I do not know, a different or a better translation.[68]

Piety as depth and dread, dead to a language that "has lost touch with true religiosity." This highly significant observation announces Carson's more recent interest in religious language and religious ideas that first surfaced in 2005, in her hybrid text, *Decreation*, a text to which I will turn for a closer analysis in the fourth chapter. Here I simply wish to highlight the manner in which Carson has presented her version of the perennial translator's dilemma. There is one word in Greek which she feels the need to translate with one word in English. This may have something to do with the lingering ideal of "transparency" that she enunciated in her Sappho translations in 2002.

But we will recall that Carson enunciated another ideal, another strategy, in that same text: creative adaptation, and a sort of authorial intrusion. I wish to recall the piling on of synonyms that so often accompanied Carson's Sapphic renderings, in the notes which I discussed earlier in this chapter.

> The word is a compound adjective, used as an epithet of Aphrodite to identify either her "chair" (*thron-*) or her "mind" (*phron-*) as *poikilos*: "many colored, spotted, dappled, variegated, intricate, embroidered, inlaid, highly wrought, complicated, changeful, diverse, abstruse, ambiguous, subtle."[69]

As we witness in her workshop reflections on piety, Carson is a compulsive reader of the *Oxford English Dictionary* (she proudly owns the last print edition, which she consults religiously). She is fascinated by shades of meaning, especially in a language with as large a vocabulary as English. By 2015, Carson occasionally opted to include this piling on of synonyms within the translation itself. Perhaps the most striking example comes in one of the most famous passages in the *Antigone*, the so-called Choral Ode on Man. Here the translational challenge hinges on the Greek word *deinos*, a word which possesses a semantic range running from the virtuous to the monstrous. The Chorus observes that there are many *deinoi* things in the world, but that nothing is more *deinos* than a human being. It might mean awful, and it might mean awe-inspiring; it might mean terrible and it might mean terribly talented. It might mean both, or neither. So how do you translate a word like that? Carson's answer is striking. There are many things in the world, she confesses, that are "strange / terrible / clever / wondrous/ monstrous / marvellous / dreadful / awful / and / weird," but nothing is more "strange / terrible / clever / wondrous / monstrous / marvellous / dreadful / awful / and / weird," than Man.[70] In such lyric moments, the translator's intrusive presence is perceived as a necessity that may enable Sophocles (like Sappho) to speak more clearly. It bears noting that this same kind of rendering, one word per verse line, also makes Sophocles look a great deal more like the Sapphic fragments with which this chapter began.

Carson's presentation of Sappho in 2002, we may recall, was one that evocatively reproduces the elusive distance which such a fragmentary literary, and papyrological, legacy creates. Avoiding the interpretive vices of skepticism and dogmatism, however, she maintained that there are indeed things we can see and say about Sappho with confident humility, mindful all the while of everything which eludes us, all that we have in fact lost for good. In Sophocles's *Antigone*, we would seem to be confronted by the opposite circumstance: a play that has been worked and re-worked with greater care and attention arguably than any other single Greek play. Perhaps in response to all the scholarly noise, Carson appears to be cultivating a subtler skepticism, due in large measure to the very extent of previous work on the play. It is an overdetermined play, and therefore a play that is very difficult to see afresh. Conscious of how Hölderlin attempted to see the *Antigone* with fresh eyes, using it as an occasion for the development of his own fairly psychedelic theory of translation as creative adaptation,[71] Carson appears to be attempting something similar here. The result is a literary hybrid, half-ancient and half-modern, a lyric Minotaur replete with deep and labyrinthine insight. There are great risks in this approach, to be sure, but they are risks that Carson feels increasingly required to run. As Will Aitken noted, "has the word *pissant* ever occurred before in a translation of Greek tragedy?," further noting the consternation that this word caused the international cast (they could not get past the 'piss'). Carson's anachronistic use of the word 'archive' displays the poetic power of such experimentation: "Archives of grief I see falling / upon this house / death on birth birth on death / there is no end to it."[72]

If any play can rival the overdetermination of translational re-readings of the *Antigone*, then it is surely Euripides's *Bacchae*. Also published in 2015, Carson's translation dispenses with a prose introduction altogether and prefaces the play simply with a poem of her own, "I Wish I Were Two Dogs Then I Could Play With Me." The poem offers a meditation on the complexity of beginnings, especially the beginnings of a god with as strange and hybrid a birth as Dionysus's. Inspired perhaps by our own age's cosmological conundrums, Carson poses the question of "the beginning before the beginning." And her analogies are all sensual, and highly eroticized: the first dizzying drink; the first paralyzing whiff of mystery; the first overwhelming fall into love.[73] These things are as amoral, or transmoral, as the god we meet on stage.

We can see how Carson's interest in themes of reaching and grasping, seeds first planted in *Eros the Bittersweet* and joined now to a fascination with mythic origins, continue to bear poetic fruit and classical insight. These interests are now armed with a new rhetoric of strikingly terse phrasings, short snippets of tight wording, the piling up of nouns or adjectives, all designed to make us see something old, anew. She has returned to the beginning first announced in *Eros the Bittersweet*, and now seems to be trying to go back further still, to "the desire before the desire,"⁷⁴ a veritable erotic Big Bang. This is the heart of the Greek god's mystery, she suggests, and the mysterious heart of Greek religion.

"The desire / before the desire" . . . the subtle links between knowing and wooing . . . these ideas have long been on her mind, but are costumed now in the fabric of an explosively violent god. When Carson speaks of the ambiguity of Dionysos's "beginning," she is thinking primarily of two mythic moments. The first concerns his ambiguous birth: Zeus struck his mortal mother, Semele, dead with a lightning bolt, rescued the fetus, sewed it up into his own thigh, then later birthed the son himself. This weird ontogeny creates deep confusion as to the god's maternity and paternity, not to mention his mortality. The second issue concerns the fact that Dionysos comes to Greece from the east in this play; he is, in this sense, a decidedly foreign god. Both confusions create resistance to the acceptance of this new divinity at Thebes. And it is this resistance that results in the explosion of murderous violence near the end of the play, the sparagmatic murder of King Pentheus at the hands of his own mother, Agave.

Carson captures some of this mythic confusion in the opening lines of the play, the Euripidean Prologue spoken by the god himself. After tracking his long course from the Asian east to the Greek west, and after posing the question of what kind of god such a god may be, Carson concludes: "In Greek they say *daimon–* / can we just use that?"⁷⁵ This is not translation in any manner we are used to, given her studied *refusal* to translate the Greek word. Those last lines burst the customary bounds.⁷⁶ It is a creative adaptation, one designed for stage performance in English, and one designed to interrogate the performative ambiguity⁷⁷ of Dionysos's mythic Greek origins in the English tongue. Carson is troubling especially over two words that Euripides uses in this one line: *teletas* (mysteries, rituals, or rites) and *daimôn* (divinity, god, or spirit).⁷⁸ And she seems increasingly drawn to the strategy of these jarring intrusions in the present as the best way to capture the Greek language's ancient strangeness on stage. "Can we just use that?"

The question of untranslatability, the fact that all translations are necessarily tentative and unfinished, as enunciated by Carson in the quotations that initialized this chapter, are relatively standard academic fare. As Mark Polizzotti puts the problem, "The stale Italian pun *traduttore, traditore* ("translator—traitor"), which has been afflicting translation commentary for centuries, derives much of its longevity from the underlying suspicion across many cultures that the middleman is either incompetent or up to no good."⁷⁹ Clearly, there is a lot more to the translator's art than serving the commercial interests of such middlemen. Cultural commerce demands an altogether different kind of exchange. Anne Carson is unusual in that she approaches these questions with the eye of an artist, an increasingly visual and performative artist. That fact accounts for much of her poetic vitality and strangeness.

We might consider the issue this way, as I believe that Carson has increasingly been inclined to do: When did Leonardo da Vinci put the last brushstroke to the Mona Lisa? When did Michelangelo daub the final pigment to the last panel of the Sistine Chapel? When did he put the chisel or sandstone to his David for the last time? When did Mozart decide that this last note sufficed? In short, when does the artist know that a work of art is finished, such that any further changes would *change* the work without *improving* the work? Carson has dedicated her entire career as a translator to reflection on that question.[80] We have seen how ancient literary tradition, modern scholarship, and her own deep awareness of the power and the limits of language have all contributed to Carson's practices as a translator. It is her awareness of the artistry of translation that has enabled the artistry of her poetic productions. It is the time and close attention that translation requires that has enabled the artistry of her readings of Sappho, Sophocles, Euripides, and the rest, as is abundantly clear in her elaborate notes and increasingly wistful introductions. If anything has changed in the course of her translational practices over the past thirty years, it is her increasingly explicit sense of the provisional nature of what she produces. Sappho in 1986 seemed far more whole than Carson's 2002 versions suggest; by contrast, Sappho has become much holier to her in the interim. Since then, we have also been given further glimpses of the translator in her workshop, deciding when (if not quite how) the last touch has been put to her own works of art. "Can we just use that?"

For my purposes, these last two essays in translating Greek tragic poetry (namely her *Antigone* and her *Bacchae*) underline Carson's enduring interest in two interrelated matters: poetics and religion . . . which is another way to say, the vast erotic arc of creation itself. We might best consider this translational convergence historically. The art of translation has a long religious pedigree, especially among the three scriptural monotheisms. The Hebrew Bible was translated into Greek, in the Septuagint, already in the Hellenistic period; it took its name from the mythical report that seventy (or seventy-two) rabbis undertook independent translations that agreed word-for-word, a mythic preference of fidelity over felicity.[81] This Septuagint would later serve as the Bible for most early members of the Jesus-movement. These Jesus-followers would subsequently add new scriptural writing, in Greek, to their inherited canon. And that canon would be translated into Latin by Jerome, patron saint of translators, in the fourth century, creating a canonical new version for the western churches, one translated with as much attention to felicity as fidelity, in the fifth century CE. Similarly, so-called Greek classical literature has enjoyed a long history of translation into Latin, Syriac, Arabic, and so on.

Given the first religious and poetic murmurings that would lead to modernity, however, we witness a significant uptick in the interest in, and production of, translations. The North Italian Renaissance, for all of its visual virtuosity, also inspired a new flourishing of translation of ancient Greek and Roman literature and philosophy. At roughly the same time, Protestant Reformers in central Europe and England made vernacular translations of the Christian Bible (and the implicit supplanting of Jerome's sacrosanct Vulgate) centerpieces of their religious reforms. It is not too much to say that Early Modern Europe witnessed a renaissance in and of translation; the disciplines of Classics and Comparative Religion were born from the innovations, insights and controversies spawned by these revolutionary changes. Anne Carson has been an eloquent, if oblique, observer of this modern terrain, and she has, like Nietzsche, proposed some notably un-modern interventions precisely here.

Poetics and religion, then: I will take up these topics in the next two chapters, respectively.

NOTES

1. Anne Carson, interview with Eleanor Wachtel, *Brick: A Literary Journal* 89 (posted on June 10, 2014). The full quote reads: "[T]he mental activity of being inside a translation is something I simply love. It's like doing an endless crossword puzzle but with a valuable product. And that puzzle mode of mind is simply the best thing."

2. For my own thinking about the challenges of translation, and the "ur-debate of fidelity versus felicity," I have profited most from Mark Polizzotti's insightful *Sympathy for the Traitor: A Translation Manifesto* (Cambridge, MA: MIT Press, 2018), 19.

Polizzotti makes especially good use of Daniel Weissbort and Astradur Eysteinsson, eds., *Translation—Theory and Practice: A Historical Reader* (New York, NY: Oxford University Press, 2006). An earlier contribution from the perspective of Reception Studies is Lorna Hardwick, *Translating Words, Translating Cultures* (London: Gerald Duckworth & Co., Ltd., 2000), esp. 9–22.

3. Anne Carson, *Nay Rather* (American University of Paris: The Cahier Series No. 21, 2013), 26.

I am indebted to Pauline Jaccon, of the Translation Studies and English Literature program at the Sorbonne Nouvelle (Paris 3), for bringing this comment to my attention. Jaccon emphasizes Carson's role as an "active reader," by which she means us to see how Carson is so actively engaged with what she reads, that she has the unique capacity to be moved by it. Such movement is what best characterizes the dynamism of her translational and readerly practices. Jaccon concludes that Carson's purpose is not simply to establish a dialogue with the author, but rather to be inspired by the author to create a new and uniquely hybrid form of writing, such that she never confines herself (or her readers) to the position of passive receptacle. In other words, Carson capitalizes on the mutual reach between text and translator, in which each side refuses simply to be grasped.

See Pauline Jaccon, "'A Strange New Kind of/Inbetween': Anne Carson et l'impulsion créative en traduction," *Ticontre. Teoria Testo Traduzione* 12 (2019): 449–467 (esp. 461–462).

4. Anne Carson, *If Not, Winter: Fragments of Sappho* (New York, NY: Alfred A. Knopf, 2002).

5. For a probing account of the mournful dimension of that riddled textual legacy, one that anticipates Carson's own later translator's mournfulness in *Nox*, see Glenn Kurtz, "What Remains: Sappho and Mourning," *Southwest Review* 95.1/2 (2010): 246–254.

6. Carson, *If Not, Winter: Fragments of Sappho*, xi.

This adventure of the imagination, like her earlier delight in understanding, are the driving impulses behind all of Carson's work—in essays, poetry and translation, alike.

7. For more on this papyrological aporia, see John Melillo, "Sappho and the 'Papyrological Event,'" in Joshua Marie Wilkinson, ed., *Anne Carson: Ecstatic Lyre* (Ann Arbor, MI: University of Michigan Press, 2015), 188–193.

8. Anne Carson, *Eros the Bittersweet*, 12–13.

9. Anne Carson, *If Not, Winter: Fragments of Sappho*, 62–63.

My italics indicate her additions to the earlier translation; additionally, one word has been removed.

10. Anne Carson, *If Not, Winter: Fragments of Sappho*, 2.

11. Anne Carson, *If Not, Winter: Fragments of Sappho*, 357.

12. The term connotes intricacy, especially in the weaving arts with which Lesbos had been associated since Homer's *Iliad* (9.128–130). It is used specifically in reference to Lesbian sandals (*poikilosambalôi*) in a famous poem by Anacreon that was reported by Athenaeus in his *Scholars at Supper* (*Deipnosophistes* 13.599c). These passages are made part of an expansive literary reception history by Kate Gilhuly, "Lesbians Are Not from Lesbos," in Ruby Blondell and Kirk Ormand, eds., *Ancient Sex: New Essays* (Columbus, OH: The Ohio State University Press, 2015), 143–176.

Another cognate of the word is used for the rich and variegated assortment of tidbits (*mezedes* or *poikilia*) that accompany a carafe of ouzo in Modern Greece, as Carson would have experienced in travels there. These, too, can "spangle" a visitor's tired mind.

13. As I noted in the Foreword, upon completing his non-conforming first book, *The Birth of Tragedy*, in 1872, Nietzsche turned to an ambitious collection of thirteen essays aiming at a thoroughgoing transformation of German culture; these were his "Untimely Meditations," or "Unmodern Observations." Extensive notes for an illuminating essay entitled *Wir Philologen* ("We Classicists") were never published, but may be found in Giorgio Colli and Mazzino Montinari, eds., KSA VIII: 1–120, and translated by William Arrowsmith as "We Classicists" in his edited volume, *Nietzsche: Unmodern Observations* (New Haven, CT: Yale University Press, 1990), 307–387.

For some initial reflection on Nietzsche's criticism of the scientific excesses, and especially the lack of lyricism, in most modern philology, see Louis A. Ruprecht Jr., "Nietzsche's Vision, Nietzsche's Greece," *Soundings* 73.1 (1990): 61-84.

14. Anne Carson, *If Not, Winter: Fragments of Sappho*, 373.

For more on the idea of the Greek woman being "a mobile unit" in the context of Greek patriarchy and Greek marriage, see Anne Carson, "Putting Her in Her Place: Women, Dirt, Desire," in David Halperin, John J. Winkler, and Froma Zeitlin, eds., *Before Sexuality: The Construction of Erotic Experience in the Ancient Greek World* (Princeton, NJ: Princeton University Press, 1990), 135–169, esp. 136. That essay has inspired a remarkable longer range essay by Carol L. Dougherty, "Why Does Aphrodite Have Her Foot on That Turtle?," *Arion, Third Series* 27.3 (2020): 25–47.

15. Evidence for potential somewheres may be found in two of Carson's own essays that develop the ritual tropes of Greek wedding ceremonies: "Wedding at Noon in Pindar's *Ninth Pythian*," *Greek, Roman and Byzantine Studies* 23 (1982): 121–128; and "Putting Her in Her Place: Women, Dirt, Desire," especially "Putting the Lid on the Bride," 160–164.

16. A further interpretive irony should be noted here. Carson may be distancing herself from a kind of feminist classicism that has made ancient Greek women's lot worse than it was. "I read somewhere once" might thus also be heard as Carson's warning to her readers not to be seduced by false assertions of "what we all know."

For a brilliant intervention in that historiography, see Cynthia B. Patterson, *The Family in Greek History* (Cambridge, MA: Harvard University Press, 1998), 5–42. For an interesting interpellation of Carson's hybrid writing style and her oblique relation to Second Wave Feminism, see Maya Linden, "'Metaphors of War': Desire, Danger, and Ambivalence in Anne Carson's Poetic Form," *Women's Studies* 43 (2014): 230–245.

17. Anne Carson, *If Not, Winter: Fragments of Sappho*, xiii.

18. Anne Carson, *If Not, Winter: Fragments of Sappho*, x.

19. Carson's locution ("I like to think") is instructive, rendering this aspiration one "she acknowledges as an illusion, perhaps a necessary fantasy or ideal within which the translator labours, but one which can never be fully or finally achieved." See Ben Hjorth, "'We're Standing in the Nick of Time': The Temporality of Translation in Anne Carson's *Antigonick*," *Performance Research* 19.3 (2014): 135–139 (quote at 138).

20. Carson, *If Not, Winter*, xii.

It bears noting that Carson was to do this same thing with her own prose in order to create a novel in verse, *Autobiography of Red*, which I will discuss in detail in the next chapter.

21. Anne Carson, *If Not, Winter: Fragments of Sappho*, xii. The fuller quotation from Benjamin goes as follows:

> Translation thus ultimately serves the purpose of expressing the central reciprocal relationship between languages. . . . Languages are not strangers to one another, but are a priori and apart from all historical relationships, interrelated in what they want to express. . . .

This, to be sure, is to admit that all translation is only a somewhat provisional way of coming to terms with the foreignness of languages. An instant and final rather than temporary and provisional solution of its foreignness remains out of the reach of mankind; at any rate, it eludes any direct attempt. Indirectly however, the growth of religions ripens the hidden seed into a higher development of language. . . .

It is the task of the translator to release in his own language that pure language which is under the spell of another, to liberate the language imprisoned in a work in his re-creation of that work. For the sake of pure language he breaks through decayed barriers of his own language. Luther, Voss, Hölderlin, and George have extended the boundaries of the German language.

Walter Benjamin, "The Task of the Translator" (1923), in *Illuminations: Essays and Reflections*, Hannah Arendt, ed. (New York, NY: Shocken Books, 1968), 69–82. Needless to say, Benjamin's Kabbalistic reference to a "pure language" met with some confusion and consternation, and has been variously interpreted.

22. Anne Carson, *If Not, Winter: Fragments of Sappho*, 342–343.
23. Anne Carson, *If Not, Winter: Fragments of Sappho*, 382.
I think Carson's assertion is overstated. The Pleiades Fragment is included in Fulvio Orsini's 1568 *Carmina Novem Illustrium Feminarum*, 10, J. Christian Wolf's 1733 *Sapphus*, 42–45, as well as David Campbell's 1982 Loeb Edition, *Greek Lyric I*, 172–173.
24. Anne Carson, *If Not, Winter: Fragments of Sappho*, 26–29.
25. Anne Carson, *If Not, Winter: Fragments of Sappho*, 362.
26. The idea that "this dissonance makes Helen who she is" was developed by Ruby Blondell in "Refractions of Homer's Helen in Archaic Lyric," *American Journal of Philology* 131 (2010): 349–391 (with pages 373–387 devoted to Sappho). She offers an even more impressive encyclopedia of such ancient readings in *Helen of Troy: Beauty, Myth, Devastation* (New York, NY: Oxford University Press, 2013), esp. 111–116 on Sappho.
27. Anne Carson, *If Not, Winter: Fragments of Sappho*, 362.
28. Anne Carson, *If Not, Winter: Fragments of Sappho*, 76–77.
29. Anne Carson, *If Not, Winter: Fragments of Sappho*, 365–366.
30. Anne Carson, *If Not, Winter: Fragments of Sappho*, 294–295.
31. See, for example, Chris Mason, "Bright Lyre Becomes Voice: Translating Sappho Into Songs," *The Antioch Review* 67.1 (2009): 109, and Thomas McEvilley, *Sappho* (Putnam, CT: Spring Publications, 2008), 200n17 and 272–273. Several studies on related themes are Barbara Hughes Fowler, "The Archaic Aesthetic," *The American Journal of Philology* 105.2 (1984): 119–149; Bonnie MacLachlan, "What's Crawling in Sappho fr. 130," *Phoenix* 43.2 (1989): 95–99; and Susan Scheinberg, "The Bee Maidens of the Homeric *Hymn to Hermes*," *Harvard Studies in Classical Philology* 83 (1979): 1–28.
32. Anne Carson, *If Not, Winter: Fragments of Sappho*, 379.
33. Anne Carson, *If Not, Winter: Fragments of Sappho*, 214–215.
34. Anne Carson, *If Not, Winter: Fragments of Sappho*, 374.

For more on the Roman-Latin configurations inspired by these fragments, see Theresa M. Krier, "Sappho's Apples: The Allusiveness of Blushes in Ovid and Beaumont," *Comparative Literature Studies* 25.1 (1988): 1–22.

35. Anne Carson, *If Not, Winter: Fragments of Sappho*, 374–375.

36. In this, she may be seen to be participating in a trend that began in earnest in the 1990s. See Lorna Hardwick, *Translating Words, Translating Cultures*, 19–20.

This work was anticipated by an even more ambitious translation effort, led by William Arrowsmith at the University of Texas at Austin in the 1960s, who arranged for the translation of the entirety of the surviving complete Greek tragedies and comedies, all of them designed for stage performance and all of them intended to draw explicit connection to then-contemporary US cultural turmoil with that of Athens during the Peloponnesian War.

37. Anne Carson, *Grief Lessons: Four Plays by Euripides* (New York, NY: New York Review Books, 2005). To my knowledge, at least two of these translations have been staged.

38. Anne Carson, *An Oresteia* (New York, NY: Faber and Faber, Inc., 2009). Carson is quick to add in her "Note from the Translator" that the conceptual idea was not hers, but rather Kulick's. Carson had already translated the *Elektra* in 1987 and the *Orestes* in 2006; Kulick asked for an *Agamemnon* in 2007 with an eye toward fashioning this newer, mingle-mangled, modern Oresteia. Kulick imagined what he called a "non-foundational Oresteia," one that might illuminate what he saw as a *tragicomic* classical movement: "a trajectory from myth to mockery" (x). He also had in mind an historical arc that takes us from Aeschylean dawn, through Sophoclean midday, to Euripidean twilight. Carson was convinced, and the result was staged for the first time Off Broadway at the East 13th Street Theater in April 2009.

39. It also provides Carson with the means to adjust Aeschylus's concern with justice and democracy, by showing how these ideas are complicated when one lifts up the very particular concern for gender also evident in these same plays and underscored by Euripides himself.

See Angela Hume, "The 'Dread Work' of Lyric: Anne Carson's *An Oresteia*," in Joshua Marie Wilkinson, ed., *Anne Carson: Ecstatic Lyre* (Ann Arbor, MI: University of Michigan Press, 2015), 206–213.

40. Anne Carson, trans., *Euripides: Iphigenia Among the Taurians* (Chicago, IL: The University of Chicago Press, 2013).

41. *Bakkhai, Euripides: A New Version by Anne Carson* (London: Oberon Books, 2015).

42. Anne Carson, *Norma Jeane Baker of Troy* (Oberon Books Ltd., 2019).

This volume is not strictly speaking a translation, so much as a wondrously creative adaptation which is among her finest and most subtle. Here Carson uses the competing myths of Helen (to whose Simonidean rendering I will return in the next chapter), together with brilliant overlaying of the mythic figure of Marilyn Monroe, to create a new heroine, Norma Jeane Baker, and thus to stage a powerful reflection on:

> women ("Rape / is the story of Helen. / Persephone, / Norma Jeane, / Troy . . . Truth is, / it's a disaster to be a girl," 11);

war ("War creates two categories of persons: those who outlive it and those who don't. / Both carry wounds," 9, and "basically nine years of cattle raids and pillaging the/ locals . . . / Then, year ten, Achilles wakes up and they take the / town. / Kill all the men, rape all the women, / pack up the boats and sail for home" 17); and

intimacy ("And I thought *Fuck! These humans! / Always finding a way to break each other's hearts!*" 6).

The translational component appears here in seven meditations on Greek words [(*eidôlon* (image), 5, *trauma* (wound), 9, *harpazein* (to take), 13, *douleia* (slavery), 21, *pallakê* (concubine), 25, *apatê* (ruse), 31, *barbaros* (barbarian), 35, *kairos* (opportunity), 39, and *tis* (someone, or who?), 43] take the place of the traditional Greek Chorus, which in this play is assigned to various individuals. The play was commissioned by "The Shed" in Manhattan and performed on April 9, 2019.

43. Anne Carson, trans., *Sophokles: Antigone* (London: Oberon Books, 2015, 2016).
44. Anne Carson, *An Oresteia*, 3–4, 7. She will return to the figure of Kassandra in some of her most provocative recent work, as we will see in the fourth chapter.
45. Anne Carson, *An Oresteia*, 77, 83, citations omitted.
46. Anne Carson, *An Oresteia*, 175–176, 178. See also *Grief Lessons*, 89. But Carson then adds this caveat:

There is another way to read Euripides, which is to forget seriousness and see him as just having a good time in the theater, creating sensation and spectacle, throwing the pieces up in the air and letting them fall. To judge from some sentences in *Poetics*, this was Aristotle's view. Still, Aristotle insists that whatever the ineptitudes of his stagecraft, Euripides is TRAGIKOTATOS, "the most tragic" of the Greek poets. A clown, but a dark clown. A child but terrific.

47. There is a telling Platonic analogy from the Middle Period to consider in this light. After presenting a fairly standard aporetic discussion of justice in Book I of the *Republic*, Socrates announces a new approach to the topic in Book II. Perhaps, he suggests, we have been looking for justice in the soul, where it is too small to be seen clearly. *Since the soul is like a city*, he observes (*Republic* 368e–369a), let us look for justice in the city to see if we can find it there, where it will appear larger. My sense is that Plato's intent (like Carson's) is ironic, since his views about what is actually seeable are not what most scholars who emphasize a "theory of the forms" allege. The *Republic*, in actual fact, puts the issue of proper seeing into question, and therefore radically in doubt, nowhere more clearly than in the so-called Allegory of the Cave.
48. Kazim Ali, "Bringing the House Down: Trojan Horses and Other Malware in Anne Carson's *Grief Lessons: Four Plays by Euripides*," in Joshua Marie Wilkinson, ed., *Anne Carson: Ecstatic Lyre*, 194–199, esp. 194.
49. Anne Carson, *Grief Lessons*, 7.
50. Anne Carson, *Grief Lessons*, 7.
51. Anne Carson, *Grief Lessons*, 8.
52. Anne Carson, *Grief Lessons*, 13–14.

I will have much more to say about myths breaking off, or ending, only to be reborn, in the conclusion.

53. Shakespeare, *King Lear*, IV.i.27–28.
54. Anne Carson, *Grief Lessons*, 90.
55. Shakespeare, *King Lear*, IV.i.36–37.
56. Anne Carson, *Grief Lessons*, 163. It bears noting that an important performance of this translation, directed by David Sachs, was staged at the Getty Villa, August 31-September 23, 2006.
57. Anne Carson, *Grief Lessons*, 168.
58. Anne Carson, *Grief Lessons*, 168.
59. Anne Carson, *Grief Lessons*, 309–311. In the ellipsis, Carson says this:

Phaidra didn't care about you. She didn't care about property. She didn't care about the game. She didn't even really care about Hippolytos—but she cared (was this what you saw?) about the core. Eros itself. She knew this was real. And she knew she would fail it. . . .

The insight may be intended to explain Euripides's self-exile too: "[he] didn't care about you. [He] didn't care about property. [He] didn't care about the game. [He] didn't even really care about Hippolytos—but [he] cared (was this what you saw?) about the core. Eros itself. [He] knew this was real."

60. (Now, again). I conclude without discussing Carson's brilliant rendering of the *Alkestis*, a play impossible to grasp within our current categories: "It is not a satyr play (no satyrs) but neither is it clearly a tragedy or a comedy. Definitions blur" (*Grief Lessons*, 247). The play is as simple as it is strange. Admetus, a man whose name (deriving from the Greek *a-damazô*) suggests that he has never been yoked to necessity of any kind, is informed that he will die unless he finds a surrogate. His parents refuse, causing him weirdly to disown them. His wife agrees to take his place. His overly theatrical expressions of grief are certainly bizarre, given that he has asked her for this. Herakles wrestles her free from (where else?) Hades, and returns her to his hand, requiring Admetus to forego a vow he made that same day not to touch another female hand. There is reconciliation here, but of a rather strange sort. Here is Carson again: "I find that I want to say less rather than more about *Alkestis*. Not because there is less in this play but because the surface has a speed and shine that evaporates with exegesis, like some of Hitchcock's plots. Or a trembling of laughter, terrible if it broke out" (*Grief Lessons*, 249). Carson could easily be describing her own prose here.

For superb insight on the deeper meaning of the *Alkestis*, see William Arrowsmith, trans., *Euripides: Alcestis* (New York, NY: Oxford University Press, 1974), 3–29. I had the pleasure of translating Greek drama with Arrowsmith during my doctoral training, including the *Alkestis*, and I find his insights about the play unparalleled.

61. Anne Carson, trans., *Euripides: Iphigenia among the Taurians*, 4–6.
62. Fuseli's "Lectures on Painting to the Royal Academy in London" were printed in 1848 by the publisher, Henry G. Bohn, in a volume edited by Ralph N. Wornum. Fuseli's verdict on his predecessor demonstrates not only the lack of scholarly charity, but also the self-serving professional meanness, against which Carson has battled throughout her own, quasi-scholarly career:

About the middle of the last century the German critics established at Rome, began to claim the exclusive privilege of teaching the art, and to form a complete system of antique style. The verdicts of Mengs and Winkelmann [sic] became the oracles of antiquaries, dilettanti, and artists from the Pyrenees to the utmost north of Europe, have been detailed, and are not without their influence here. Winkelmann [sic] was the parasite of the fragments that fell from the conversation or the tablets of Mengs, a deep scholar, and better fitted to comment on a classic than to give lessons on art and style: he reasoned himself into frigid reveries and Platonic dreams on beauty.... To him Germany owes the shackles of her artists, and the narrow limits of their aim; from him they have learnt to substitute the means for the end, and, by a hopeless chase after what they call beauty, to lose what alone can make beauty interesting,—expression and mind. (344-345)

63. See George Steiner, *Antigones* (New York, NY: Oxford University Press, 1984), 231–232.

64. Carson produced this extraordinarily ambitious and unconventional adaptation of Sophocles's *Antigone* in 2012, *Antigonick* (New York, NY: New Directions, 2012). The play is very difficult to summarize but the opening lines give something of the larger dramatic idea.

Antigone: We begin in the dark and birth is the death of us

Ismene: Who said that

Antigone: Hegel

Ismene: Sounds more like Beckett

Antigone: He was paraphrasing Hegel

Ismene: I don't think so

Antigone: Whoever it was whoever we are dear sister ever since we were born from the evils of Oidipous what bitterness pain disgust disgrace or moral shock have we been spared and now this edict you've heard the edict

Ismene: I've heard no edict. That our two brothers are dead by one another's hands and the Argive army gone from this city is all I know

(there are also no page numbers in this artfully produced book version).

The play was performed as a stage reading (billed as a "Distinguished Faculty Lecture") at NYU-Gallatin on February 22, 2013, under the direction of Kristin Horton, with Judith Butler in the role of Creon, and Carson herself playing the Chorus.

For a fascinating review of the event, see Mary Maxwell, "Questions & Comments from the Audience," *Arion, Third Series* 21.1 (2013): 175–192. She notes: "Carson the translator has created for herself a kind of no-man's land: In critical terms, classicists go easy on her poetics while most poets don't dare to question her philological credentials" (181).

65. George Steiner was quite critical in his review of *Antigonick*, feeling that Carson's work lacked sufficient reverence for the Sophoclean original; see his "Anne Carson Translates Antigone,' *Times Literary Supplement* (1 August 2012).

Three more sympathetic reviews may be read in Joshua Marie Wilkinson, ed., *Anne Carson: Ecstatic Lyre*: Bianca Stone, "Your Soul is Blowing Apart: *Antigonick* and the Influence of Collaborative Process" (152–155); Andrew Zawacki, "'Standing in / the Nick of Time': *Antigonick* in Seven Short Takes" (156–164); and Vanessa Place, "What's So Funny About *Antigonick*?" (165-171). A more probing analysis, and defense of Carson's effort, may be found in Ben Hjorth, "'We're Standing in the Nick of Time': The Temporality of Translation in Anne Carson's *Antigonick*," *Performance Research* 19.3 (2014): 135–139.

66. The history of this collaboration is nicely laid out by Will Aitken in *Antigone Undone: Juliette Binoche, Anne Carson, Ivo van Hove and the Art of Resistance* (Saskatchewan: University of Regina Press, 2018), 78–95.

67. Anne Carson, trans. *Sophokles: Antigone* (London: Oberon Books Ltd., 2015), 5–8. This paradox of untranslatability (paradoxical because we do in fact continue to translate Greek drama) has been a significant preoccupation in poetical and philosophical circles since the Second World War and especially in the twenty-first century.

Two representative recent discussions may be found in Barbara Cassin, ed., *Vocabulaire européen des philosophies: Dictionnaire des intraduisibles* 26.2 (Paris: Seuil, 2004), and Emily Apter, *Against World Literature: On the Politics of Untranslatability* (London: Verso, 2013).

68. Anne Carson, trans. *Sophokles: Antigone*, 6.

69. Anne Carson, *If Not, Winter: Fragments of Sappho*, 357.

70. Anne Carson, trans. *Sophokles: Antigone*, 23.

Later, the Chorus uses the same word in relation to fate suggesting that, whatever fate is, it is a "strange / terrible / clever / wondrous / monstrous / marvellous / dreadful / awful / weird," power (Carson, *Antigone*, 42).

71. For Hölderlin's version, see *Sophokles: Antigone* (Altenmünster: Jazzybee Verlag and North Charleston, SC: Createspace, 2017).

72. Aitken, *Antigone Undone*, 25, 34, 88–89, 101.

73. *Bakhai: Euripides*, a new version by Anne Carson (London: Oberon Books Ltd., 2015), 5.

74. *Bakhai: Euripides*, 8.

75. *Bakhai: Euripides*, 13.

76. Carson, for her part, appears to reject this idea, insisting on a continuity in her approaches to translation, now spanning four decades. I propose comparing two other equally poetic versions of the passage, for a point of literary reference:

The Bacchae of Euripides, C. K. Williams, trans., with an Introduction by Martha Nussbaum (New York, NY: Farrar Straus and Giroux, 1990):

> When I had taught my dances there, established
> the ritual of my mystery, making
> my divinity manifest to mortals,
> I came to Greece, to Thebes, the first Greek city
> I've caused to shriek in ecstasy for me (4);

and *Euripides Bacchae*, Robin Robertson, trans., with a Preface by Daniel Mendelsohn (New York, NY: HarperCollins Publishers, 2014):

> There I established my rites and mysteries,
> revealed myself as a god. I set all Asia dancing,
> and now I have come to Greece.
> Returned to the place of my first birth:
> come back, here, to Thebes. (2)

77. In this play, the ambiguity hinges centrally on gender performance. When Dionysus convinces Pentheus to dress in drag and to spy upon his Maenads on Mount Kithaeron, we know that Pentheus is doomed.

For a highly critical review of Carson's play with transgender themes in this translation, see Kay Gabriel, "Specters of Dying Empire: The Case of Carson's Bacchae," *Tripwire: A Journal of Poetics* (2018): 315–323.

78. For the Greek text I am using E. R. Dodds, ed., *Euripides Bacchae*, 2nd Edition (Oxford: Clarendon Press, 1960), 4:

τελετάς, ἵν' εἴην ἐμφανὴς δαίμων βροτοῖς.

79. Mark Polizzotti, *Sympathy for the Traitor*, 12.

80. Pliny the Elder (*Natural History*, Book 35.36.79–80) says this of Apelles of Kos (fl. 330 BCE), whom he deemed the finest of all painters up to his own day: "He knew how to take his hand away from a picture." In fact, *manum de tabula* became a Latin truism, meaning "it is enough."

81. See Abraham Wasserstein and David J. Wasserstein, *The Legend of the Septuagint: From Classical Antiquity to Today* (New York, NY: Cambridge University Press, 2006).

Chapter 3

Poetry, Madness and Markets, or, The Ancients and the Moderns

I must say it's a false story (*etymos logos*) that would suggest that a non-lover should be given preference over a lover, since the lover is mad (*mainetai*) and the non-lover is moderate (*sôphronei*). If madness (*to manian*) were bad (*kakon*), pure and simple, then this would be well said. And yet the greatest of goods come to us through madness (*dia manias*), when it is given as a divine gift.

—Plato, *Phaedrus* 244a

If prose is a house, poetry is a man on fire running quite fast through it.

—Anne Carson, interview with Kate Kelleway (*The Guardian*, 2016)

* * * * *

In *Eros the Bittersweet*, we encountered a classical scholar who was also a self-styled philosopher, a winsome translator, and a gifted poet. I have explored the implications of Carson's philosophical and translational musings on reach and grasp at some length in the previous two chapters. In this chapter, I turn to her own wide-ranging and fast-running poetic practices.

As her translator, the first thing that Carson observes about Sappho is that she was a *musician*.

> Her poetry is lyric, that is, composed to be sung to the lyre. She addresses her lyre in one of her poems (fr. 118) and frequently mentions music, songs and singing. Ancient vase painters depict her with her instrument. Later writers ascribe to her three musical inventions. . . . All Sappho's music is lost.[1]

The second thing that Carson says about her is that Sappho was a *poet*.

> There is a fifth century *hydria* in the National Museum of Athens that depicts Sappho, identified by name, reading from a papyrus. This is an ideal image; whether or not she herself was literate is unknown. But it seems likely that the words to her songs were written down during or soon after her lifetime and existed on papyrus rolls by the end of the fifth century B.C. . . . Of the nine books of lyrics that Sappho is said to have composed, one poem has survived complete. All the rest are fragments.[2]

That a poet should be musical may seem a commonplace in ancient Greek; the Muses are the goddesses of artistic inspiration after all: one of them, Euterpe, was dedicated specifically to flutes and lyric poetry; and another, Erato, was dedicated exclusively to erotic verse. The combination of the two—the lyricism, sheer musicality and eroticism of Carson's own poetry—will preoccupy me in this chapter. But here once again, given my preoccupation with the classical re-readings lying at the heart of Carson's oeuvre, I will approach her poetry, as she does, from an oblique angle.

On the face of it, Carson's poetic production may seem the least "classical" portion of her corpus. She appears to gesture in her own poems to more modern poetic influences, especially the Romantic influences, such as Keats and Shelley (especially evident in *The Beauty of the Husband*), the Brönte sisters (major figures in "The Glass Essay"), Hölderlin, and even Wordsworth. To be sure, each of these Romantic authors was classically informed, deeply so. Thus their literary formation contributes to Carson's own. Yet Carson plumbs more deeply, recognizing that these Romantic poets, wrenching in their poignancy and self-disclosure, participate in a lyric-erotic tradition with ancient Greek roots and a particularly intimate relation to Sappho's lyrics. The central question, as Carson made clear in her first book, is how to render the erotic loss of self as something other than lyric death or poetic dissolution.

There is one classical genre that is rarely attempted these days: epic poetry. Arguably the most singular exception to this apparent modernist rule[3] is the late Derek Walcott's (1930–2017) rhythmed verse epic, *Omeros*,[4] setting the vast Homeric world in a small contemporary Caribbean fishing village, and then situating that place within a post-colonial history of mingled imperial and interpersonal griefs and triumphs. The poem is breathtakingly beautiful and unbearably sad, both in its humane cadence and its vast humanistic ambition.[5]

Anne Carson ventured something similar in the later 1990s, conceiving a classically inspired novel in verse,[6] a prose-poetic hybrid[7] entitled *Autobiography of Red*.[8] Whether Walcott was an inspiration for this venture is uncertain.[9] Nevertheless, this book represents one of Carson's most extensive poetic interrogations of Greek mythology, specifically the mythic cycle of Herakles and Geryon as related in some surviving fragments of the Archaic Greek poet, Stesichorus (c630-c555 BCE), who was Sappho's rough contemporary.

Stesichorus is one of the many elusive, quasi-historical figures whom Carson finds so fascinating, some stories and fragments of whose we have inherited from the spotty remains of the Greek lyric tradition. He is remembered as one of the earliest representatives of that mysterious period in Greek history we call Archaic—a complex period in which mainland Greek cities extensively colonized in southern Italy and Sicily (that is, in *Magna Graecia*), as well as throughout Asia Minor and the Black Sea. Sappho came from one end of that expansive Greek world (Lesbos) and Stesichorus from the other (Sicily).

The Greek arts were changing in this period, too. Doric temple architecture erupted at Syracuse and rapidly became a panhellenic canon of architecture.[10] The tradition of three-dimensional statues in carved and often painted marble was coming into its own. Greek poetic traditions were evolving even more dramatically in this period: from epic, to the lyric and erotic verses at which Sappho excelled. We have already seen how Sappho playfully exploited the heroic traditions embodied in the Homeric poems, to do far more personal work in her own lyrics. If others think infantry, or cavalry, or naval fleets, represent the most beautiful sight on the dark earth, then Sappho prefers the beauty of the beloved. A number of other poets came to be associated with that same preference.

An interesting collection of general information about Stesichorus may be found in the *Suda*, a Byzantine encyclopedia which represents an exhaustive compilation of varying literary traditions as they had evolved in the later Roman period.[11] One of the many fascinations of the *Suda* is the way it gathers various contradictory stories together, without rendering a final judgment as to their comparative validity.[12] The *Suda* lists five possible names of Stesichorus's father (Euphorbus, Euphemus, Eucleides, Hyetes, and Hesiod) and two possible homelands (Himera on Sicily and Matauria in southern Italy).[13] But it dates the poet with great specificity, noting that he was born in the 37th Olympiad (632–629 BCE) and died in the 56th (556–553 BCE).[14] The *Suda* also recalls Stesichorus as a lyric poet (*lyrikos*), whose work was compiled in twenty-six books, all of it written in the Doric dialect. Finally, the *Suda* claims that his original name was Teisias, but that he was re-named due to his formative role in creating lyric poetry designed for choral performance that he himself set to music:

> ἐκλήθη δὲ Στησίχορος ὅτι πρῶτος κιθαρῳδίας χορὸν ἔστησεν.
> ---

> eklêthê de Stêsichoros hoti prôtos kitharôidias choron estêsen.
> ---
> He was called Stesichorus because he was the first to set up (*estesen*) a chorus (*choron*) of singers for the lyre (*kitharôidias*).

One of the most interesting stories rehearsed about Stesichorus's poetic production is one to which Plato refers in the *Phaedrus*: namely, his Palinode, the famous "retraction" he was forced to make regarding a poem in which he reviled Helen for creating all the carnage at Troy. Helen, now divinized, blinded him for this poetic libel and, when the poet realized what had happened, he wrote some new verses (literally a "now-again song"), in which he reversed himself, and his judgment on Helen.

The same story is related by Horace,[15] by Zonaras,[16] and by Aelius Aristides,[17] but only Plato quotes the substance of the new verses (at *Phaedrus* 243a)[18]:

> That story (*logos*) is not right (*etymos*):
> You did not board the well-benched ships,
> You did not go to the towers of Troy (*pergama Troias*).[19]

The story is interesting for many reasons, but one should be underscored here. Stesichorus has been remembered as a poet who stands in an uneasy relationship to the Homeric tradition. He is rewriting Homeric myths in a new and different verse idiolect, creating new war music as it were. Anne Carson considers this the literate and literary revolution that gave birth to lyric and erotic poetry, first with Archilochus, and then far more artfully in Sappho.[20]

Stesichorus also lived on the edge of that same sea-change. Antipater of Thessaloniki, in the *Palatine Anthology*,[21] notes that Pythagoras (another native son from *Magna Graecia* who subscribed to belief in the reincarnation of the human soul) believed that Homer's soul "found a second home" (*deuteron ôikisato*) in Stesichorus's chest. Longinus links Herodotus, Stesichorus, Archilochus, and Plato together in "that Homeric stream" (*Homerikou keinou namatos*).[22] And Quintilian recalls that Stesichorus sang on the large themes of wars and heroes "with great clarity and beauty, sustaining the weight of epic poetry with a lyre."[23] He was, in short, remembered as one of the first and the very finest of Greek lyric poets. The *Suda* associates him in various places with rough contemporaries like Alcaeus, Pittacus, Sappho, and Simonides (Carson will have much more to say about this last poet on the list, as we will see later in this chapter). Dionysus of Halicarnassus describes the emerging lyric traditions in this way: Alcaeus and Sappho wrote in short stanzas (*mikras strophes*) whereas Stesichorus and Pindar made their verses longer (*meizous ergasamenoi*) and in a variety of meters (*polla metra*).[24]

The situation is similar to the one Carson faced first in translating Sappho, and then later in trying to reconstruct Euripides's first play about Phaedra and Hippolytos: we have a few fragments of various lengths, and tantalizing later discussions of them among literary critics and philosophers. In this instance, we possess some 325 fragments which are likely ascribable to Stesichorus; the vast majority of them are too short to be of much use.[25] Most are believed to belong to thirteen quasi-epic verse cycles he composed, including: The Funeral Games of Pelias, Tales of Geryon, Helen (and the *Palinode*), Eriphyle, Europeta, Thebais, The Sack of Troy, Cerberus, Cycnus, The Homecomings, The Oresteia, Scylla, and The Boarhunters. Carson is specifically interested in the *Tales of Geryon*, of which we possess roughly seventy-eight fragments,[26] twenty-six of which are legible enough to be suggestive.[27]

Our knowledge of the myth of Geryon and Herakles is due primarily to a brief mention in Hesiod, a longer one in Apollodorus, and a number of vase paintings whose find-sites span the entire eastern Greek Mediterranean. It bears noting that the context of Greek colonization is crucial for understanding the role played by Herakles in Greek mythology, especially in southern Italy and Sicily. Unlike most Greek heroes, Herakles was a wanderer, a wanderer who killed monsters and wild animals more often than men. He serves as the originary Greek defender of order who pushed chaos to the margins so that Greek civilization could flourish and later extend its borders across the entire Mediterranean world.[28]

Geryon, then, was a monster, a signature of chaos: a strange figure with three heads, wings and a tail; later renderings like Stesichorus's give him three bodies, six arms and six legs as well (an image that is weirdly echoed by Aristophanes's myth of originally paired, titanic human beings in Plato's *Symposium*). Hesiod reports Geryon's pedigree, and his death at Herakles's hands, though he seems somewhat unclear as to whether Geryon was a monster or a man:

> Chrysaor then lay with Kallirhoe, daughter of glorious Okeanos,
> and sired the three-headed Geryones
> whom the might of Herakles slew
> beside his shambling oxen at sea-girt Erytheia
> on the very day he crossed Ocean's stream
> and drove broad-browed cattle to holy Tiryns.
> Then he also slew Orthos and the oxherd Eurytion
> out at that misty place, beyond glorious Ocean. . . .
> (*Theogony* 287–294)

And again:

> Kallirhoe, Ocean's daughter, spell-bound by golden Aphrodite,

> coupled in love with stout-hearted Chrysaor
> and bore a son surpassing all men in strength,
> Geryones, whom brawny Herakles slew
> in sea-stroked Erytheia, to win the ambling oxen.
> (*Theogony* 979–983)[29]

Apollodorus discusses this story at greater length in prose:

> In respect of the 10th labor, he [Herakles] was ordered to bring the kine of Geryon from Erytheia. Erytheia was an island lying near to Okeanos, which is now called Gadeira. Geryon, son of Chrysaor and Kallirhoe, daughter of Okeanos, inhabited this island. He had the body of three men grown together, and joined into one at the waist, these were divided into three from the flanks and thighs. He had red kine, of which Eurytion was the herdsman, Orthos was the guard-dog, a twin-headed hound, begotten by Typhon on Echidna. And so he [Herakles] journeying through Europe in quest of the cattle of Geryon and destroying many wild beasts, set foot in Libya, proceeding to the Tartessos and erecting [as] tokens, two pillars constructed in opposing rows over the boundaries of Europe and Libya. But being hated by Helios on his journey, he [Herakles] bent his bow at the god. And he [Helios] marveled at his boldness and gave him a golden cup, in which he crossed Okeanos. Arriving in Erytheia he camped on Mount Abas. But the hound, perceiving him, rushed towards him; but he [Herakles] smote this beast with a club and killed the herdsman, Eurytion, [when] helping the hounds. Menoites, pasturing the kine of Hades there, reported what happened to Geryon. And he [Geryon] checking Herakles beside the river Anthemos [as] he was leading off the herd, joined battle with him and he [Geryon] died being shot. And Herakles, having put the herd into the cup, sailed across to the Tartessos, and returned the cup to Helios.[30]

In the surviving fragments of Stesichorus, it appears that he preserved the accounts of the killing of Geryon by Herakles, and of Herakles's subsequent return of the Sun-cauldron. But Stesichorus also appears to have made Geryon more sympathetic—much as Hektor, and Helen, were made to be by Homer. Consider this stunning simile among the longer fragments which survive:

> and the arrow went straight into the crown of his head, and his armor and gory limbs were stained with blood; and Geryon tilted his head like a poppy when spoiling its gentle body suddenly drops its petals . . .[31]

This should remind us of Sappho's Fragment 105B, where a flower, trampled by violent men, bleeds its colors sadly into the earth. This echo of a Sapphic stanza, utilized in a delicately eroticized image of death, may also provide a clue as to what Carson has seen in the Geryon myth, and how she has elected to exploit it in a quasi-epic poem of her own design.

Imagining the two mythic heroes as a gay couple,[32] Carson returns to some of the deepest insights from her first book, utilizing this novelistic poem as a way to illustrate points made in a more philosophical idiom there. Here she will show us, rather than tell us, about the agony of erotic possession. Carson subtly suggests that the couple's sexual identity is not nearly as significant, from a poetic point of view, as the intense vulnerability, the shattering psychic agony, of desire itself. That the book is a novel in verse is fitting—blurred genres, once again.

We meet Geryon first as an extremely sensitive young boy of kindergarten age, one who is comforted and comprehended deeply by his mother, but tormented and sexually exploited by an older brother subject to inexplicable bouts of heedless cruelty. If his body seems monstrous, then the situations in which Geryon finds himself are more monstrous by far. Like many sensitive children, Geryon withdraws inward, and finds a peace there unavailable to him in the outside world.

> and he thought about the difference
> between outside and inside.
> Inside is mine, he thought. The next day Geryon and his brother
> went to the beach. . . .
> That was also the day
> he began his autobiography. In this work Geryon set down all inside
> things
> particularly his own heroism
> and early death much to the despair of the community. He coolly
> omitted
> all outside things.[33]

Of course, the boy cannot write yet, so his creative inner work takes the form of impromptu sculpture made from pieces of found art. But when he learns literacy he, much like the Archaic Greek poets who discovered the power of vowels, changes his tune.

> His mother's friend Maria gave him a beautiful notebook from
> Japan with a fluorescent cover.
> On the cover Geryon wrote *Autobiography*. Inside he set down the
> facts.
>
> > *Total Facts Known About Geryon.*
> > *Geryon was a monster everything about him was red. Geryon*
> > *lived on an island in the Atlantic called the Red Place.*
> > *Geryon's mother was a river that runs to the sea the Red Joy*
> > *River Geryon's father was gold. Some say Geryon had six*

> hands six feet some say wings. Geryon was red so were his
> strange red cattle. Herakles came one day killed Geryon got
> the cattle.

He followed Facts with Questions and Answers

QUESTIONS *Why did Herakles kill Geryon?*
1. Just violent.
2. Had to it was one of His Labors (10th).
3. Got the idea that Geryon was Death otherwise he could live forever.

FINALLY
Geryon had a little red dog Herakles killed that too.

Where does he get his ideas, said the teacher. It was Parent-Teacher Day at school.
They were sitting side by side in tiny desks.
Geryon watched his mother pick a fragment of tobacco off her tongue before she said,
Does he ever write anything with a happy ending?
Geryon paused.
Then he reached up and carefully disengaged the composition paper from the teacher's hand.
Proceeding to the back of the classroom he sat at his usual desk and took out a pencil.

> *New Ending.*
> *All over the world the beautiful red breezes went on blowing hand in hand.*[34]

Where he has learned these things we do not know, but it is as if he is rewriting his own Greek myth, drawing out the contours of his own scripted identity, or destiny. There is more to say about this quasi-Euripidean rewriting of Herakles's myth, though there is that, too.

By the time he reaches adolescence, Geryon has landed upon photography as his preferred autobiographical medium.[35] He meets Herakles by accident at 3:00am in a bus station (evidently, his mother permits a great deal of her son's insomniac wandering); he is fourteen and Herakles sixteen. It is not long before Herakles convinces Geryon to take a trip with him to the other end of the island of Hawai'i—to see his hometown, to meet his grandmother, and to see a volcano up close ("a healthy volcano is an exercise in the uses of pressure"[36]).

> Herakles' hometown of Hades
> lay at the other end of the island about four hours by car, a town
> of moderate size and little importance
> except for one thing. *Have you ever seen a volcano?* said Herakles.
> Staring at him Geryon felt his soul
> move in his side. Then Geryon wrote a note full of lies for his mother
> and stuck it on the fridge.[37]

The soul moving in his side is driven by eros, of course, and playing on one of the most moving images from Plato's *Phaedrus*, Carson notes that Geryon has now lost control of his own wings.

> These days Geryon was experiencing a pain not felt since childhood.
>
> ———
>
> His wings were struggling. They tore against each other on his shoulders
> like the little mindless red animals they were.
> With a piece of wooden plank he'd found in the basement Geryon
> made a back brace
> and lashed the wings tight.
> Then he put his jacket back on. *You seem moody today Geryon anything wrong?*[38]

As the two men explore their newfound sexual symmetries, Geryon feels a new sense of power, which is tragically fleeting, of course. This idyllic phase of raw adolescent passion cannot last; eros's sweetness swiftly turns bitter. Geryon's mother tracks the boys down and demands that Geryon return home. Unexpectedly, Herakles hands him a bus schedule, opting to stay behind with his grandmother.

> *Freedom is what I want for you Geryon we're true friends you know that's why*
> *I want you to be free.*
> Don't want to be free want to be with you. Beaten but alert Geryon organized all
> his inside force to suppress this remark.[39]

Herakles's desire for freedom clearly tells us more about his own desire, not Geryon's.

And so "Geryon's life entered a numb time, caught between the tongue and the taste."[40] That is to say, he has been assaulted by Kafka's raw erotic lesson, the terrible tension between reaching and grasping, between desiring and having or holding. Even the magical period of transition from sleep to waking, which he had always loved before now, is disturbed.

> It was raining on his face. He forgot for a moment that he was a brokenheart
> then he remembered. Sick lurch
> downward to Geryon trapped in his own bad apple. Each morning a shock
> to return to the cut soul.[41]

Years pass, and Geryon moves from grief and heartbreak, through anger, to departure (or perhaps flight). He moves to Buenos Aires at the age of twenty-two, consumed by two questions: "How people get power over one another/ this mystery"; and time, "which was squeezing Geryon like the pleats of an accordion."[42] He studies German philosophy for three years (mostly Heidegger, on moods[43]), but this course of study proves of little help.

> It was not the fear of ridicule
> to which everyday life as a winged red person had accommodated
> Geryon early in life,
> but this blank desertion of his own mind
> that threw him into despair.[44]

And then he accidentally bumps into Herakles again: another random bus station; another accident of fortune inclining toward fate.

Herakles is traveling with a friend named Ancash, a Quechua-speaking native of Peru and "a man as beautiful as a live feather."[45] They are traveling around the world taping and filming volcanoes for a documentary. . . . on Emily Dickinson, of all people. Geryon, still exercised by the question of what time is made of, will experience new aesthetic difficulties in trying to fit this image of a newer, older Herakles onto the one he had known and grieved.[46] Drawn to Ancash's beauty as well as Herakles's now, Geryon accepts the two men's invitation to join them on a trip to Lima to visit Ancash's mother, then make a trip to another volcano at Huaraz. Time is circling back (now, again); Geryon has made this trip before.

On the plane to Lima, seated between the two men, and with Ancash sound asleep, Herakles returns to his body.

> The smell of the leather jacket near
> his face and the hard pressure of Herakles'
> arm under the leather sent a wave of longing as strong as a color through Geryon.
> It exploded at the bottom of his belly.

> Then the blanket shifted. He felt Herakles' hand move on his thigh
> and Geryon's
> head went back like a poppy in a breeze
> as Herakles' mouth came down on his and blackness sank through
> him.[47]

This stunningly beautiful rendition of a fragment from Stesichorus raises many questions. Why is this kiss the beginning of the end? If eros is like death, a radical loss of self, then is Herakles killing Geryon with a kiss? That seems to be the case, as far as it goes. But we are dealing here with an arrow through the heart, not the head. Carson is exploring the same issues which she has already investigated in philosophical prose, but now in epic verse. What is emptying Geryon is not Herakles, nor his love for Herakles; it is a new triangle that has emerged through the mysterious presence and pressure of Ancash. Carson has told us all about this, too—or rather, she showed us the ways in which Sappho has.

The point of the triangle, we will recall, is not the three persons who constitute the points; it is the empty space defined by their geographical relation. It is a hole that only eros may reveal.

> Even when they were lovers
> he had never known what Herakles was thinking. Once in a while
> he would say
> *Penny for your thoughts!*
> and it always turned out to be some odd thing like a bumper sticker
> or a dish
> he'd eaten in a Chinese restaurant years ago.
> What Geryon was thinking Herakles never asked. In the space
> between them
> developed a dangerous cloud.
> Geryon knew he must not go back into that cloud. Desire is no light
> thing.[48]

It is Ancash, the mysterious third point of this triangle with a distinctive third point-of-view, who will provide the pivot to this dramatic poem. When he sees Geryon's wings for the first time, he alone has the means to see them as something other than monstrous. Ancash recognizes Geryon as a *Yazcol Yazcamac*:

> it means
> the Ones Who Went and Saw and Came Back–
> *I think the anthropologists say* eyewitnesses. *These people did exist.*
> *Stories are told of them still.*

> *Eyewitnesses*, said Geryon.
> Yes. People who saw the inside of the volcano.
> And came back.
> Yes.
> How do they come back?
> Wings.
> Wings? Yes that's what they say the Yazcamac return as red people with wings,
> all their weakness burned away—
> and their mortality.[49]

When Ancash learns that Geryon has returned to Herakles's bed, he strikes Geryon to the ground, then relents as grief replaces rage, asking him if he still loves Herakles. Tellingly, Geryon does not know. If he does not know what time, or dreams, are made of, then he certainly cannot know what to make of his memories (other than a photographic essay). Ancash rises to leave, then pauses; there is one thing he wants from Geryon: "*Want to see you use those wings.*"[50]

Geryon does so, for Ancash. And thus it is Ancash who has ironically enabled him to fly. Late that evening, he takes Ancash's tape recorder, together with his own camera, and records the secret at the heart of the volcano of Icchantikas, marrying sound to sight at last.

The next day, the three men are quarreling. It is not jealousy exactly, but something deeper, the differentness of different souls, perhaps. Such things can happen to intimate travelers, and especially to travelers who are intimate. They visit one of the mysteries of this mountain village: open crevices through which you can look inside the volcano. Bakers use these vents as ovens.

> *Do you see that*, says Ancash.
> *Beautiful*, Herakles breathes out. He is looking at the men.
> *I mean the fire*, says Ancash.
> Herakles grins in the dark. Ancash watches the flames.
> We are amazing beings,
> Geryon is thinking. We are neighbors of fire.
> And now time is rushing towards them
> where they stand side by side with arms touching, immortality in their faces,
> night at their back.[51]

A happy ending? Perhaps. A new ending, certainly. That is what talented and non-conforming poets do with old myths, after all. Euripides did that; so does Anne Carson. "This text is trickier, more subversive, more deeply parodic of scholarly authority and readerly and critical passivity than most reviewers and critics yet acknowledge."[52] All we know with certainty is that this ending serves as the somatic confirmation of Geryon's poetic premonition at the ripening age of seven: *"New Ending. / All over the world the beautiful red breezes went on blowing hand / in hand."*[53] Geryon had already re-written his own myth.

* * * * *

This idea, that poets do new things with old myths, is especially important to the Greek lyric tradition with which Carson most clearly identifies.[54] We have seen Sappho artfully re-write Homeric mythology. We have learned that Stesichorus was blinded for doing the same thing, until he composed his Palinode. There are a great many other figures in the Archaic lyric tradition—all of them fragmentary, all of them mythically creative—with whom Carson has engaged creatively over the years.[55]

Cicero reports that Stesichorus died on the same day that another important lyric poet, Simonides, was born.[56] We know as little about the latter poet as we do the former; everything is left to us in fragmentary papyri, or else through often contradictory ancient testimonia, and quotations by other authors. Yet out of these fragments Carson has been so bold as to construct a persona. She did it with Sappho; she did it with Geryon. And she does it again with Simonides.

Autobiography of Red is not only a unique book, generically speaking, but it is also a unique hybrid: one part the translation of Stesichorus's Greek fragments; and one part the creative adaptation of a supremely gifted English language poet. In a closer study of Carson's Sappho translations in the last chapter, I noted the paradoxical attempts she identifies to keep herself out of the fragments, to render them more transparent, coupled with the felt need to supplement the fragments, the creative adaptations and intrusions necessary to make them more fully meaningful. It may be that the Greek lyric poets, every one of them fragmentary and piecemeal, provide the particular occasion for these kinds of paradoxical and lyrical encounter.

As she turned her attention to Simonides and his poetic legacy, Carson crafted a brief "Note on Method," one which deepened her thinking about this problem. First, she returned to the question of transparency.

> There is too much self in my writing. Do you know the term Lukács uses to describe aesthetic structure? *Eine fensterlose Monade*. I do not want to be a windowless monad—my training and trainers [i.e., classicists and philosophers] opposed subjectivity strongly, I have struggled since the beginning to drive my

thought out into the landscape of science and fact where other people converse logically and exchange judgments—but I go blind out there. So writing involves some dashing back and forth between the darkening landscape where facticity is strewn and a windowless room cleared of everything I do not know. It is the clearing that takes time. It is the clearing that is a mystery.

> Once cleared the room writes itself. I copy down the names of everything left in it and note their activity.

> How does the clearing occur? Lukács says it begins with my intent to excise everything that is not accessible to the immediate experience (*Erlebbarkeit*) of the self as self. Were this possible, it would seal the room on its own boundaries like a cosmos. Lukács is prescribing a room for aesthetic work; it would be a gesture of false consciousness to say academic writing can take place there. And yet, you know as well as I, thought finds itself in this room in its best moments—[57]

And so, with transparency become either a false idol or merely a stultifying scholarly approach to writing that should aim to be more lyrical, Carson strives to find a different method to generate truly creative poetic work. She lands here on the method of *comparisons*, fashioning another kind of hybridity in the process:

Attention is a task we share, you and I. To keep attention strong means to keep it from settling. Partly for this reason I have chosen to talk about two men at once. They keep each other from settling. Moving and not settling, they are side by side in a conversation and yet no conversation takes place. Face to face, yet they do not know one another, did not live in the same era, never spoke the same language. With and against, aligned and adverse, each is placed like a surface on which the other may come into focus. Sometimes you can see a celestial object better by looking at something else, with it, in the sky.[58]

In this particular case, Carson proposes to compare Simonides of Keos (556–468 BCE) and Paul Celan (1920–1970).[59] I think it fair to say that, for Carson, Simonides is the celestial object whom Paul Celan will help her see better, though she weaves the two poets together in an artful and seamless presentation that positively glitters with galactic insight. Carson has audaciously proposed to look at two poets, one writing in ancient Greek and one in modern German, and to render them both legible in English—no mean feat, no matter how fine the poet. In this proposition, she is constructing another poetic/erotic triangle.

Carson's comparative attentions reveal three moments of stunning insight borne of such close literary attention; they involve two of Simonides's fragments, and one testimonial about him. The fragments are these:

> ὁ λόγος τῶν πραγμάτων εἰκών ἐστιν
> ---
> *ho logos tôn pragmatôn eikôn estin.*
> ---
> The word is a picture of things.

and again

> θανάτῳ πάντες ὀφειλόμεθα
> ---
> *thanatôi pantes opheilometha*
> ---
> We are all debts owed to Death.[60]

I will turn to what Carson has to say about both of these aphoristic observations shortly. But first, I would like to turn to the testimonial. The story is that Simonides was the very first Greek lyric poet to receive money for his work, the first poet-for-hire, as it were.[61] How to hold these three ideas together in the same lyric sky?

Simonides had become a stock comic character of the miser by the fourth century BCE in Athens. Aristotle used him as an exemplum of "miserliness" in the *Nicomachean Ethics*[62] and in the *Rhetoric*[63]; the word he uses is *aneleutheria* (ἀνελευθερία), literally "un-free-ness."[64] We have thus been placed on notice that Anne Carson, the poet-philosopher, will be exploring the strange semantic field that links art, to politics, to economics.[65] We may refer to things, not just people, as "free." Liquidity accounts for cash as well as character.

Carson suggests that Simonides lived in and between two incompatible worlds, in a time of seismic transition in the eastern Mediterranean: from the heroic world of the Homeric poems, with their gift-and-patronage exchange systems, to a monied economy in the colonies of Greater Greece. This is as significant to understanding Simonides's poetry as the invention of writing was to Archilochus's.[66] Carson tells us that, according to Herodotus, coins were invented in Lydia around 700 BCE.[67] By the 550s, both Athens and Corinth had entered the monied economy in dramatic fashion, minting the silver coins that were to make them legendary.[68] Simonides traveled the length and breadth of the Greek-speaking world in search of this new coinage. And he *thought* about money, about its symbolic value as well as its exchange value.[69] Coins were given in trade for ephemera as well as for things: for words, for poetry, and the like.

> You cannot eat money. You can, on the other hand, sell food. In fact you can sell anything. Marx called this fact "commodity form" and believed it to

characterize the life of all objects in a money economy. "Selling is the practice of alienation," he says, "and the commodity is its expression."[70]

Marx, in fact, will serve as the ironic modern mediator between the poetry of Simonides and Celan in Carson's comparative study.

> It is often said that money is like language. Marx thought this comparison weak. . . . Marx suggests an alternate model: money is not like language but is like *translated* language. "Ideas which have first to be translated out of their mother tongue into a foreign (*fremde*) language in order circulate, in order to become exchangeable, offer a somewhat better analogy. So the analogy lies not in language but in the foreign quality or strangeness (*Fremdheit*) of language."
>
> This simple striking notion, that money makes our daily life strange in the same way translation makes ordinary language strange, seems a helpful one for exploring the *Fremdheit* of Paul Celan. We have already seen how Simonides' alienation began with his historical situation. . . . He is analogous to Paul Celan, after the model suggested by Marx, insofar as Celan is a poet who uses language *as if he were always translating*.[71]

If money is a translator's medium (and a very strange one, at that), then the question of how to inhabit the world it creates (the coin of the realm[72]) becomes poetically paramount.

Simonides was attempting to translate between two worlds: between gifts and cold cash, between poets and their patrons, and he did so in the name of a new idea, *the poetic vocation*. Paul Celan also had a poetic vocation, one built upon the ash-heap of the Second World War: to bring dead and death-dealing language back to life, after Nazism and the Shoah. His long-awaited visits with Martin Buber and Martin Heidegger disappointed him; neither scholar could help him articulate the texture of his own postwar linguistic vocation, his desire to shake the (German) language awake.[73] What had put it to sleep, or rather into coma, was the enormity of millions of human bodies turned to ash, the scale of physical suffering and trauma which can seem to make language break under the strain. Death is a bodily fact. Death under torture or worse transforms human beings into things. How can poetry provide an image of such a thing?

What Simonides and Celan share most fundamentally, according to Carson, is an acute sense of loss, of literal and bodily negation.

> Words like "no," "not," "never," "nowhere," "nobody," "nothing" dominate their poems and create bottomless places for reading. Not white but red. Was it not Aristotle who said, "A mistake enriches the mere truth once you see it as that." Both Simonides and Celan are poets who see it as that. And ask us to see it as that.[74]

When Paul Celan used a curious double-negation in 1958 ("reachable, near and unlost amid the losses"[75]) as a description of his own understanding of language (*die Sprache*), then we see the deeper implication of Carson's title: "Economy of the Unlost" may also be translated as "Economy of Language." This is yet another twist or play of language, the first of many plays on words Carson will unveil as her lyrical comparisons proceed. Why do we speak of price-less things, or things that are not for sale, as "free"? Why is the Greek word for the gift (*charis*) also the Christian word for grace? When and how can a gift ever be truly free? Carson's tentative answer appears to be: *in poetry*. And perhaps in the fine arts or religion more generally.

Turning now to the two Simonidean fragments quoted above, I wish to highlight what these painstaking comparative insights have enabled Carson to see with astonishing clarity.

> Simonides is Western culture's original literary critic, for he is the first person in our extant tradition to theorize about the nature and function of poetry. The central dictum of his literary critical theory is well known, much celebrated and little understood. "Simonides says that painting is silent poetry while poetry is painting that talks," Plutarch tells us. What did the poet mean? Why did Simonides choose to inaugurate literary criticism by setting his own verbal art against the ground of painting?
>
> It is true he was a most painterly poet, using proportionately more color words than any writer of his time and congratulated by Longinus for his pictorial power (εἰδωλοποίησε). His poems are well described as miniature canvases where each word is as meticulously placed as a brushstroke. In real life he seems to have enjoyed the society and patronage of painters. . . .[76]

Hence the aphoristic genius of the line: "the word (*logos*) is a picture (*eikôn*) of things (*pragmatôn*)." It proposes a paradoxical linkage of what should presumably be kept apart[77]: the visual and the textual; the picture and the word.

> True to itself, the statement does what it says. It shows us λόγος and εἰκών poised on either side of the world of τῶν πραγμάτων in a syntactic tension that precisely pictures their ontology. "Things," in the genitive case, depend for their meaning on "word" and "picture" at once: both nominatives vie for the attention of the genitive πραγμάτων, which is placed to read in either direction and unite all three words like the hinge of a backsprung bow. . . . When we consider Simonidean sentences, we see appearances engaged in a dialectic with one another, by participation of λόγος and εἰκών at once. We overhear a conversation that sounds like reality. No other Greek writer of the period, except perhaps Heraklitos, uses the sentence in this way, as a "synthetic and tensional" unit that enacts the reality of which it speaks. This is mimesis in its most radical mechanism. This is the bone structure of poetic deception.[78]

According to Carson, Simonides lived in a world where poets and painters received money for their art. So what did the buyer think he or she was getting for the money? The above discussion suggests that they were getting a slice of reality, a picture of reality painted from an unexpected angle. Painters in Simonides's generation discovered modes of perspectival rendering that made the painting seem more real, more alive. The rich array of colors on Simonides's poetic palette helped his poems come alive, too (we might well say the same thing for Sappho's). The point is that, as the social status of the artist grew in this new, for-hire economy, the Greek-speaking world was buying in to a new way of looking at reality, one in which the creative role of human beings—their words, and their pictures—provided the essential mediating and depictive role. Inanimate things are brought to life by artistic people and their arts. Creation is our common, sacred labor.

And yet these same people are mortal. "We are all debts owed to Death." Hence the creation of another for-hire genre at which Simonides allegedly excelled: *the epitaph*.

> No genre of verse is more profoundly concerned with seeing what is not there, and not seeing what is, than that of the epitaph. An epitaph is something placed upon a grave—a σῶμα that becomes a σῆμα, a body that is made into a sign. . . . Simonides was the most prolific composer of epitaphs in the ancient world and set the conventions of the genre. The formal sale of pity contributed substantially to his fame and became inseparable from his name. . . . What did they get for their money, the mourners who bought tears from Simonides?[79]

At one level, the epitaphic poet is a conjuror, one who calls back to life a being who is gone, or in Carson's chosen parlance, *lost*. If paid for the conjuring, such a poet participates in the "economy off the unlost," an economy of language. A creator who is one part poet and one part painter, Simonides marked the grave with an image of (lost) life, a point of view taken from the before and placed in the (ever) after. Simonides thereby brilliantly captured the essence of the new money economy: people make things that are not real but that come to have real value, symbolic value. Money is nothing, save in relation; it comes to signify and generate things only through its exchange, or transfer, or *translation*.

> The idea that human life is not a gift but a loan or debt, which will have to be paid back, originated with Simonides. It became a cliché on gravestones throughout Hellenistic and Roman times; numerous examples are extant. But in Simonides' phrasing the idea has a bleakness that sets it apart. Facts of stone and money alone cannot account for this sentence.[80]

Our lives are on loan, and the note will come due; this is a very bleak vision indeed, except for the fact that Simonides takes it upon himself to paint images of these lost bodies in words . . . and so to un-lose them. Celan struggled with the enormity of this same challenge, on a tragic and far more massive scale, after the Second World War. Conjuring seems too quaint a term for that kind of unlosing. Carson calls it "radical mimesis."[81]

One of the most famous of Simonides's many epitaphs was the one composed for the Spartan dead who served under Leonidas at Thermopylae.[82] The agonizing challenge about this commission was that the tomb itself was an empty mound; tragically, no bodies were recovered from the battlefield at Thermopylae. Simonides, then, is culling an epitaph entirely from his imagination, one designed for an empty tomb built for bodies that literally are not there. Poetic conjuring, married to this empty cipher, "generate[s] a surplus value that guarantees poetic vocation against epistemological stinginess. To make 'paintings that talk' is to engage in a conversation that is more than words and beyond price."[83]

To think epitaphically about an empty tomb calls up a Christian resonance that warrants further refection. What renders the tomb "empty" is, precisely, the absence of Christ's body. In the "Note on Method" with which *Economy of the Unlost* begins, Carson offered one further example of the insights provided by her mode of poetic comparisons. It goes like this.

> Think of the Greek preposition πρός. When used with the accusative case, this preposition means "toward, upon, against, with, ready for, face to face, engaging, concerning, touching, in reply to, in respect of, compared with, according to, as accompaniment for." It is the preposition chosen by John the Evangelist to describe the relationship between God and The Word in the first verse of the first chapter of his Revelation:
>
> πρὸς Θεόν
>
> "And The Word was with God" is how the usual translation goes. What kind of withness is it?[84]

We have seen this strategy of piling on synonyms become more prominent in Carson's subsequent works of translation. Here we should note that one of the synonyms she offers for *pros*'s kind of "withness" is *comparison*. Carson has accomplished two things here, things that conjoin her interest in poetry—an interest of long standing—with her interest in religion which, I believe, really came to the fore in the first decade of the twenty-first century.

And make no mistake: if *pros* can also mean "compared to," then John, perhaps the most lyrical of the Greek evangelists in the prose New Testament, may be suggesting that the Word be *compared* to God. If the word is "an image of things," as Simonides claims it to be, then Christ is an image (or icon, *eikôn*) of God. And not only Christ, but all of the embodied people, now lost, who consumed Simonides's poetic imagination. When God first creates a human being, we read an interesting description of the act in the Greek Septuagint: "Let us make (*poiêsômen*) a human being (*anthrôpon*) according to our image (*eikona*) and according to a similarity (*homoiôsin*) with us" (*Genesis* 1:26).[85] It is all *poiêsis*,[86] all a form of poetic creation, and what are created here are explicitly bodies of various kinds.[87] Both the poet and God are creators. And both stand in a decidedly complex relation to what they create. Even God's Word, that which was "with or compared to (*pros*) God," was embodied. The conundrums raised by this type of "withness," this kind of body, inspired a set of indelibly religious questions, during the Christological controversies that consumed several of the early centuries of the Jesus-movement, and that may well haunt the poet who dares to lyricize this kind of withness.

It is to the question of religion, then, and its haunting, yet generative, place in Carson's more recent work, that I turn in the next chapter. The issue hinges on the complex quality of Greek *poêsis*, that is, creation of literary and other kinds, as well as their eventual undoing.

NOTES

1. Anne Carson, *If Not, Winter: Fragments of Sappho*, ix.
2. Ibid. As I noted in the first chapter, this all changed two years after Carson published her Sappho volume, then again even more dramatically a decade later. Two important new poems were discovered and published in 2004 (one on old age, and one about her brother); a new set of five papyri, containing portions of nine poems, came to light next and were published one decade later.
3. One might think of Jorge Luis Borges, HD (Hilda Doolittle), James Joyce, Nikos Kazantzakis, and Ezra Pound as important exceptions to this rule. See Barbara Graziosi and Emily Greenwood, eds., *Homer in the Twentieth Century: Between World Literature and the Western Canon* (New York, NY: Oxford University Press, 2005), and Leah Flack, *Modernism and Homer: The Odyssey of HD, James Joyce, Osip Mandalstam and Ezra Pound* (New York, NY: Cambridge University Press, 2015).

More recent examples of the channeling of Homeric epic include Christopher Logue's *War Music* (New York, NY: Farrar Straus Giroux, 1981, 1987) and Alice Oswald's *Memorial: A Version of Homer's Iliad* (New York, NY: W. W. Norton & Company, 2011).

4. Derek Walcott, *Omeros* (New York, NY: Farrar Straus and Giroux, 1990). This text was the primary inspiration for the award of his Nobel Prize for Literature in 1992. See his Nobel Address as well, *The Antilles: Fragments of Epic Memory* (New York, NY: Farrar Straus and Giroux, 1992).

5. An excellent discussion of Walcott's poetic achievements may be found in Gregson Davis, special ed., "The Poetics of Derek Walcott: Intertextual Perspectives," *South Atlantic Quarterly* 96.2 (1997). Also see the final chapter, entitled "The Sea Is History," in Ian Baucomb, *Specters of the Atlantic: Finance Capital, Slavery and the Philosophy of History* (Durham, NC: Duke University Press, 2005), 309–333.

6. In an interview with John D'Agata, Carson coyly confesses: "Well, there's a novel I've written that was all prose at first and very thick. Then I thought, 'What if I break these lines up a bit? Maybe they'd move along more smartly.' So now the novel's in verse."

See John D'Agata, "A Talk with Anne Carson," *Brick* 57 (1997): 14–22 (quote at 22), and John D'Agata, "A____ with Anne Carson," *The Iowa Review* 27.2 (1997): 20.

7. John D'Agata emphasizes the etymological foundation, and thus the classical pedigree, of this ambiguous hybridity as follows:

Some history: The word *prose* came into English use by way of the Latin *prosus*, the Vulgate's paired-down simplification of *prorsus*, itself the contracted form of *proversus*, "to move forward," as in Cicero's *prosa oratio*, "speech going straight ahead without turns." Notice, however, that the Latin root of *prose* has in it the word *versus*, which comes from the Greek *verso*, the little mechanism on a plow that allows a farmer to manually turn a furrow—or, for our purposes, a "line." In Latin, *verso* became *versus* and its verb form *vertere*, meaning "to turn"—hence the English *vertex, vertigo*, and even the word *conversant*, "one capable of spinning an interesting tale." *Verse*, in other words, is etymologically both the root of *prose* as well as its direct opposite in meaning. No wonder this scholar of classical texts is blurring genre distinctions.

John D'Agata, "Review of *Men in the Off Hours* by Anne Carson," *Boston Review* (Summer 2000) [http://bostonreview.net/BR25.3/dagata.html] (accessed July 19, 2018)

8. Anne Carson, *Autobiography of Red: A Novel in Verse* (New York, NY: Alfred A. Knopf Inc., 1998).

9. While many literary critics have seen the connection, or read the two works against one another, the only suggestion of actual influence I have located is Katherine Burkett, *Literary Form as Postcolonial Critique* (London: Ashgate Publishing, 2012), but even here, the link is presented as more political than explicitly literary.

10. See Phil Sapirstein, "The First Doric Temple in Sicily, Its Builder, and IG XIV 1," *Hesperia* 90 (2021): 411–477.

11. For this reading of the *Suda*, I am using David A. Campbell, ed., *Greek Lyric III: Stesichorus, Ibycus, Simonides, and Others* (Cambridge, MA: Loeb Classical Library of Harvard University Press, 1991), 28–31.

12. The strategy is put to very different effect by Patrick Finglass in the Introduction to Malcolm Davies and Patrick J. Finglass, *Stesichorus: The Poems* (New York, NY: Cambridge University Press, 2014).

13. Plato appears to be more certain, claiming him as the son of Euphemus from the Sicilian colony of Himera (*Phaedrus* 244a).

14. Pliny (*Natural History* Book II, chapter 9) recalls that both Stesichorus and Pindar wrote about total solar eclipses, which we now know took place in 585, 557,

and 463 BCE. Lucian (*On Longevity* 26) recalls that Stesichorus lived to be eighty-five years old.

15. Horace, *Epodes* 17.38.

16. Zonaras, *Lexicon* 1338.

17. Aelius Aristides, *Orations* 2.572.

18. Ammianus Marcellinus (*History* 38.4) tells an interesting story in which Socrates heard one of Stesichorus's songs while he was in prison, and was determined to learn it, "in order to die knowing something more."

19. Note that the phrase "false story" (*etymos logos*) is repeated by Plato in the quotation with which I begin this chapter. Carson provides some hilarious meditations on this story in three Appendices that come, ironically enough, just before the body of her own narrative poem (*Autobiography of Red*, 15–20).

20. Anne Carson, *Eros the Bittersweet*, 46–52.

21. *Palatine Anthology* 7.75.

22. (Pseudo)Longinus, *On the Sublime* 13.3.

23. Quintilian, *Elements of Oratory* 10.1.62: *maxima bella et clarissimos canentem duces et epici carminis onera lyra sustinentem.*

24. Dionysus of Halicarnassus, *On Literary Composition* 19.

A helpful compendium of these ancient testimonia about Stesichorus may be found in David A. Campbell, *Greek Lyric III: Stesichorus, Ibycus, Simonides, and Others* (Cambridge, MA: Loeb Classical Library of Harvard University Press, 1991), 28–59.

25. See the critical edition of Davies and Finglass, *Stesichorus: The Poems*, 99–205.

What makes Sappho's equally fragmentary literary legacy more "useful" is no easy question to answer.

26. Davies and Finglass, *Stesichorus: The Poems*, 100–121.

27. For more on this material, see Paul Curtis, *Stesichoros's Geryoneis* (Leiden, Boston: E. J. Brill, 2011); Volume 333 of Mnemosyne Supplements, Monographs on Greek and Latin Language and Literature.

28. This adds poignancy to the irony that Euripides describes, whereby Herakles's return to his homestead proves to be his undoing, whereby his storied career should end in such murderous and uncivilized disorder, with the shocking murder of his own family.

29. *Hesiod: Theogony, Works and Days, Shield*, Apostolos N. Athanassakis, trans. (Baltimore, MD: Johns Hopkins University Press, 1983), 20, 37.

30. Apollodorus, *Library of Mythology* 2.5.10, as quoted by Curtis in *Stesichoros's Geryoneis*, 63–64.

31. Fragment 12, in Curtis, *Stesichoros's Geryoneis*, 84. Carson renders the fragment, which she calls "Herakles' Arrow," thus:

> Arrow means kill It parted Geryon's skull like a comb Made
> The boy neck lean At an odd slow angle sideways as when a
> Poppy shames itself in a whip of Nude breeze.
> (*Autobiography of Red*, 13)

The Loeb Classical Library includes a fragment of seventeen lines in all:

S15 ... (bringing) the end that is hateful (death), having (doom) on its head, befouled with blood and with ... gall, the anguish of the dapple-necked Hydra, destroyer of men; and in silence he thrust it cunningly into his brow, and it cut through the flesh and bones by divine dispensation; and the arrow held straight on the crown of his head, and it stained with gushing blood his breastplate and gory limbs; and Geryon drooped his neck to one side, like a poppy which spoiling its tender beauty suddenly sheds its petals and ...

(David A. Campbell, ed., *Greek Lyric III*, 74–77, notes omitted).

See also Diane Rayor, trans., *Sappho's Lyre: Archaic Lyric and Women Poets of Ancient Greece* (Berkeley, CA: University of California Press, 1991), 46:

> then Geryon bent his neck
> at an angle, as when a poppy,
> dishonoring its delicate body,
> suddenly sheds its petals ...

32. Dina Giorgis, in "Discarded Histories and Queer Affects in Anne Carson's *Autobiography of Red*," *Studies in Gender and Sexuality* 15 (2014): 154–166, reminds readers of this verse novel that "the noun 'gay' is never uttered" (155) in it, and thus, she re-figures Geryon as a "queer" literary type, one defined by his unaccountable physicality: red, winged, monstrous. She concludes: "To write the history of discarded lives therefore requires a different historiography" (165).

I take her point, but as I emphasized at the conclusion of the first chapter, I believe that Carson's avoidance of the terminologies of sexual (or queer) identity has another, and potentially more radical, purpose: to recover the agony of *the desiring subject* as a perennial matter for philosophy and religion and literature, alike.

33. Anne Carson, *Autobiography of Red*, 29.
34. Anne Carson, *Autobiography of Red*, 37–38.
35. Later we will learn that the autobiography on which Geryon labored for nearly forty years had settled into the form of "a photographic essay" (*Autobiography of Red*, 60).

In an imagined interview which she conducts with Stesichorus as an appendix to this novel-in-verse, Carson has him say, "I was (very simply) in charge of seeing for the world after all seeing is just a substance" (148). The manner in which Geryon takes his substantial manner of seeing from inside (journal) to outside (photography) stages a crucial gesture for Carsons's understanding of his work, and her own. "Stesichorus released being. All the substances in the world went floating up" (5). This is a remarkably ambitious statement of the power of art.

36. Anne Carson, *Autobiography of Red*, 105. Chris Jennings expands on this point brilliantly:

> The volcano is the exemplar. An image of a boundary between interior and exterior, a normally placid surface punctuated by intense bursts from its core, it mirrors the pressure that builds within Geryon himself, his interior always threatening, or promising, to surface. It also mirrors the structural relationship between narrative and lyric in the book's central romance.

Chris Jennings, "The Erotic Poetics of Anne Carson," *University of Toronto Quarterly* 70.4 (2001): 923–936, quote at 932.

37. Anne Carson, *Autobiography of Red*, 46.
38. Anne Carson, *Autobiography of Red*, 53.
39. Anne Carson, *Autobiography of Red*, 74.
40. Anne Carson, *Autobiography of Red*, 72.
41. Anne Carson, *Autobiography of Red*, 70.
42. Anne Carson, *Autobiography of Red*, 79–80.
43. See Stuart J. Murray, "The Autobiographical Self: Phenomenology and the Limits of Narrative Self-Possession in Anne Carson's *Autobiography of Red*," *English Studies in Canada* 31.4 (2-0-5): 101–122, for a most helpful extension of insights from Heidegger's and especially Merleau-Ponty's respective phenomenological accounts to Carson's verse novel.
44. Anne Carson, *Autobiography of Red*, 83–84.
45. Anne Carson, *Autobiography of Red*, 112.
46. Anne Carson, *Autobiography of Red*, 108.
47. Anne Carson, *Autobiography of Red*, 118–119.
48. Anne Carson, *Autobiography of Red*, 132–133.
49. Anne Carson, *Autobiography of Red*, 128–129.
50. Anne Carson, *Autobiography of Red*, 144.
51. Anne Carson, *Autobiography of Red*, 146.
52. Bruce Beasley, "Who *Can* a Monster Blame for Being Red? Three Fragments on the Academic and the 'Other' in *Autobiography of Red*," in Joshua Marie Wilkinson, ed., *Anne Carson: Ecstatic Lyre*, 74–81 (quote at 77). This image of Carson as a "subversive" scholar in a Nietzschean vein is one that I find most helpful in assessing her classicizing (and other) literary achievements.
53. Anne Carson, *Autobiography of Red*, 38.
54. Carson has even done it herself by composing a sort of sequel to *Autobiography of Red*, entitled *Red Doc>* (New York, NY: Alfred A. Knopf, 2013). Her explanation of the central idea is one she underlined in her rendering of Euripides's *Herakles*, namely that "to live past the end of your myth is a perilous thing"; she has observed this about the tragic figure of Herakles before. I note this one descriptive detail of her own Herakles-figure:

> He is a person always in motion he needs to be kept vibrating. Between any two activities he plunges. Can't stand to be alone hates quiet time has little interest in introspection let alone other people as individuals. Or rather he doesn't care for people he cares what flows through them. And usually takes it. His teacher at med school called him a minotaur who swallows other people's labyrinths. Good I'll do psychiatry he said. (127)

For a judicious and insightful review of the book's flaws and enduring poetic power, see Roy Scranton, "Estranged Pain: Anne Carson's *Red Doc>*," *Contemporary Literature* 55.1 (2014): 202–214. Building upon the former novel in a verse where "[t]he buzzing mystery of adolescence connects with erotic desire and erotic loss, with a sophisticated scholarly riddle of how we make historical narratives out of fragments and lies" (207), now in this sequel-of-sorts, "[c]aprice is a topic that Carson seems to be thinking about" (209). The poetic results are indeed capricious in their way.

55. See for example, "Mimnermos: The Brainsex Paintings," in *Plainwater: Essays and Poetry* (New York, NY: Vintage Books, 1995), 3–26; and the translation of Ibykos in *Nay Rather* (American University of Paris: The Cahiers Series No. 21, 2013), 34–40.

The fragments of Mimnermus may be found in Douglas E. Gerber, ed., *Greek Elegiac Poetry from the Seventh to Fifth Centuries BC* (Cambridge, MA: Loeb Classical Library of Harvard University Press, 1999), 72–105.

The fragments of Ibycus may be found in David A. Campbell, ed., *Greek Lyric III: Stesichorus, Ibycus, Simonides, and Others* (Cambridge, MA: Loeb Classical Library of Harvard University Press, 1991), 208–293.

56. Cicero, *Republic* 2.20.

57. Anne Carson, *Economy of the Unlost (Reading Simonides of Keos with Paul Celan)* (The Princeton University Press, 1999), vii.

This might almost serve as the credo for a non-conforming and subversive scholar like Carson who ultimately identifies with a more Nietzschean, Neoclassical pedigree.

58. Anne Carson, *Economy of the Unlost*, viii.

59. Celan was an artful and gifted poet-translator in his own right, which makes him an intriguing counterpoint to the stricter Greekness of Simonides. A brief biography of Celan may be found at https://www.poetryfoundation.org/poets/paul-celan (accessed August 24, 2017). His given name was Paul Antschel which, together with Carson's discussion of an "economy" of poetic losses, offers a suggestive echo of the figure of Ancash in *Autobiography of Red*.

Other valuable studies include: Israel Chalfin, *Paul Celan: A Biography of His Youth*, Maximilian Bleyleben, trans. (New York, NY: Persea Books, 1991); Amy Colin, *Paul Celan: Holograms of Darkness* (Bloomington, IN: University of Indiana Press, 1991); Jerry Glenn, *Paul Celan* (New York, NY: Twayne Publishers, Inc., 1973); Ruven Karr, *Die Toten im Gespräch: Trialogische Strukturen in der Dichtung Paul Celans* (Hannover: Wehrmann Verlag, 2015); and Clarise Samuels, *Holocaust Visions: Surrealism and Existentialism in the Poetry of Paul Celan* (Columbia, SC: Camden House, Inc., 1993).

Peter Szondi offers a fascinating analysis of Celan as a translator (specifically of Shakespeare) in "The Poetry of Constancy: Paul Celan's Translation of Shakespeare's Sonnet 105," in *On Textual Understanding and Other Essays*, Harvey Mendelsohn, trans. (Minneapolis, MN: University of Minnesota Press, 1986), 161–178, one which uses Benjamin's "The Task of the Translator" to demonstrate how Celan utilizes language *to perform poetically* the very things that Shakespeare was content to describe in verse.

60. Anne Carson, *Economy of the Unlost*, 47, 80.

The Greek text may be found in David A. Campbell, ed., *Greek Lyric III*, 362–363 and 584–585.

61. Anne Carson, *Economy of the Unlost*, 10–46, 73ff.

62. Aristotle, *Nicomachean Ethics* 1121a25–27.

63. Aristotle, *Rhetoric*, Book II, chapter 16, and Book III, chapter 13.
64. Anne Carson, *Economy of the Unlost*, 15.
65. In an interview with Kevin McNeilly [*Canadian Literature* 176 (Spring 2003): 15], Carson observes the following:

> I think that the gift-exchange circuit is more or less broken down in our culture, simply because our culture is too big. When you're writing a book nowadays for Knopf which is owned by Random House, which is owned by Viacom which is owned by the Bertelsmann brothers in Germany, the context is too expanded to grasp, whereas somebody like Pindar was speaking to twenty-five people he'd known all his life. An exchange of gifts is very abstract when you're talking to an audience that might include people you'll never even know about. So I don't think in any real sense that it's an exchange anymore, except in a reading situation. There's something that happens there when you're physically present doing a reading that's an exchange, but the multiple copies going out to a zillion people, it's hard to have a sense of that as a sensual and emotional experience, whereas someone like Pindar did have that, and felt the burden of it.

That fertile idea, that the "reading situation" represents the most unsullied site of modern exchange, is an enormously fruitful one with which to approach her artistic practices, especially as relating to live staged performance.

66. See Anne Carson, *Eros the Bittersweet*, 46–52.
For the fragments of Archilochus, see Douglas E. Gerber, ed., *Greek Iambic Poetry from the Seventh to the Fifth Centuries BC* (Cambridge, MA: Loeb Classical Library of Harvard University Press, 1999), 14–293.
67. Herodotus, *Histories* I.94; see also relevant stories told at *Histories* I.50–54, I.92, V.49 and VI.125.
68. Anne Carson, *Economy of the Unlost*, 11.
69. "Simonides was born on the island of Keos: a barren, rocky, impoverished place where the calculus of sheer survival demanded of its inhabitants an economy both radical and obvious. It was the custom on Keos for every male citizen who reached the age of sixty to voluntarily drink the hemlock, in order that there be enough supplies of life to go around. The historian Strabo records the rationale for this custom in a sentence as cold and clear as an epitaph: *The man who cannot live well shall not live poorly*. Simonides chose to live elsewhere." (Anne Carson, *Economy of the Unlost*, 80–81, note omitted.)
In sum, making money had become a matter of life and death. . . .
70. Anne Carson, *Economy of the Unlost*, 24; tellingly, the quotation is taken from Marx's essay "On the Jewish Question."
71. Anne Carson, *Economy of the Unlost*, 28, notes omitted.
72. For a fascinating study that situates some of Carson's most challenging twenty-first century poetic endeavors (he calls them "banditry") within the equally seismic shift from a money economy to the world of Wall Street "derivatives," see Oran McKenzie, "Spillage and Banditry: Anne Carson's Derivatives," in Martin Leer and Genoveva Puskás, eds., *Economies of English* (Tübingen: Narr Francke Attempto Verlag, 2016), 225–242. This analysis generates a very appreciative reading of one of her most difficult texts, *Decreation*, to which I will turn in the next chapter.

73. Anne Carson, *Economy of the Unlost*, 28–38.

On the relationship with Heidegger, see James K. Lyon, *Paul Celan and Martin Heidegger: An Unresolved Conversation, 1951–1970* (Baltimore, MD: Johns Hopkins University Press, 2001); Hadrien France-Lanord, *Paul Celan et Martin Heidegger, le sens d'un dialogue* (Paris: Fayard, 2004); and Pablo Oyarzun Robles, *Entre Celan y Heidegger*, 2nd Edition (Santiago: Ediciones/ Metales Pesados, 2013).

Other Continental philosophers have profited from their engagement with Celan's poetry as well, including: Jacques Derrida, *Sovereignties in Question: The Poetics of Paul Celan*, Thomas Dutoit and Outi Pasanen, eds. and trans. (New York, NY: Fordham University Press, 2005); Hans-Georg Gadamer, *Gadamer on Celan*, Richard Heinemann and Bruce Krajewski, eds. (Albany, NY: State University of New York Press, 1997); and Philippe Lacoue-Labarthe, *Poetry as Experience*, Andrea Tarnewski, trans. (Palo Alto, CA: Stanford University Press, 1999).

74. Anne Carson, *Economy of the Unlost*, 9.

75. Anne Carson, *Economy of the Unlost*, 29: *Erreichbar, nah und unverloren blieb inmitten der Verluste...*

76. Anne Carson, *Economy of the Unlost*, 46, notes omitted.

77. And such a linkage creates the possibility of deeper metaphoric thinking, thinking which *reaches out* to know, actively, and thus sees things in their complex hybridity. See Monique Tschofen, "'First I Must Tell about Seeing': (De)monstrations of Visuality and the Dynamics of Metaphor in Anne Carson's *Autobiography of Red*," *Canadian Literature* 180 (2004): 32–34, 47-49.

78. Anne Carson, *Economy of the Unlost*, 51–52, notes omitted.

79. Anne Carson, *Economy of the Unlost*, 73.

80. Anne Carson, *Economy of the Unlost*, 80, note omitted. For more on the idea of the cliché and its religious valence, see *Nay Rather*, 4ff.

81. Anne Carson, *Economy of the Unlost*, 52.

82. Anne Carson, *Economy of the Unlost*, 52-55.

83. Anne Carson, *Economy of the Unlost*, 55.

84. Anne Carson, *Economy of the Unlost*, viii.

For more on the concept of *with-ness* in Carson's work, see: Kristi Maxwell, "The Unbearable Withness of Being: On Anne Carson's *Plainwater*," in Joshua Marie Wilkinson, ed., *Anne Carson: Ecstatic Lyre*, 56–62; and Andre Furlani, "Reading Paul Celan with Anne Carson: 'What Kind of Withness Would That Be?,'" *Canadian Literature* 176 (Spring 2003): 84–104. Furlani suggests quite brilliantly that the kind of "withness" in play is precisely the poetic proximity we see Carson establish between herself and Celan, a sort of playful pilfering out of which novelty may erupt.

A more general examination of the way in which Carson's work as a Greek translator has forced her to attend to the power of prepositions is Chris Jennings, "The Erotic Poetics of Anne Carson," esp. 926–929.

I should note finally, albeit pedantically, that this is the first line of John's Gospel, not the Revelation.

85. Alfred Rahlfs, ed., *Septuaginta* (Stutttgart: Deutsche Bibelstiftung, 1935), 2.

86. True to the philosophical strategy of making a distinction to resolve a dilemma, later Christian theologians would distinguish between *genesis*-creation and

poiêsis-creation in order to distinguish the manner in which God *generated* Christ from the way God *made* human beings. They would also distinguish between those things which were made of a substance similar (*homoi-ousios*) to God, from that unique being, Christ, who was alleged to be made of the same substance (*homo-ousios*) as God. In this latter view, human bodies were made similar to God whereas Christ's body was generated the same as God. These are some very complex kinds of withness, indeed.

87. In her "Short Talk on the Withness of the Body," *The New Republic* (October 4, 2013), which Carson appears to have written to console a friend on the death of her dog, we read the following elliptical remark: "What departs at death is 19 grams (=7/8 ounce) of you shedding a soft blue light. What remains behind is various." Later, playing now with crude empiricism, she paints us a character who notes:

> There's no test for soul. You may be familiar with the story of Dr. Duncan MacDougall, who in 1901 attempted to discover the weight of the S-O-U-L by calculating the mass lost by a human body at the moment of death. His experiments gave him an average result of twenty-one grams but these could never be replicated by anyone else and are regarded as scientifically meaningless. More recently an Oregon rancher tried a similar experiment on eight sheep, three lambs, and a goat, who all gained weight at death. He continues to puzzle over this result.

["We've Only Just Begun," *Harper's Magazine* (January 2016), 73].

Chapter 4

Hybrid Genres Between Body and Spirit, or, Righting the Self and Writing God

The thirteen volumes of Marcel Proust's *À la Recherche du temps perdu* are the end-result of a synthesis, impossible to replicate, in which the mystic's trance, the prose writer's art, the satirist's verve, the scholar's knowledge, and the hermit's self-absorption have all been woven together into an autobiographical work. It has properly been said that all great works of literature either fashion a genre (*Gattung*) or else they unravel one—in a word, they are singularities (*Sonderfälle*). Among such singularities, however, this one is among the most impossible to grasp (*unfaßlichsten*).

—Walter Benjamin, "The Image of Proust" (1929)

* * * * *

If Sappho was a musician as well as a poet, then she was also a decidedly religious writer. The first (and until recently, the only) complete poem that has survived is her so-called Hymn (*Asma*) to Aphrodite ("hymn," together with "ode" or "song," is one of the shades of meaning that the Greek word, *asma*, contains). This is an underexamined fact to which Anne Carson has devoted a great deal of time and attention. Most poets in the Greek lyric tradition wrote in a great many genres as well as in varying dialects. Such poets wrote love lyrics, quasi-heroic mythic cycles, personal polemics, reflections on nature and the gods, epinikian victory songs of praise, traditional hymns, and epitaphs. Simonides, as we saw, was an early exemplar of this latter genre, though two significant epitaphs are ascribed by the tradition of Greek Anthology to Sappho as well. If suffering and death are perennial aspects of the embodied condition, and if tragedy was a poetic genre born in Greece, and so long as aspiring desire (*eros*) remains bittersweet, then religion will be an essential part of the poetic landscape for all such Greek lyric poets.

The same holds true for Anne Carson. If *Eros the Bittersweet* is an unexpected and daring first academic monograph, and if *Antigonick* is not, traditionally speaking, a translation of the most perennially popular of Sophocles's tragedies, then four more of Carson's works announce themselves as even more radically non-conforming works, texts which explode the traditional categories and expectations of literary production by combining multiple genres in a single textual corpus.

In 1992, Carson published a series of texts in an unusual format. *Short Talks*[1] has the feel of the fragmentary lyric tradition itself, offering crisp, one-paragraph meditations on an extraordinarily wide range of lyric topics. Three years later, she published two even more hybrid literary endeavors: *Glass, Irony and God*[2] mingles poetry and poetic essays with more traditional prose to great effect, organized around a complex array of religious ideas; *Plainwater*[3] mingled her poetry and prose again with an even more ambitious array of topics. Fifteen years after that, Carson published what is arguably her most genre-defying text, *Nox*,[4] the reproduction of an emotionally shattering and complex collage that Carson created after the unexpected death of her brother in Copenhagen in 2000. The piece is organized around an extended meditation on Catullus's Lyric Poem #101,[5] with its strong echo of Simonidean epitaph; Carson's translation of the poem is as follows:

> Many the peoples many the oceans I crossed
> I arrive at these poor, brother, burials
> so I could give you the last gift owed to death
> and talk (why?) with mute ash.
> Now that Fortune tore you from me, you
> oh poor (wrongly) brother (wrongly) taken from me,
> now still anyway this—what a distant mood of parents
> handed down as the sad gift for burials[6]—
> accept! Soaked with tears of a brother
> and not forever, brother, farewell and farewell.[7]

Carson concludes her raw testament to sibling grief simply, and with agonizing brevity, observing coolly that "repent means 'the pain again.'" It is difficult to know where to go further after reading a statement like that. When grief is so fresh, raw even, lessons may be wanting, despite Carson's attempt to make the mourning "festive."[8]

In this chapter, I take up the place of religion, and particularly of desiring bodies in religious thought, in Anne Carson's remarkable body of literary works, especially as it emerged in the early twenty-first century, by looking more closely at another one of her experimental hybrids, one I consider to be among the richest and most provocative of all her works. That text is entitled *Decreation*.[9] In all of these hybrid texts, it is as if Carson wishes to blur the standard emotional registers—bitter to sweet, and back again—much as she has blurred literary genres throughout her career.[10] The frontispiece to *Decreation* offers a delightful line from John Florio's 1603 translation of what she identifies as Montaigne's "Essay on Some Verses of Virgil": "I love a poetical kind of marche, by friskes, skips and jumps."[11] Carson is once again after something as elusive as a Sapphic fragment, as self-lacerating as a Greek tragedy, as moving as a lyric poem. As she never tires of reminding us, the spiritual challenge for such a quest lies in reaching without grasping . . . else the mystery slips through the fingers, like water, like tears.

In this ambitious collection, Carson's first such hybrid endeavor in a decade (as I illustrated in the previous chapter, she devoted much of her attention to *translating* a large body of Greek drama in the intervening years), she returned to some of her most delightfully genre-bending tricks. As the subtitle and table of contents tell it, this book consists of various pieces including poems, essays, an operatic libretto, as well as the suggestive outline for a short film entitled "Longing." Channeling Simonides perhaps, this was also her most visual book to date (though now superseded by the ornate production of several works, including and subsequent to *Nox*). Carson appears to be painting on a larger canvas now, and there are some startling new colors on her palette. There is nothing else quite like *Decreation* in the entirety of her daunting body of work. How, then, to write about this book's central topic, spiritual strangeness and soulful estrangement, without becoming strange, oneself? That, as the reader soon discovers, is an essentially *religious* question . . . and it may not be possible to answer it in a traditional literary manner.

Carson takes her title from Simone Weil (1909–1943), the French mystic whom Albert Camus called "the only great spirit of our time,"[12] and Andre Gide "the most truly spiritual writer of this [twentieth] century."[13] We should be called to wonder what Carson, a poet of raw erotic desire and a philosopher of such restless reaching, could possibly have to say about the seemingly bloodless kinds of Christian self-erasure to which Simone Weil apparently aspired.[14] Weil described her spiritual aspirations in a vaguely autobiographical body of essays, of which most were published posthumously;[15] they are as eclectic as Carson's own hybrid works, works in which we find an uncanny range of philosophical and mathematical and religious meditations, as well as one especially important essay on the *Iliad*.[16] Simone Weil eventually achieved the invisibility she desired, through the unpromising route of apparent self-starvation in a London sanitorium, in 1943.[17]

Yet Carson manages to describe Weil, whom she recalls with curt irony as a "twentieth century French classicist and philosopher,"[18] and her core spiritual insights, with poetic brilliance and deep sympathy:

> I am excess.
>   Flesh.
>   Brain.
>   Breath.
>   Creature who
> breaks the silence of heaven,
>   blocks God's view of his beloved creation
>   and like an unwelcome third between two lovers
>   gets in the way.
> It is creation that God loves—
>   *mountains and seas and the years after—*
>   blue simple horizon of all care.
>   World seen as it is when I am not there.
> Undo this creature!
>   Excess.
>   Flesh.
>   Brain.
>   Breath.
>   Creature.
> Undo this creature.[19]

This moving mingling of lyrics, erotics, and theology recalls Carson's previous work on the Love Triangle, especially in *Eros the Bittersweet* and *Autobiography of* Red . . . only now, God is one of the three points of the triangle, and the World is another, definitive lovers who defines the empty space inside and between people and also the material world they inhabit. When Carson speaks (in Weil's voice) of feeling "*like an unwelcome third between two lovers*" (italics mine), she is attempting to resolve the Archaic Greek lyric poet's dilemma, one she highlighted to great effect in her first book: "change of self is loss of self to these poets."[20]

Might it be that this perception is sexed, Carson is now put to wonder, that from the perspective of sex difference men in the Greek lyric tradition, like Archilochus (whom she compares to Ernest Hemingway[21]), associated passionate loving with dying, whereas women like Sappho gave themselves to the experience with something more closely approaching reverent awe? This appears to be one of the central questions broached in this hybrid volume on religious visionaries. Carson had already contributed several important essays on gender, especially in the ancient Greek context, that pursue such questions with stunning originality and insight.[22] In the latter half of *Decreation*, she elects to focus on three women who were all lyrical writers, philosophical lovers of a very particular sort, and great spiritual adepts: Sappho of Lesbos (c630–580 BCE), Marguerite Porete (c1250–1310), and Simone Weil (1909–1943). To capture some of the strangeness of these women and of their writing, Carson concludes the book with three complex performative entries: a lyric essay entitled "DECREATION: How Women Like Sappho, Marguerite Porete and Simone Weil Tell God,"[23] a libretto entitled "DECREATION: An Opera in Three Parts,"[24] and some filmic notes for "LONGING, A Documentary."[25] We can see, in these elusive new offerings, how Carson's entire writerly career has been bookended by longing, of various kinds.

And yet, we are put to wonder: what can Sappho's erotic and lyrical insights really have to do with the mystic and quasi-Christian self-abnegation that Simone Weil imagined and to which she clearly aspired? A great deal, Carson suggests, once we drop our superficial notion of spiritual "decreation" as bloodless, and our secular conceptions of mysticism as anti-worldly, and our cynical sense of mystics as company-men and -women whose company just so happens to be a temple or a church. Not so the lyrical women whom Carson lauds, for each of whom embodied spirituality is the heart of the matter: not Sappho ("a Greek poet of the seventh century BC who lived on the island of Lesbos, wrote some famous poetry about love and is said to have organized her life around worship of the god Aphrodite"[26]); not Simone Weil ("twentieth century French classicist and philosopher"); and perhaps most emphatically, not Marguerite Porete ("who was burned alive in the public square of Paris in 1310 because she had written a book about the love of God that the papal inquisitor deemed heretical"[27]).

One would be hard-pressed to say that any of these three women's lives was a happy one. Sappho was reputedly exiled from Lesbos for a decade,[28] and a later Ovidian tradition claimed that she committed suicide over a failed love affair (I will examine this Ovidian tradition more closely at the end of this chapter). Simone Weil, as I have already noted, died near the bombarded city of London in the middle of the carnage of the Second World War, refusing rations any greater than what was available to her starving comrades in Occupied France. Marguerite Porete's case was extreme, even by these standards. She was put to death at the end of the second ecclesiastical investigation to which she had been subject, burned alive in Paris together with copies of her book, *The Mirror of Simple Souls* [*Le Mirouer des Simples Ames*],[29] a "swirling exploration of spiritual nonbeing"[30] which here becomes a sort of (self?)reflecting pool in which to catch glimpses of what Carson, too, is after. "In the history of book burning, it is the first known instance of an inquisitorial procedure ending with the burning both of a book and the accused author."[31] A clearer and more tragic connection between corpus and corpse is scarcely imaginable. Clearly, these lines of spiritual self-erasure create complicated webs of signification, as well as hybrid writing, and real danger (Marguerite Porete also composed her work in poetry, dialogue, and prose, and Carson began working on an operatic libretto inspired by this hybrid text at the University of Michigan in 1999). Carson earlier noted, in a poetic meditation on Sappho, that we can be sure that the law exists . . . because of the "daily burnings."[32] Repression, to her eye, is antithetical to true religion.

The central paradox with which Anne Carson is concerned here is the writerly self's reflection on its own selfhood, as well as the relative expansion or contraction of the borders of such a self. The question lying at the heart of the paradox concerns how much disorder one is prepared to allow into a life that aspires to some kind of order. Carson has been tugging at this philosophical thread since 1995, in *Glass, Irony and God*, whose final essay concludes with this puzzle: "I wonder if there might not be another idea of human order than repression, another notion of human virtue than self-control, another kind of human self than one based on dissociation of inside and outside. Or, indeed, another human essence than self."[33] She essayed, in that same text, to blur the sacred border between I and Thou.[34] In a mysterious manner not yet explained, writing both intensifies and enables the religious aspiration toward *decreation*, by highlighting the creativity which such self-effacement may produce. That is to say, the question concerns how best to enable the "righted" soul to write God. Carson herself has faced this spiritual challenge throughout her career as a translator, attempting to get out of the way so as to be more transparent to the texts (and the authors) she loves best; we have also seen that such aspirations to transparency were necessarily supplemented by some fairly audacious intrusions by that same translating self. Such paradoxes multiply and amplify in this challenging text. It will not do to say that such an aspiring religious soul must disappear; *that* would be "quietism," and in any case, then the writing really would cease. The challenge is rather, to echo Diotima's observation in Plato's *Symposium*, to mirror God's creativity with one's own pregnant spiritual powers. Marguerite Porete could not be clearer about this paradox in what may have been her Prologue to *The Mirror*: "I Creature made of the Maker, by me that the maker hath made, [do make] of him this book."[35] That observation could virtually serve as the credo for *Decreation,* were it slightly friskier.[36]

Marguerite Porete's first four chapters announce the stunning originality of the work's conception and design with great lyricism. Its subject is simply and supremely *love* (love of God, yes, but love that finally transcends all attachment to any being, floating free in space and time). Porete begins with the allegorical story of an anonymous princess who falls in love after hearing of the virtues and renown of a distant (that is, absent) King named Alexander. She loves him completely, but the distance between them causes her acute spiritual agony: "But this lady was so far from this great lord, in whom she had laid her love, that she might neither have him nor see him. Wherefore she was full oft discomforted. . . ."[37] So the princess commissions an image (*ymage*), referred to also as "a figure" (*figure*) and "a semblance" (*semblablement vrayement*, which phrase is also used to describe the literary image itself), of this perfect lover, and she salves her soul with the sight of it (this all echoes the iconic and mimetic language of creation in *Genesis* 1:26, as well as Simonides's observation on the power of the right kind of icon). Marguerite Porete suggests that this image (both the painting and her story about it) is the best analogy for the free Christian soul's relationship to God, and she subsequently choreographs a triangulated dialogue between Love, and Soul, and Reason to explore its subtle (and often shocking) implications. The aim is a self-less relationship of pure love, she suggests. This involves "the martyrdom of will and love" as Porete will observe near the end of the book,[38] one focused on absent presence and anguished desiring, but also on a kind of spiritual freedom that transcends virtue's and reason's lesser claims. Marguerite Porete was presumably well aware of the potential scandal here, and this casual, wave-of-the-hand dismissal of "virtue" was, in any case, one of the claims specifically mentioned in her final condemnation. In this book, the free (or "noble") soul is described as the soul fully sundered, no longer merely "sad" or "annihilated," and thereby rendered supremely transparent to divine love. Such a soul is wingéd, she suggests; it has six wings, in fact (like Geryon), and may be capable (if persistent and fortunate enough) of ascending through seven stages of self-annihilation into the loving plenitude of God. That such self-annihilation is viewed *as an ascent* is the paradox of this entire poetic proposal. Echoing Carson's lyrical logic of eros, involving the unbridgeable space between two beings, Marguerite Porete shows her readers how the perception of this gap is actually the beginning of the soul's final ascent, that is to say, the perception of the infinite gap "between the wickedness of me and the goodness of him" and how to come to peace with this infinite distance you cannot grasp.[39] These same spiritual analogies—the loving, the descending, the reaching and the rising—may be found in Sappho and Simone Weil, Carson informs us.

But these figures can be given voice only up to a point. For the images, like the vision in this provocative and engaging book, are all filtered through Carson's own spiritual meanderings. Carson begins *Decreation* with a start, a kind of miniature shock-to-self. This shock is nothing other than the brute fact of sleep. The first poem in the first schedule of readings (entitled "Stops") is called "Sleepchains." On the face of it, sleep might seem a fruitful and auspicious example of a temporary and altogether benign type of "decreation," calling us to wonder where the soul goes when it dreams, and even more so, where it goes when it does *not* dream. "In the ancient struggle of breath against death, one more sleep given."[40] Carson's use of such aspirated language (breath, sleep, death) calls the soul (*anima*) to mind, but one might also ask where *the body* goes when one sleeps. The nighttime observation of the sleeping beloved is an issue to which I will turn in the conclusion.

Carson returns to this image of somnolence throughout the book, and in the next cycle of readings, entitled "Every Exit is an Entrance (In Praise of Sleep)," she reminds us that Crito,[41] in the Platonic dialogue which bears his name,[42] could not sleep and so came early to the prison on the day which he knew was to be Socrates's last. But Crito did not wake his friend, who was sleeping soundly. And Socrates, who has been dreaming, is confident now of an imminent bliss.[43] A beautiful white-clad woman visited him in his sleep and pronounced it so: "on the third day you shall reach rich Phthia" (a quote, Carson is careful to note, which comes from the weirdly insomniac Homeric poems).[44] In reading this, we may also recall that, somewhat later on that same day, in his final conversation with most of his closest friends,[45] Socrates reminds them that death, in the worst-case scenario, is a painless sleep without dream. In other words, a *blissful loss of self* (since there was no perdition or hellfire to cloud this philosopher's cosmic horizons).

Sleep, then, as a temporary kind of decreation; so far, so good. But why refer to "chains"? Why the *chains* of sleep? The answer which suggests itself in this book is that sleep is but a temporary, stop-gap measure for the soul which desires actual liberation from . . . it-self. We are still chained to the body, to the earth, and to their inescapable demands, in sleep. We will inevitably awaken to self (now, again).

We might well assume this to be the lyric lesson of Carson's weighty meditations. But what we learn in this first poetic series of readings takes us elsewhere. We learn that the poet's mother is dying. And now we are meant to recall one of Homer's most memorable poetic images, that of men who grieve their friends fallen in battle. At some point, and surprisingly soon in most cases, bodily needs re-assert themselves. "When they had had their fill of tears, their thoughts turned to food and wine and sleep."[46] We will recall the scene in *Autobiography of Red*, when Geryon is restored, from sleep, to grief. Anyone who has experienced the loss of life, or lover, will know this moment well: you hunger, and yet do not want to eat; you tire, and yet do not want to sleep.[47] To submit to the indignant reassertion of the individual self and its material needs, what can seem such a selfish kind of desire and wanting, would be to cease to be filled with the absence defined by the loss. The soul has been shorn, "decreated," and we do not really want to be re-created. At least not now, not yet. Great grief occupies the bittersweet temporality of *deûte* (now, again). As Carson has asked of us many times in the face of such paradoxes, "Let us see what that feels like."

Up to now, we have seen sleeping as an anticipation of dying, in miniature, a "little death" which does not require an epitaph. Reveling in the sensual-erotic word-play here, Carson appears to be hinting to any readers schooled on ancient Greek erotic poetry (as opposed to the Latin parallels), which is so surprisingly devoid of explicit sexual content, that desire (and not sex) is the spiritual matter most at issue in the lyric tradition of which Sappho is emblematic. It will then become clear that the orgasmic loss of self is but a momentary mapping of an infinitely larger losing, the crushing of self which culminates in the harsh new vintage of the erotic divine. Carson had described this all brilliantly, already, in her first book. I reiterate the central lesson of it here:

> Eros is an issue of boundaries. He exists because certain boundaries do. In the interval between reach and grasp, between glance and counterglance, between "I love you" and "I love you too," the absent presence of desire comes alive. But the boundaries of time and glance and I love you are only aftershocks of the main, inevitable boundary that creates Eros: the boundary of flesh and self between you and me. And it is only, suddenly, at the moment when I would dissolve that boundary, I realize I never can. . . .
>
> If we follow the trajectory of eros we consistently find it tracing this same route: it moves out from the lover toward the beloved, then ricochets back to the lover himself and the hole in him, unnoticed before. Who is the real subject of most love poems? Not the beloved. It is that hole.[48]

We are now caught in the thick weave of a strange constellation of ideas, ideas with which Carson has been grappling quite literally for decades. The soul is holy because the self is hole-y and incomplete (puns, she has told us, may be necessary here, one part of language's restless desire to capture what it can only ever chase). There is an absence in us, and because of this there is a desire in us, a hunger that food and wine cannot quench. *It is a desire, not for fullness, but for emptiness.* Gradually (and I have not yet finished with her first circuit of readings here), a set of interlocking topics is beginning to crystallize: sleep, death, sex, death, eros, death, the self lost in God, in mysticism, in Gnosticism . . . the unifying theme in all of this is seems to be some subtler conception of soulful "decreation." The self longs to disappear, yet re-asserts itself in this very mode of longing. To render that paradox poetically is an essentially spiritual undertaking.

Carson returns to several of the most significant philosophical themes she developed in *Eros the Bittersweet* in this text, but lends them an explicitly religious resonance, which seems altogether new and strange. One issue concerns triangulation (there is a great deal of playful dancing around various trinities in this text), and its erotic cognate, jealousy. These two combine to inspire ecstatic soul-states in which one literally stands outside of oneself: "not so much to an *undoing of the self as to an outdoing of it.*"⁴⁹

> Jealousy is a dance in which everyone moves. It is a dance with a dialectical nature. For the jealous lover must balance two contradictory realities within her heart: on the one hand, that of herself as the centre of the universe and in command of her own will, offering love to her beloved; on the other, that of herself off the centre of the universe and in despite of her own will, watching her beloved love someone else. Naked collision of these two realities brings the lover to a sort of breakdown—as we saw in Sappho's poem—whose effect is to expose her very Being to its own scrutiny and to dislodge it from the centre of itself. It would be a very high test of dialectical endurance to be able to, not just recognize, but consent to this breakdown. Sappho seems to be entering on a mood of consent when her poem stops. Marguerite faints three times before she can manage it. But then, with a psychological clarity as amazing as Sappho's, Marguerite pushes open the implications of her own pain. . . . Simone Weil was also a person who wanted to get herself out of the way so as to arrive at God.⁵⁰

What is most striking here is the triangulated metaphor for jealousy, observing someone we love who loves someone else, and how this metaphor has now been taken to involve the love of (a triune) God who may love a more faithful rival for His affection more than me.

Time and tense haunt this text, much as they haunted the second half of *Eros the Bittersweet*: "thinking there aren't enough tenses for all of this to happen in, the past and present fragmenting as they bop off one another."⁵¹ *Decreation* thus demands patience, and a slow reader. It is tender in some places, excruciating in others—very much like a love affair in its sweetbitterness. It builds slowly, gains momentum, then turns on a dime, taking on the subtle character of a seduction as it develops, grabbing its reader roughly then letting go again. "Out goes 'I,'" Carson winks at her readers, in the imagined voice of Simone Weil.⁵² She does not say where this outgoing may be.

The section headings of *Decreation* may be read cumulatively. "Stops" offers further meditations on sleep, tragedy, and death—in short, further grief lessons that burnish the soul. "Every Exit is an Entrance" contains more musing on sleep, inspired by Virginia Woolf and Homer. "Foam" and "Sublimes" takes up the historically delicate matter of the *philosopher's* way of thinking about *religious* things, from Plato thinking about the eternity of the soul, to Longinus thinking about the sublime, to Kant thinking about beauty. "Gnosticism" contains the most explicit material on the mystical extinguishing of the singular soul in favor of the universal spirit.⁵³ Then comes an inspiring series of Carson's own poetic "friskes, skips and jumps" which culminate in the two most shattering sections of the book (both of them entitled "Decreation") to which I have already alluded. From poetry, to essay, to opera and film; the journey inscribed in this book is epic in both scale and scope, well worthy of Dante.[54]

It is only at the end of the book that Carson's three spiritual lodestars are fully revealed: Sappho (about whom she says the least, perhaps because she has already said so much and so well elsewhere); Marguerite Porete (about whom she says the most, perhaps because she is so elusive, so unknown, and so fascinating[55]); and Simone Weil (whose titular coinage has perhaps already said it all).[56] These women are all speaking the same subtle spiritual language, Carson suggests, one which seeks ultimately to "tell God"—an hybristic arc of self-annihilation which also necessarily involves the writing, or else the lyricizing, of God. They are so bold as to speak *for* God. And they all use the same poetic tools to tell It: written images like Simonidean *eikones* which speak of eros, tragedy, sleep, loss, and death. Simone Weil puts the idea in its pithiest and most haunting terms when she suggests that the soul's circuitously philosophical passage runs "from atheism through affliction to love of God."[57]

Bringing her readers to this somewhat shocking impasse is already an uncanny spiritual achievement. But Carson has one last card to play, and this final ruse makes her own essays sublime. *You must have a self in order to give it away; the larger the soul, the greater the gift.* Such an insight calls for a great deal of reconsideration of what we mean by "self" in the first place. We will recall her puzzlement over selfhood and the limits of the virtue of self-control: "I wonder if there might not be another idea of human order than repression, another notion of human virtue that self-control, another kind of human self than one based on dissociation of inside and outside. Or indeed, another human essence than self."[58] Now, Carson suggests that this will also call for a reconsideration of the Greek preposition, *pros*, and how such a revised self may be imagined as "with" God.

> It seemed odd to me that Marguerite Porete puts the quotation marks around the "with" rather than around one of the pronouns. But Marguerite knows what she is doing: the people are not the problem here. Witness is the problem. She is trying to use the simplest language and the plainest marks to express a profoundly tricky spiritual fact, viz. that I cannot go toward God in love without bringing myself along. And so in the deepest possible sense I can never be alone with God. I can only be alone "with" God.[59]

Even a self that aspires to reconsideration through decreation brings herself along for the ride.

The moment of greatest awakening comes in part four of the "Decreation" essay,[60] an essay which had coyly promised its reader only three parts.[61] "We should brace ourselves for some inconsequentiality," Carson smiles at her reader.⁶² Why? Because all of these women—heroically trying to let go, even to let go of God, and in their most reckless moments seeming to celebrate this extinction of self—*these same women are the ones who write it all down*, and do so in works that are so utterly strange and distinctive, so marked by their unique soul-signature, that it would seem to undermine the very nature of their desire to decreate themselves.⁶³ "I don't feel the cause of this inconsequence is me," Carson muses. "Rather it originates with the three women we are studying and the cause of it is the fact that they are writers."⁶⁴ Here we are brought face-to-face with a paradox (arguably the central paradox) that has preoccupied Anne Carson from her first book to the present. Shouldn't the decreated soul *stop* creating? Shouldn't it cease *wanting* to create? Or at least, if it must speak, then shouldn't it do so in a more muted and less self-centered manner? Shouldn't such a soul at the very least refuse to sign its name? In his (written) meditation on Simone Weil, T.S. Eliot noted a related paradox: "A potential saint can be a very difficult person; I suspect that Simone Weil could be at times insupportable. One is struck, here and there, by a contrast between an almost superhuman humility and what appears to be an almost outrageous arrogance."⁶⁵ This is a very Homeric, a very lyric, perhaps simply a very Greek, paradox. It is also the essential paradox of the poet, where poetic creation is religious in its purest and broadest sense.

Carson draws special attention to Marguerite Porete's poetic coinage of a new name for God (*le Loing-prés,* "the FarNear")⁶⁶ in order to assist with her conclusion that describing that image of, and relationship to, God is only possible in writing. The "withness" is literary, writerly, creative. An object that is FarNear almost perfectly accords with Kakfa's elusive tops, which initiated the reach after which we can see Carson is grasping still. Perhaps the longing (loing-ing?) princess needed a poet in the end, not a painter. Or both.⁶⁷

> For the writer of a kletic hymn [an invitation of the god's arrival, such as Sappho wrote⁶⁸], God's absence is something tricky, perhaps impossible, to tell. This writer will have to invoke a God who arrives bringing her own absence with her—a God whose Farness is the more Near. It is an impossible motion possible only in writing.⁶⁹

"I have no idea what this means," Carson confesses, "but it gives me a thrill."⁷⁰

The kletic poem Carson has in mind is one of the longest of Sappho's surviving fragments (Fragment #2), and justifiably one of her most famous. The poet urges the goddess Aphrodite to "'come here from Krete/ to this holy temple." And, to Carson's point and current purpose, the last line of the poem, which is set off by itself, says simply "pour." So the "calling" is framed by two verbs, one present and one absent, two strange images of kenotic divine motion: coming forth, and pouring out. It is all very fluid, slippery and elusive. And it really makes no logical sense, Carson reminds us, because the goddess is always already here: "there is no climactic moment of God's arrival"[71] in this poem. The poem is also erotically arrogant, utterly self-possessed, assuming that a mortal poet can force a goddess to come pour herself out for the poet's own mortal desires. The poem is also selfish and egotistical, asking the goddess for favors and special attention—an issue that will recur in Marguerite Porete's startling conclusions and eventual condemnation. The claim to be the object of divine affection, to be divinely loved, demands a certain hybris after all. Yet the same poem also overflows with graceful thanksgiving. It hymns the goddess and the poet in equal measure, that is, what they are creating together; Sappho and Aphrodite actually appear to switch places in the final chapters of this book. Thus these two beings create something new together: what can be more divinely erotic than this? Diotima, as we have seen, spoke famously of our capacity for spiritual pregnancy in the *Symposium*.[72] "God has entire need of me. . . . Where else can God put God?"[73]

It is also significant that Sappho's invocation calls upon Aphrodite, whose priestess Carson assumes her to have been; the whole arc of this imaginary spiritual flow is erotically charged, passionately desiring, reaching and grasping, with virtual inexhaustibility. In such a way, this long Sapphic fragment eerily mimics a jarring image from the very last page of Simone Weil's notebooks, which were also published posthumously:

> He entered my room and said: "Poor creature, you who understand nothing, who know nothing. Come with me and I will teach you things which you do not suspect." I followed him.
>
> He took me into a church. It was new and ugly. He led me up to the altar and said: "Kneel down." I said "I have not been baptized." He said "Fall on your knees before this place, in love, as before the place where lies the truth." I obeyed.
>
> He brought me out and made me climb a garret. Through the open window one could see the whole city spread out, some wooden scaffolding, and the river on which boats were being unloaded. The garret was empty, except for a table and two chairs. He bade me be seated.
>
> We were alone. He spoke. From time to time someone would enter, mingle in the conversation, then leave again.
>
> Winter had gone; spring had not yet come. The branches of the tree lay bare, without buds, in the cold air full of sunshine.

> The light of day would arise, shine forth in splendor, and fade away; then the moon and the stars would enter through the window. And then once more the dawn would come up.
>
> At times he would fall silent, take some bread from the cupboard, and we would share it. This bread really had the taste of bread. I have never found that taste again.
>
> He would pour out some wine for me, and some for himself—wine which tasted of the sun and of the soil upon which this city was built.
>
> At other times we would stretch ourselves out on the floor of the garret, and sweet silence would enfold me. Then I would awake and drink in the light of the sun.
>
> He had promised to teach me, but he did not teach me anything. We talked about all kinds of things; in a desultory way, as do old friends.
>
> One day he said to me: "Now go." I fell down before him, I clasped his knees, I implored him not to drive me away. But he threw me out on the stairs. I went down unconscious of anything, my heart as it were in shreds. I wandered along the streets. Then I realized that I had no idea where the house lay.
>
> I have never tried to find it again. I understood that he had come for me by mistake. My place is not in that garret. It can be anywhere—in a prison cell, in one of those middle-class drawing-rooms full of knick-knacks and red plush, in the waiting room of a station—anywhere, except in that garret.
>
> Sometimes I cannot help trying, fearfully and remorsefully, to repeat to myself a part of what he said to me. How am I to know if I remember rightly? He is not there to tell me.
>
> I know well that he does not love me. How could he love me? And yet deep down within me something, a particle of myself cannot help thinking, with fear and trembling, that perhaps, in spite of all, he loves me.[74]

Two months after penning this mystic vision of a spiritually shattering love triangle, Simone Weil died. Carson reminds us that, in her last letter to her parents, she said "everything was fine."[75]

As we struggle to digest these difficult spiritual exercises, we cannot escape a worrisome question, one that we likely cannot answer, but one which Carson clearly means us to ask and to ask in earnestness. In the High Middle Ages, radically nonconforming women addressing heterodox ideas in jumbled, hybrid genres could easily find themselves on trial. Or worse. This was true of Joan of Arc (d.1431),[76] true of Margeurite Porete (d.1310), and true of many others whose stories have been brilliantly told by Caroline Walker Bynum, in whose inspired wake many others have followed.[77] Now, to be sure, state-sponsored immolation is one way to de-create a sentient being, though it is hardly a laudable strategy for any of the parties involved. But what, are we to make of it when public acclaim and notoriety—rather than condemnation—come to these virtuosi of spiritual decreation? If she is wise, Carson seems to suggest, then such a spiritual adept will flee from that kind of acclaim and the temptation to that kind of notoriety. Carson herself took up a rather strange signature in the years when she was working on this book: "Anne Carson lives in Canada and teaches Greek for a living"—so good luck tracking her down, or writing her a fan letter. Now *that* is an economy of unlosing. Decreation in the vast lands of celebrity.

A new spiritual problem comes into focus through these implicit concerns: *temptation*. In the modern west, we rightly congratulate ourselves on several genuinely historic achievements: of promoting religious tolerance and religious liberty in the face of increasing religious pluralism, on the one hand; and of feminism and women's liberation, on the other. Inquisitions and witch trials are, for the most part, a thing of the past. And yet, given our increasing comfort, Carson's challenging women put her reader to wonder if we may unwittingly have made the world impossible for the Sapphos, the Marguerites, the Joans, the Simones, all of these strange and inconvenient, non-conforming women who still wish to right themselves by *decreating* themselves in order to write God. The arc they all trace runs from affection through affliction to redemption. Sappho wrote in a period of tremendous political turmoil on her home island of Lesbos, and was herself exiled for quite some time. Marguerite Porete faced down one Inquisition in Valenciennes (in 1306), a second one in Paris (in 1309–1310), and suffered the lethal consequences of her bravado. Simone Weil would be unthinkable apart from the revolutionary turmoil of fascism, communism, and the Second World War. By contrast, Carson seems to imply, what do we really suffer?[78]

That seems an unfair question, especially in light of Carson's earlier reflections on Paul Celan's poetry in the horrific aftermath of the Shoah, and yet it is not, I do not think, precisely because Celan and Weil lived a long time ago, in a very different world. Anne Carson has placed her poetic finger on precisely this sensitive spot throughout her career: "the hole in us, unnoticed before." Or rather, she *discovered* the question there, in that holy place, and then she too wrote it out. She has done so again here in this text through some rather unlikely examples: of Sappho, legendarily settled, then unsettled, then suicidal; of Marguerite Porete, burned together with her book; and of Simone Weil, self-starved in the midst of a brutal London bombardment in a second World War.[79] It has something to do with tragedy, something to do with erotic intrusion, something to do with the ways rage and grief may be combined, or even self-reinforcing. It has something to do as well with erotic self-emptying and the soulful affliction which results.

> and as
> for the scandal of our abandonment
> in a universe of "sudden trembling love," blondes
> being
> always
> fatally
> reinscribed
> on an old cloth
> faintly,
> interminably
> undone, why
> does Plato
> call Necessity
> a "wandering cause" isn't it because
> you can
> 't
> tell
> where
> she got in?–men steady on the rock
> now they have put that gilded night
> down
> a little rip in their minds.[80]

That "little rip in their minds" echoes of one of William Carlos Williams's (1883–1963) most shattering poetic passages, from his "Tribute to the Painters" of 1955. The passage I have in mind begins with an invocation of dancing satyrs, then pirouettes inward to the poet's own dancing mind. It is there that he discovers "the tyranny of the image," which prompts men to iconoclastic violence, "that the trouble/ in their minds/ shall be quieted," and put to bed in the end.[81]

Williams is paying tribute to the painters, but he is well aware of the iconoclastic religious energies these figures have also unleashed. A word may be "an icon of things," but what then is a painting? Monotheists have often been uncertain of the proper reply to that question. In the "Book of Isaiah,"[82] Carson meditates on the paradox of people smashing the things that they love best, then justifying the action as "piety" or "sacrifice." Prophets, she adds, call these names and this whole spiritual economy into question. So, we should add, do poets . . . hence the need for another language to capture the pain and violence we do. Tyrannous or not, art's central issues are still intrusion, affliction, tragedy, all of which can both trouble and spangle the mind. Change of self is loss of self, for lyrical men. But what is it for these lyrical and spirited women? As Carson put this conundrum in 1995, well before her Sappho translations and this text, perhaps there is a better virtue than self-control to which we may aspire. In any case, this mingling of sexed bodies and spirituality, matters which have always "frisked, skipped and jumped" across the pages of Carson's poetry and prose, seem to obtain a gravity and poetic density in the labyrinthine spiritual course of *Decreation*. As the avant garde filmmaker, Maya Deren (1917–1961), came to see it, the central paradox of all artistic-and-spiritual creativity is the following: "the self must exit so that [spirit] may enter."[83] Hence Deren's interest in spirit possession and Haitian Vodou. "Out I go," Carson has Weil tell us. And so she did.

It is here, in the context of Carson's most explicitly religious writing, that I would like to explore the possible role played by a Roman, rather than a Greek, poet in the fashioning and reframing of these spiritual reflections, one she rarely mentions by name: I am speaking of Ovid.[84]

* * * * *

If ever there were an ancient poet who understood the paradox of reach and grasp, then that would be Ovid. One need think only of his canonical description of Apollo and Daphne[85] to see this clear. Apollo, fresh from his conquest of the Python and seeing young Cupid (Eros) arming his significantly smaller bow, insults the boy and tells him to leave such arms to men. Cupid responds strangely, observing that souled creatures (*animalia*) are less than deity (*deo*), and that by just so great a degree does Apollo's glory fall short of his own. He pierces Apollo with a golden arrow, but Daphne, with one made of lead. So the enamored god pursues and Daphne, committed to her perpetual virginity (*mihi perpetua . . . virginitate*), flees him. He runs in hope of reaching her, she in fear of his grasp. And so in the end, as he approaches her in mid-chase, she prays for release and is transformed into a laurel tree. Apollo, his erotic desire wedded now to tragedy, wears her leaves as his ornament, a perpetual memory of what he could not have or hold. Bernini's sculptural rendering of the scene captures the moment perfectly, from the frozen tears to the blossoming fingertips.[86] It is an ominous story, an erotic cautionary tale of great power and sadness, one suggesting that the gap between the ensouled human and the divine is potentially unbridgeable. Yet Ovid commonly refers to these rapacious pursuits of the Greek gods as more humorous than amorous.[87] In the end, the dance of erotic love he attempted to frame as a game turned serious, and eventually swallowed him, like a wave.

Publius Ovidius Naso (43 BCE–17 CE) composed a justly famous collection of fantastical letters written by Classical mythical heroines, the *Heroides*, presenting it (fittingly, for my interests in this book) as a new genre of his own invention. The fifteenth and last letter[88] in the original collection is one allegedly composed by "Sappho to Phaon," the legendary ferryboat operator who deflected her amours and allegedly inspired her suicidal leap from the cliffs of Leucadia (the Ionian Greek island of Leukas). Some have questioned the authenticity of this Sapphic epistle,[89] though I find the arguments in favor of Ovid's authorship still fairly persuasive.[90] Regardless of how one views the status of that question, the fact is that this Sapphic epistle makes the question of authorship an explicit topic at the very outset, such that one may remain agnostic on the question and still be rewarded with deep insight by examining it closely in relation to Ovid's other works.[91] In its heterosexualizing of Sappho's poetic persona,[92] and in its cultivation of the image of a Romantic poet who gave her all, including her life, for love,[93] Ovid's work may seem an unpromising source of insight for a poet and a philosopher of Carson's rare discernment regarding Sappho, her musical passions, and her soaring lyrical universe.

Still, we should suspend judgment until we have looked more deeply into the body, and the context, of Ovid's own writings, which are traditionally conceived in three phases defined by the interrelated topics of love, of transformation, and of exile. That, I will suggest, offers the most familiar point of comparative convergence to Carson's ouevre: the interest in love, in transformation, and in spiritual exile. In phasing him this way, readers have linked Ovid's biography to his poetry, in ways that more recent studies of Sappho's fragments have cautioned against. The history of reading Ovid, and its differences from the history of reading Sappho, are perhaps relevant here. In a word, Ovid's reception was far more discontinuous. Ovid was not consistently recognized as a part of the Latin literary firmament as Sappho was in Greek. Remarkably, Ovid, unlike other classical Latin writers such as Cicero, Seneca, Virgil, and the moral historians (Livy, Sallust, and Tacitus), had dropped out of the curriculum in Late Antiquity, a situation which was reversed only in the twelfth and thirteenth centuries in Europe. In the Middle Ages and Renaissance, "Lives of Ovid" were to inspire the same sort of cottage industry which "Lives of Sappho" had created in antiquity, and would again in the nineteenth century. By the fifteenth century in Italy, "Lives of Ovid" were actually being produced independently of editions of his poetry, that is, no longer serving merely as the preface to their poet's own works. By the High Renaissance, Ovid had become every bit as popular as Virgil throughout Europe and was taught extensively in the schools, especially his *Heroides* and the *Metamorphoses*. And by the nineteenth century, there was a robust international market for the buying and selling of Ovid's various manuscripts and print editions.[94] In the twentieth century, Ovid's star was almost continuously on the rise, such that he came to be seen as the most sensible, the most intelligible, and the most contemporary, of the old Roman poets. In short, by the time that Carson was conceiving of her first book on Sappho and Plato, Ovid had been mainstreamed.[95]

But why? The reasons are various and varying, a fact especially in line with Ovid's rather liquid literary personality. Was he a sexual libertine? a reckless seducer? a world-weary observer of imperial *Realpolitik*? an overly ambitious self-promoter? eventually the victim of his own success? Was he smart, or simply clever? And how do these questions inform our reading of his remarkable words and works? In putting the interpretive questions in this way, I am highlighting the fact that versions of many of these same questions have been put to Carson and her work as well. And indeed, since Sappho and Simonides, the relation between personality and poetics has been an open question.[96]

From the art of love, through spiritual transformation, to exile . . . how do we make sense of this trajectory, in a corpus or in a life?[97] I have found the work of a more contemporary creative writer of rare emotional range to be essential in my attempts to come to terms with the paradoxes of Ovid's erotic universe.[98] Jane Alison's first novel[99] seeks to imagine how Ovid composed his now-lost version of *Medea*, simultaneously and imaginatively resolving the historical mystery of how the poet came to be exiled by Augustus to Tomis, a Roman outpost on the western coast of the Black Sea. In brief, Ovid played the role of creative "love artist," twice over. First, he manipulated the violent jealousy of his own foreign lover, observing how she responded to the anguish he deliberately caused her, then he wrote it all down. That is, like a cruel Pygmalion in reverse, Ovid created a Medea in reality, in order to render another in verse. When his lover came to understand the dark game the poet was playing, she responded with a tragic and murderous game of her own, sifting through Ovid's papers and sending some incriminating excerpts to Augustus, who promptly banished the poet. The novel ends with the two gazing out at the Black Sea from opposing coasts, fully aware that the other is gazing similarly, mirror-fashion, on the other side of the sea. The prose here is as haunting as the story.

Later, Alison returned to Ovid's *Metamorphoses*, translating twenty-six narrative sequences in which someone's sex was changed in the poem (as well as six related passages from the *Amores*).[100] In between these two texts—one lost (*Medea*), one found (*Metamorphoses*)—we have the rich body of Ovid's masterful erotic works, like the *Loves* (*Amores*) and the *Heroides*,[101] as well as *The Art of Love* (*Ars Amatoria*) and *The Cures for Love* (*Remedia Amoris*).[102] These texts divide the insights of Carson's first book in two, presenting eros sweetly at the first, and then more sourly as time runs its subtle course through us.[103] Ovid well understood the ecstasies, the agonized self-sacrifices, the ruses, the emotional triangulations, that constitute eros's all-conquering power and endless fascination. Later, in the *Metamorphoses*, Ovid will even come to view eros, and the myths that enframe it, in a more spiritual manner. In this text, metamorphosis—that is to say, transformation, in all of its manifold and mystifying variety—is presented as the eternal principle of the universe, in matter as it is in mind. This startling realization will have large erotic and religious consequences. Here, arguably for the first time in Rome, we meet a lyric poet who does not experience change of self simply as loss of self, but rather as something bountiful and beautiful, all the more beautiful the more finely it may be wrought.[104] That Ovid's life spanned the bridge which leads us into Christian time is also highly suggestive, as I hope to demonstrate shortly.[105]

This new genre, as I am reading it, nonetheless played innovatively with established Roman ideas and recognizably Roman themes: we meet the endless fascination with Greece, in its literary and its philosophical modes; and still more importantly, we meet the encyclopedic arrangement of these modes into more inclusive and expansive wholes. It is here that we can see how Ovid did far more than enhance the Roman encyclopedia of Greek mythology; he virtually added new subject headings. Ovid *organized* a massive amount of Greek mythological material into themes, tropes, and thrills . . . he also permitted them to undergo metamorphosis in his own wizened poetic hands. The results are dazzling, and we owe a great deal of what we think we know about Greek myth to Ovid's alternately transgressive and transformative poetic powers.

Thus far, I have focused on Ovid's erotic and primarily bittersweet erotic reflections. "There is far more that bruises lovers than heals them;/ let them steel their souls to trouble";[106] so he cautions his readers early on. I am intrigued by the overlap between these cautious sentiments and Carson's more recent decreative meditations. If erotic agony may be read as spiritual affliction, then the poetry changes, too. After his exile in 8 CE, Ovid will enunciate his own version of tragic "grief lessons," in the *Tristia* and his *Poems from Exile*. It is here that his biography seems inseparable from the poetics:

> Desperate (*flebiles*) is our current state, and desperate (*flebile*) our song,
>   the matter and the writing intertwined (*materiae scripto conveniente suae*).[107]

In these works we make the acquaintance of a different sort of writer, one who seems unable to accept such a change as anything other than loss, even a form of symbolic death, and the obsequious pleading to the emperor for reprieve[108] can make for some difficult reading, almost as if we were being forced to read a private journal, or a love letter—something akin to the dangerous circumstance Jane Alison imagined in her first novel devoted to this Latin poet, and the literary thrust of his own ideas in the *Heroides*.

As to the reasons for his exile, Ovid is oblique, perhaps necessarily so. He famously speaks with suggestive vagueness of "a poem and an error."

> Two crimes (*crimina*) brought me down, a poem and an error (*carmen et error*),
>   yet I cloak my guilt (*culpa*) in silence:
> I am not so bold as to revive your pain, o Caesar;
>   it is enough I did so once.[109]

Seeking comfort from pain in lyric poetry, Ovid speaks of the Muse as his only faithful companion in exile, as she had once been his partner in the crime:

> She knows very well the error (*error*) that led me to ruin,
>   that the fault (*culpa*) is mine, yes, but no crime (*scelus*).
> So she is fair to me now, she who injured me then,
>   since her work is judged as criminal (*criminis*) as mine.[110]

In fact, Ovid will never speak of the "error," but only of the poem, which is presumed by many to have been his *Ars Amatoria*. But this was likely the pretense for an exile that had darker and more obscure political causes.[111] And in any case, it is only in a song, not in a criminal error, that the Muse may have been Ovid's co-conspirator.

Anne Carson dedicated a "Short Talk" to Ovid, and in it, she takes up this endlessly fascinating literary question of his poetic exile.

> I see him there on a night like this but cool, the moon blowing through black streets. He sups and walks back to his room. The radio is on the floor. Its luminous green dial blares softly. He sits down at the table; people in exile write so many letters. Now Ovid is weeping. Each night about this time he puts on sadness like a garment and goes on writing. In his spare time he is teaching himself the local language (Getic) in order to compose in it an epic poem no one will ever read.[112]

Carson seems utterly uninterested in the forensic question of what crime led to Ovid's banishment. She is solely interested in his experience of isolation, the lessons to be gleaned from profound and well-nigh paralyzing grief. And she is interested in how the exiled poet, much like the abandoned lover, finds solace in lyric poetry. "Each night about this time he puts on sadness like a garment and goes on writing." Loves are won and lost, the soul changes much as love and life do, but the writing endures, offering the poet a weird sort of constant companionship. There is more than a subtle hint in the entire body of Carson's work to suggest that the poetic *fragment* captures the truth of such writing (and such experiences) best, much as it captures the truth of the soul in love: we are, we fall, to pieces. And no Roman poet, presumably, knew that better than Ovid.

Carson also teases out the unique form of torture which exile may represent for a poet: namely, *the loss of language*. She imagines Ovid composing a new epic in the Getic tongue, an epic for which there will be no readers. The Romans will not be able to read this new verse, and the "Scythians" among whom Ovid now lives have no taste for, nor tradition of, lyric poetry. This politically inspired change of venue, Ovid's final metamorphosis, thus put an end to the *Metamorphoses*. It severed the bridge between the writer and his formerly enamored audience.[113] It is a terrifying poetic prospect, one Ovid confronts explicitly.

> Often now when I try to speak–such shameful confession (*turpe fateri*)!—
>> words fail me and I have unlearned speech (*verba mihi desunt dedidicique loqui*).
> Thracian and Scythian sense-surround me now,
>> and I think I could write in the Getic mode.
> Honestly, I fear that there may be mixed up in my Latin (*inmixta Latinis*)
>> writings (*inque meis scriptis*), the very language of the Pontus.
> Howsoever you find my book, indulge it and excuse it,
>> given this my current state (*sortis et excusa condicione meae*).[114]

There is something funny about this confession; something seems wrong. Something nags at us as we read Ovid's theatrical nostalgia for his lost homeland, together with these hyperbolic complaints about his new location where nothing—not the weather, not the food, and certainly not the people—possess anything of interest, inspiration, or of lasting value. Nostalgia is often a falsifying and debilitating emotion, one that requires the romantic (and largely antiseptic) overestimation of what was left behind in the past.[115] Ovid himself had made that caution a virtual canon of his love-cures. At an earlier point in his career, he had advised self-exile as the surest cure for a failed love affair, and the surest antidote to nostalgia of any kind, whether for places or for people:

> Do not count the hours (*tempora nec numera*), do not keep looking back at Rome,
>> but fly away (*sed fuge*): in such flight even the Parthian is safe from us.
> Some may call my precepts hard (*dura*); and hard (*dura*) they are;
>> to recover your health requires the shock of pain (*multa*

> *dolenda feres*). . . .
> Once you have set out, a hundred distractions will bring solace (*centum solatia curae*):
> country scenes, companions, the long road.
> Do not tell yourself that flight is enough; prolong the exile (*lentus abesto*)
> until burning flame fades to ember, and dead ash (*igne cinis*).[116]

Ovid, we may note, was not from Rome, originally; he grew up in Sulmo, in the Abruzzo, roughly ninety miles north of the capitol. He remembers nothing particularly special or worthwhile about his homeland and he transitioned easily enough to the capitol at the age of twelve. He seems to have adapted fairly easily to change and circumstance then. But no longer. His suppleness seems at an end.

We might construe this all the more sympathetically, of course. And the latest generation of Ovid scholars have turned to this important task.[117] He had worked very hard to achieve poetic success and notoriety in Rome; to lose such an audience was to lose a world, for such a poet. Yet Ovid somehow manages to make the isolation and despair even worse than it is.[118] He left a dutiful and long-suffering third wife behind in Rome, lobbying for his return, then complained bitterly about the distance between them, as well as his desperate personal isolation and cultural starvation. He can sound almost like Admetus, theatrically mourning the very loss of Alkestis that he commissioned. To be sure, Ovid was older by then, such that the energy he might have brought to a situation of this kind at the age of twelve or twenty-five was lacking at the age of fifty. His hair was graying already when he left Rome, he admits, but now the experience of exile has grayed his hair and addled his mind at an accelerated rate. He simply lacked the spiritual resources to face this change, to pick up and start over (now, again).[119] Tellingly, he did continue to write though, and with a furious increase in pace—what else is an exile to do?[120]

According to the Parian Marble,[121] Sappho was exiled as well—for over a decade, from Lesbos to Sicily. The unstated reasons must also have been political, at a highly volatile moment in the political life of Archaic Lesbos. But the Marble says no more; we may reasonably suppose that Sappho did not belabor the exile in her poetry. The reason there is so much modern discussion of Ovid's exile, by contrast, is that he talked about it so obsessively himself, creating yet another genre—that of "exile writings"—along the way.[122]

While sympathetic with Ovid's poetic plight, of course, I would like to suggest that what is missing in Ovid's description of his exile, and his experience of it, is the apparent lack of sensibility to the power and possibilities of *translation*. For all of the genre-bending and transgressive overlap between Ovid and Anne Carson, the one thing that Ovid does *not* share is the prominence of language translation in his profile. He was in Rome, and of Rome, and when absent from Rome, he suffered the absence. That seemed to make all the difference, in Tomis. As I noted in the second chapter, Carson accepts Walter Benjamin's conception of translation in terms of linguistic *reciprocity*: "Translation thus ultimately serves the purpose of expressing the central reciprocal relationship between languages. . . . Languages are not strangers to one another, but are a priori and apart from all historical relationships, interrelated in what they want to express."[123] There is a reciprocity lacking here, somehow, not only in Augustus's harsh banishment of the poet to the very edges of the empire, but also in the poet's assessment and experience of his new homeland.

A poet with Ovid's feeling and flair for language might have applied himself passionately to the acquisition of a new language, to translating some classical Scythian poetry into Latin, or even to translating his own verse into Getic. He might have performed a dramatic adaptation into Latin of some western Black Sea myths, much as he had done with the myth of Medea. He does appear to have toyed with the idea,

> For shame (*pudet*)! I have written a poem in the Getic tongue,
>   setting barbarian words to Roman cadence:
> I even seem to have pleased as a poet (*kudos to me*),
>   earning that name among these uncivilized (*inhumanos*) Getae.
> My theme? You'd approve: I sang of Caesar (*de Caesare dixi*).[124]

But clearly this is offered in ironic jest: Ovid expresses shame at the venture; he demeans the praise of his barbarian, and scarcely human, audience; and he was clearly well past singing Caesar's praises in Tomis. More to the point, the barrier between languages appears to have been insurmountable for Ovid, perceived as an unbridgeable cultural chasm. Here, a new language can deform the old one, he seems to suggest, but never enhance it ("small wonder if my poems putter, as I am virtually remade in Getic verse"[125]). Change of language is loss of language for this poet; and as such, Ovid appears incapable of the soaring flights of transformative (and translational) fancy that have animated most of Carson's deepest erotic and spiritual insights. It is not just that translations are central to her resume; *Carson utilizes the image of erotic triangulation to theorize her practice of translation*. In Carson's view, poets such as Sappho, Marguerite Porete, and Simone Weil even aspired to translate the ways of heaven to the world, and vice versa.[126]

We now may hear something more than playful avoidance in Carson's coy self-description: "Anne Carson lives[127] in Canada and teaches Greek for a living." In a word, Anne Carson has devoted a lifetime to translating Greek and Latin into English, and that linguistic practice has been absolutely essential to her formation as a poet in the English tongue (as well as a reader of medieval and modern French mystics, of German poets and philosophers, and of ancient Greek lyricists). It is the most un-Ovidian thing about her. (We can't quite imagine Ovid ever saying "Publius Ovidius Naso lives in Tomis and teaches Latin for a living." But he might have done).

As Carson's work in *Decreation* and since then suggests, this may well have deeper spiritual consequences. Many of the women to whom Carson gave poetic voice in *Decreation* went so far as to conceive of embodied life itself as a form of the soul's exile. If change of self (that is, metamorphosis) is to be perceived as anything more than loss of self, if transformation is to be re-claimed as an indelible personal experience in which the gains compensate for the losses, then the unwillingness, or the inability, to embrace these facts is almost surely to result in a serious spiritual deficit. Then there is no getting over an insult, an injury, a heartbreak, a dislocation, a re-location, a new language added to the repertoire.

> I should need ten months, and just as many tongues,
>   To tell all the sacrilegious ruses Roman beauties employ.[128]

The self is rendered as static as the world it wishes to inhabit, much like Lysias's frigid non-lover, and something runs aground. Not for nothing does Ovid compare himself obsessively to shipwrecked Odysseus in these many works of exile. But Odysseus, of course had his homecoming.

It is to Anne Carson's supple mingling of poetic images for romantic and spiritual homecoming that I would like to turn in conclusion. I suspect that she is reaching after an anti-nostalgic type of homecoming (*nostos*), one which *embraces* temporal change, spatial change, and ultimately change of self—unlike Archilochus, or Ovid—even to the point of self-annihilation.

> To stay human is to break a limitation.
> Like it if you can. Like it if you dare.[129]

NOTES

1. Anne Carson, *Short Talks* (Ontario: Brick Books, 1992). This collection was reprinted in *Plainwater* (29–45), in 1995.

It is remarkable that Carson has recently returned to this self-defined genre (if that is what it is); see her "Short Talk on Homer and John Ashbery," *The New Yorker* (December 24 & 31, 2018). She announced her intention to return to the form in a "Short Talk" dedicated to the contemporary translator and her close friend, Stanley Lombardo.

2. Anne Carson, *Glass, Irony and God* (New York, NY: New Directions Publishing Corporation, 1992, 1995).

3. Anne Carson, *Plainwater: Essays and Poetry* (New York, NY: Vintage Books, 1995).

4. Anne Carson, *Nox* (New York, NY: New Directions Publishing Corporation, 2010), which has the form of a cardboard accordion, such that page numbers are not available for this extraordinary piece of visual art, either.

All I know to say about this overwhelming piece is this: It is, loosely speaking, a literary memoir of sorts, replicating a collage which Carson produced to commemorate and to mourn the death of her brother. But this essay in poignant self-disclosure borders on the unbearable, the textual and visual production of tragic states of such extremity as to exceed what is naturally bearable. It is as if Carson wishes to blur the standard emotional genres, much as she has blurred literary ones throughout her career. This, too, is a grief lesson of singular power and poignancy.

A profound and insightful examination of the psychological depths in *Nox* is Joan Fleming, "'Talk (Why?) With Mute Ash': Anne Carson's *Nox* as Therapeutic Biography," *Biography: An Interdisciplinary Quarterly* 39.1 (Winter 2016): 64–78. For a superb analysis of the materiality of this boxed archive of mourning, see Tatiani G. Rapatzikou, "Anne Carson's *Nox*: Materiality and Memory," *Book 2.0* 7.1 (2017): 57–65. Finally, Jane Alison offers a brilliant reading of *Nox* in her passionate plea for non-teleological forms of narration, *Meander, Spiral, Explode: Design and Pattern in Narrative* (New York, NY: Catapult, 2019), 230–234.

5. Kiene Brillenburg Wurth, "Re-vision as Remediation: Hypermediacy and Translation in Anne Carson's *Nox*," *Image & Narrative* 14.4 (2013): 20–33 connects these two matters in a deeply insightful way: "If *Nox* is a book about Carson's remembrance of Michael, it is as much about her translation of Catullus 101. Remembering and translating: two related gestures that revolve around incorporations and re-creation" (22). Tellingly, Carson notes that she had loved both poem and brother since her adolescence; both remained elusive. "I have loved the poem since the first time I read it in high school Latin class and I have tried to translate it a number of times. . . . But over the years of working on it, I came to think of translating as a room, not exactly an unknown room, where one gropes for the light switch. I guess it never ends" (quoted at 30).

The link between Carson's practices of translation and of mourning (both demanding a reach without the possibility of grasping) is also noted in Gillian Sze, "The Consolatory Fold: Anne Carson's *Nox* and the Melancholic Archive," *Studies in Canadian Literature* 44.1 (2019): 66–80.

6. The two-fold repetition, *ad inferias*, poignantly reminds us of what Carson was not able to do, since the ashes of her brother's body were scattered in the North Sea, well before Carson had even learned of his passing.

7. Carson had published an earlier venture at Catullus 101 in *Men in the Off Hours* (New York, NY: Alfred A. Knopf, 2000), 45.

8. Fleming, "Talk (Why?) With Mute Ash," 77.

9. Anne Carson, *Decreation: Poetry, Essays, Opera* (New York, NY: Alfred A. Knopf, 2005). Dan Disney aptly describes the book "as a pastiche, a trans-genred and surrealistic ready-made which explores interstices between a selection of tracts, treatises, mediums and artefacts." Dan Disney, "Sublime Disembodiment? Self-as-Other in Anne Carson's *Decreation*," *Orbis Litterarum* 67.1 (2021), 25–38 (quote at 26).

10. This same claim might be ventured for her first hybrid collection, *Glass, Irony and God*. On that topic, see Jessica Fisher, "Anne Carson's Stereoscopic Poetics," in Joshua Marie Wilkinson, ed., *Anne Carson: Ecstatic Lyre* (Ann Arbor, MI: University of Michigan Press, 2015), 10–16:

> Of all the boundaries Anne Carson works to dissolve in her allusive, intergeneric work, the most trenchant is that of the self. A strong line of philosophical inquiry runs through her writing, which frequently addresses the startling question she first poses in *Glass, Irony and God*: "I wonder," she asks, "if there might not be . . . another kind of human self than one based on dissociation of inside and outside. Or, indeed, another human essence than self." (10)

I will have much more to say about this passage later in this chapter.

See also Brian Teare, "Reading Carson Reading Brontë RE *The Soul's Difficult Sexual Destiny*," in Wilkinson, ed., *Anne Carson: Ecstatic Lyre*, 30–35.

11. In point of fact, Ian Rae notes, the quote does not come from that essay, but rather from "Of Vanitie," an *erratum* he takes to be "a scholarly joke since the sentence preceding the Montaigne citation states, in the original, that 'the titles of my chapters, embrace not always the matter'" (Ian Rae, "Verglas: Narrative Techniques in Anne Carson's 'The Glass Essay,'" *English Studies in Canada* 37.3/4 (2011): 165n2).

Rae erroneously claims that the citation appears at the beginning of Carson's volume of poetry, *Men in the Off Hours* (2000), rather than the beginning of *Decreation* (2005). Nonetheless, Rae is correct; the passage from "Of Vanitie" reads as follows, and we should note that its initial prompting is Plato's *Phaedrus*:

> I have heretofore cast mine eyes upon some of Platoes Dialogues: [bemotled] with a fantasticall variety: the first part treateth of love, all the latter of Rhetorick. They feare not these variances: and have a wonderfull grace in suffering themselves to bee transported by the wind; or to seeme so. The titles of my chapters, embrace not allwayes the matter: they often but glance at it by some marke: as these others, Andria, Eunuchus: or these, Sylla, Cicero, Torquatus. I love a Poeticall kinde of march, by friskes, skips and jumps. It is an art (saith Plato) light, nimble, fleeting and light braind.

I am using the text edited by Ernest Rhys, *The Essayes of Michael Lord of Montaigne Translated by John Florio*, (London & Toronto: J. M. Dent & Sons, Ltd., 1910), Volume III: 244.

Why Carson should have assigned the passage to the essay "Upon Some Verses of *Virgil*" is a difficult question on which to speculate, whether it was due to deliberate humor, or a more unconscious juxtaposition. Either way, it is worth noting that

Montaigne's overall purpose in the essay on Virgil is to decry the excesses of jealousy and envy, especially in relation to sexual and marital relations, the final point of which seems especially germane to the erotic hypothesis proffered in *Decreation*:

> *I say, that both male and female, are cast in one same moulde; instruction and custome excepted, there is no great difference betweene them*: Plato calleth them both indifferently to the society of all studies, exercises, charges and functions of warre and peace, in his Commonwealth. And the philosopher *Antisthenes* took away all distinction betweene their vertue and ours. It is much more easie to accuse the one sexe, than to excuse the other. (Ibid., III: 128)

12. Anne Carson, *Decreation*, 157.

13. This unattested observation is quoted together with Camus's in nearly every discussion of Weil, excluding Carson's. For more on Weil's connection to Camus, see Robert Zaretsky, "The Logic of the Rebel: On Simone Weil and Albert Camus," *Los Angeles Review of Books* (March 7, 2020).

14. That said, one suggestive point of entry concerns Weil's reflections on the arts of writing and translation, in which she echoes Carson's own aspirations to transparency through a clearing away of what Emerson called "all mean egoism." Weil notes:

> The real way of writing is to write as we translate. When we translate a text written in some foreign language we do not seek to add anything to it; on the contrary, we are scrupulously careful not to add anything to it. That is how we have to try to translate a text which is not written down.

This remark appeared in a letter Weil wrote to her friend, Gustave Thibon, one which he quotes in his Introduction to *Gravity and Grace*, Arthur Wills, trans. (New York, NY: Octagon Books, 1983), 8.

15. Of particular interest to me are the following: *Gateway to God*, David Raper, ed. (New York, NY: Crossroads, 1982); *Gravity and Grace*, Arthur Wills, trans. (New York, NY: Octagon Books, 1983); *Lectures on Philosophy*, Hugh Price, trans. (New York, NY: Cambridge University Press, 1978); *The Need for Roots: Prelude to a Declaration of Duties toward Mankind*, Arthur Wills, trans. (New York, NY: Octagon Books, 1984); *Oppression and Liberty*, Arthur Wills and John Petrie, trans. (Amherst, MA: University of Massachusetts Press, 1973); and *Waiting for God*, Emma Crauford, trans. (New York, NY: Harper & Row, Publishers, 1951).

16. Simone Weil, "l'*Iliade*, ou, le Poème de la Force," was originally written in 1943 for *Cahiers du Sud*, then translated into English twice: as "The *Iliad*, or the Poem of Force" by Mary McCarthy (Pendle Hills Pamphlets, 1974) and as "The *Iliad*, Poem of Might," in a posthumous collection entitled *Intimations of Christianity among the Ancient Greeks* (London: Routledge & Kegan Paul, 1957), 24–55.

17. The secondary bibliography on Simone Weil has grown quite large. I have profited especially from analyses of her Christian classicism by: Robert Coles, *Simone Weil: A Modern Pilgrimage* (Reading, MA: Addison-Wesley Publishing Company, Inc., 1987); Henry Leroy Finch, *Simone Weil and the Intellect of Grace* (New York, NY: Continuum, 1999); Francine du Plessix Gray, *Simone Weil* (New York, NY:

Penguin Books, 2001); John Hellman, *Simone Weil: An Introduction to Her Thought* (Philadelphia, PA: Fortress Press, 1984); and Eric O. Springsted, *Christus Mediator: Platonic Mediation in the Thought of Simone Weil* (Chico, CA: American Academy of Religion Series No. 41, 1983).

Finally, I note Megan Terry's wonderful play, "Approaching Simone: A Drama in Two Acts" (Samuel French, Inc., 1970).

18. Anne Carson, *Decreation*, 157.

19. Anne Carson, *Decreation*, "Decreation Aria [sung by Simone alone in an empty place]," 235.

20. Anne Carson, *Eros the Bittersweet*, 39.

21. Anne Carson, "The Gender of Sound," in *Glass, Irony and God*, 121–125.

22. See, for example: "The Justice of Aphrodite in Sappho Fr. 1," *Transactions of the American Philological Association* 110 (1980): 135–142; "Wedding at Noon in Pindar's *Ninth Pythian*," *Greek, Roman and Byzantine Studies* 23 (1982): 121–128; "Putting Her in Her Place: Women, Dirt, Desire," in David Halperin, John J. Winkler, and Froma Zeitlin, eds., *Before Sexuality: The Construction of Erotic Experience in the Ancient Greek World* (Princeton, NJ: Princeton University Press, 1990), 135–169; "The Gender of Sound" in *Glass, Irony and God*, 119–142; "The Anthropology of Water," in *Plainwater*, 117–260; and the entirety of *Men in the Off Hours* (New York, NY: Alfred A. Knopf, 2000).

23. Anne Carson, *Decreation*, 155–183.

24. Anne Carson, *Decreation*, 187–240. A version of this opera was performed for the first time on September 8, 2001 at the California College of Arts and Crafts in San Francisco.

See Peter Streckfus, "Collaborating on *Decreation*: An Interview with Anne Carson," in Joshua Marie Wilkinson, ed., *Anne Carson: Ecstatic Lyre*, 214–221.

25. Anne Carson, *Decreation*, 243–245.

26. Anne Carson, *Decreation*, 157.

27. Anne Carson, *Decreation*, 157.

28. This is stated on the Parian Marble, for which see D. A. Campbell, ed., *Greek Lyric I: Sappho and Alcaeus*, 8–9.

29. For the Old French (and Italian) version, I have used Margherita Porete, *Lo Specchio delle Anime Semplici*, Giovanni Fozzer, trans. (Firenze: Editoriale De Lettere, 2018). I have also consulted three Latin manuscript versions of *The Mirror* which are housed at the Vatican Library (*Vat. lat.* 4355, *Rossiani* 4, and *Chigiani* IV.85 ff96r–143v).

A useful English edition is Marguerite Porete, *The Mirror of Simple Souls*, Ellen L. Babinsky, trans. (New York, NY: Paulist Press, 1993).

The book was (re)connected to Marguerite Porete's authorship in 1946 by Romana Guarnieri, as recounted in "Quando si dice, il caso!" *Bailamme: Rivista di spiritualità e politica* 8 (1990): 45–55. For more on the translation history of the *Mirror*, see Richard Methley, *Speculum Animarum Simplicium, A Glossed Latin Version of the Mirror of Simple Souls* (Salzburg: Institüt für Anglistik und Amerikanstik, 2010), II: 1–9, and Robert E. Lerner, "New Light on *The Mirror of Simple Souls*," *Speculum* 85 (2010): 91–116.

Lerner's work offers a fascinating and far-reaching analysis of the Middle English translation of the *Mirror*, which, he concludes, "stands for the most pristine surviving version in every respect" (100), and is "closest to Marguerite's own intentions" (116), demonstrating how the major French and Latin versions have been cleaned up, theologically. That version is available in *The Mirror of Simple Souls* (London: Burns Oates and Washburne Ltd., 1927), which publication was ironically approved by the Holy See, and which refers to its author as "an unknown French mystic of the thirteenth century" (and assumes her to be male); it was translated by an anonymous figure identified as "M. N.," who added extensive commentary to defend the book's orthodoxy. Lerner assembles the available evidence to suggest that this translator was none other than Michael Northburgh (d.1361), a lawyer/clerk to Edward III, and that the unadulterated French text he translated had been spirited out of Marguerite's home region of Valenciennes in the retinue for Edward's bride, Philippa of Hainaut (103–107).

The introduction and notes compiled by Claire Kirchberger in 1927 trace the manuscript history of the English and Latin versions of *The Mirror*, which were arguably less tumultuous than the Old French original's, and also defend the book's orthodoxy against charges of "Pantheism and Quietism." Since Anne Carson appears to have consulted with Lerner on several performance pieces inspired by Marguerite's *Mirror* in 2001 and thereafter, I suspect that she worked closely with this 1927 version. It is by far the most adventurous and non-conforming of the available versions, and I will make significant use of it as well.

30. I take this wonderful phrase from a superb study of Marguerite Porete's interrogation and condemnation: Sean L. Field, *The Beguine, the Angel, and the Inquisitor: The Trials of Marguerite Porete and Guiard of Cressonessart* (Notre Dame, IN: University of Notre Dame Press, 2012), 2 (of particular interest are his discussions at 1–26, 85–166, and 209–231). Field nicely captures the sense of the book, as indicated by the Latin title in the Vatican Chigiani manuscript: *Speculum [animatum] simplicitum i voluntate et desiderio morantur / ATS anima adnihilata.*

Of additional interest is the collection of essays in Sean L. Field, Robert E. Lerner et Sylvain Piron, *Marguerite Porete et Le Miroir des Simples Âmes: Perspectives Historiques, Philosophiques et Littéraires* (Paris: Librairie Philosophique J. Vrin, 2013).

31. Sean L. Field, *The Beguine, the Angel, and the Inquisitor*, 3. One can scarcely imagine a more compelling way of illustrating the thick weave of connection Carson the classicist sees between a corpus, a body, and a corpse.

32. Anne Carson, "TV Men: Sappho," in *Glass, Irony and God*, 71–72.

33. Anne Carson, "The Gender of Sound," in *Glass, Irony and God* (New York, NY: New Directions Publishing Corporation, 1995), 136–137.

For more on this provocative idea, see Christine Wiesenthal, "The 'Impossible Truth' of Writing Off the Subject: Anne Carson's Decreation Poetics and 'The Glass Essay,'" *TEXT*, Special Issue 50 (2018): 1–10. What Wiesenthal notes with rare and admirable clarity is the degree to which Carson's ideal of "glass" is sundered by the very text that attempts to make it transparent: it is smudged with authorial fingerprints, turns dark as black ice, and is eventually dirtied to the point of being clear as mud.

34. Carson, "Thou," in *Glass, Irony and God*, 31–38.

In addition, she will also blur boundaries between waking and sleep, writer and reader, seer and things seen . . . all of this culminating in a blurring, or expanding, of the trim borders of self.

See Helena Van Praet, "Recalibrating Categorisation: A Semiological Reading of Anne Carson's *Decreation*," *English Text Construction* 12.2 (2019): 169.

35. *The Mirror of Simple Souls*, lxv.

The Italian critical edition of the Old French edition (2018, pages 454–455) and the modern English translation by Ellen Bandinsky (1993, page 221) place this Latin "Approval" (*Approbatio*) at the conclusion of the work, not the beginning, and emphasize God's role in it as Author: "I [am] a creature from the creator by whose mediation the Creator made this book of Himself for those whom I do not know nor do I desire to know, because I ought not to desire this" [*ego creatura a creante condita, mediante qua Creator de se facit hunc librum, pro quibus nescio nec scire volo, quia hoc non debeo velle*].

The connection to Diotima's speech in the *Symposium* is suggestive, since both women are allegorizing the soul's ascent to some sort of "divine" vision. The "ladder of love" image from that speech would give birth to a great deal of spiritual speculation over ensuing millennia, of which *The Mirror*, with its seven stages of soulful purgation, is clearly one example.

For more on the ladder of love's subsequent mystical and poetic career, see Martha C. Nussbaum, *Upheavals of Thought: The Intelligence of Emotions* (New York, NY: Cambridge University Press, 2001), esp. 457–500.

36. And were it more certainly true to Marguerite Porete's own phrasing. As I observed in the previous Note, this section appears as the Prologue only in the Middle English version of *The Mirror* printed in 1927; elsewhere it is made part of an "Approval" placed at the end of the book which only appears in the Latin and Middle English versions of *The Mirror*.

It bears mention that the Italian critical edition of the Old French edition (2018, pages 84–87) and the modern English translation by Ellen Bandinsky (1993, page 80) both describe a manuscript that begins with a poem and identify chapter one as the Prologue. In that Prologue, we find a reference to "the high [sublime] love of the Unencumbered Soul [and] how the Holy Spirit has placed his sail in her as if she were his ship" [*la haulte amour de l'Ame Enfranchie, et comment le Saint Esperit a mis son voille en elle comme en sa naif*].

That remarkably oceanic image might serve as a credo of sorts, too. The second century Christian apologist, Athenagoras, famously noted that the holy spirit "used the prophets as a flautist plays a flute."

37. *The Mirror of Simple Souls*, 2.

The Italian critical edition of the Old French edition (2018, pages 88-89) and the modern English translation by Ellen Bandinsky (1993, page 80) say this: "But this maiden was so far from this great lord, in whom she had fixed her love from herself, that she was able neither to see him nor to have him. Thus she was inconsolable in herself, for no love except this one would suffice her" [*Mais si loing estoit ceste damoiselle de ce grant seigneur, ouquel elle avoit mis son amour d'elle mesmes, car veoir ne avoir ne le povoit; par quoy en elle mesmes souvent estoit desconfortee, car nulle amour fors que ceste cy ne luy souffisoit*].

38. *The Mirror of Simple Souls*, 284–285 ("Thus my will is martyred, and my love martyred; ye have them to martyrdom brought").

The Italian critical edition of the Old French edition (2018, pages 436–437) and the modern English translation by Ellen Bandinsky (1993, page 214) say this: "And thus, Lord, my will has ended in saying this; my will is martyred, and my love is martyred: You have guided these to martyrdom" [*Et ainsi, sire, ma voulenté prent sa fin en ce dire; et pource est mon vouloir martir, et mon amour martire: vould les avez a martire amenez*].

39. *The Mirror of Simple Souls*, 278.

The Italian critical edition of the Old French edition (2018, pages 428–429) and the modern English translation by Ellen Bandinsky (1993, page 211) say this: "After this, I pondered, in light of my wretchedness and in light of His goodness, what I could do to calm myself about Him" [*Après donc je regarday parmy la mauvaistié de moy et parmy la bonté de luy quelle chose je pourroie faire pour moy apaiser de luy*].

40. Anne Carson, *Decreation*, 7.
41. Anne Carson, *Decreation*, 36–40.
42. Plato, *Crito* 43a–b.
43. Plato, *Crito* 43d–44b.
44. For an altogether brilliant analysis of the role of insomnia in ancient epic, one which suggests that the relatively new phenomenon of citied life had disturbed natural sleep patterns in ways that created psychic turmoil which epic poetry sought to resolve, see Andrea Deagon, "The Twelve Double-Hours of Night: Insomnia and Transformation in 'Gilgamesh,'" *Soundings* 81.3/4 (1998): 461–489.
45. Plato, *Phaedo* 71c–73a.
46. See the paradigmatic episode of the meeting between Achilles and Priam at *Iliad* 24: 597–628, with its rich constellation of evocative nouns: *dakru* and *dakrua* (tear and tears), *eros* (desire), *posis* or *posios* (drink), *oinos* (wine), *edêtus* (meat or food) and *sitos* (grain or bread).
47. See *Iliad* 23: 231ff.
48. Anne Carson, *Eros the Bittersweet*, 30.
49. Cole Swensen, "Opera Povera: *Decreation*, An Opera in Three Parts," in Joshua Marie Wilkinson, ed., *Anne Carson: Ecstatic Lyre*, 127–131 (quote at 129).
50. Anne Carson, *Decreation*, 165, 167.
51. This elegant phrase is from another one of Carson's poetic adepts, Susan Mitchell, in her poetic rendition of the myth of Eros and Psyche entitled "Erotikon."
52. Anne Carson, *Decreation*, 230.
53. This is a very large claim, which hinges on an understudied aspect of the early spirituality of the Jesus movement, as influenced by "Gnosticism" and as evidenced both inside and outside of the New Testament, one which put a premium on something they began to call "holy spirit." In short, a philosophical interest in the body and the soul led these people to the spirit—and eventually to a bolder, Trinitarian theology. Here, I will simply itemize the way in which "holy spirit" is at issue in nearly every book in the New Testament.

In the Gospel according to Mark, when Jesus is baptized by an ascetic figure named John, that is when *holy spirit* comes upon him, and that is when he is identified as "son of God."

In the Gospel according to Matthew, for all the ways in which Jesus is shown preaching that people should be more forgiving than the Law of Moses is, he is reported to have said that there is one, and only one, crime his followers may commit that will not be forgiven: blasphemy against *holy spirit*.

In the Gospel according to Matthew, when Jesus prays in the Garden of Gethsemane that he will not have to go through with the crucifixion, he observes that "*the spirit* is willing, but *the flesh* is weak."

In the Gospel according to Luke, when Jesus dies on the cross, his final words are "Father, into your hands I commit *my spirit*."

In the Gospel according to John, when Jesus is first seen by his disciples after the Rising, he will not let people touch him because he has not ascended yet, and so had not yet become *a spirit body*.

Paul also distinguishes between "*spirit bodies*" and "*soul bodies*" in his letters, insisting that understanding this difference is essential for the followers of the new faith.

In the history of the first generation of the Jesus-movement, we are told that, after the Rising, Jesus spent forty days with his followers, and then left them for the final time. He said that his absence would be compensated for by *holy spirit*.

When that *holy spirit* descended on them afterwards in Jerusalem, at what was later recalled as Pentecost, those who were not touched by this holy spirit thought everyone was drunk. But in reality, they had been enabled to understand each other in whatever language they spoke. In other words, they escaped the problem of an "ethics after Babel."

And that *possession by holy spirit* is what launched the evangelizing movement that later became Christianity.

Peter, James, and John all claim to have written letters while "*in the spirit*."

The book of Revelation was also written on "the Lord's Day" when its author was "*in the spirit*."

Clearly, sorting out the relationship between the individual body, the soul that drives it, and holy spirit had become a deep concern for these people. I take it to be a poetic, and personal, concern for Anne Carson in this text as well, one to which I hope to devote a future book.

54. In terms of poetic influence, we may recall that Dante also performed a re-staging of Geryon, in Canto XVII of the *Inferno*. See Monique Tschofen, "'First I Must Tell about Seeing': (De)monstrations of Visuality and the Dynamics of Metaphor in Anne Carson's *Autobiography of Red*," *Canadian Literature* 180 (2004): 31-50, esp. 34–37.

55. For an excellent summary of the post-War historiography that assigned authorship of *The Mirror of Simple Souls* to the condemned heretic, Marguerite of Hainaut, called "Porete," see Sean L. Field, *The Beguine, the Angel and the Inquisitor*, 248–250nn2–3.

As I noted earlier, the attribution was made first by Romana Guarnieri in the *Osservatore Romano* (July 1946).

56. In an interview, Carson says this about her conception of the opera: "I had already worked on an academic lecture about Simone Weil, Marguerite Porete, and Sappho. The analytic level was there. The libretto was the fumes coming off that analytic effort, the sort of intoxicating fumes left in the room by mashing up all the grapes of the academic part."

As quoted by Peter Streckfus in "Collaborating on *Decreation*: An Interview with Anne Carson," in Joshua Marie Wilkinson, ed., *Anne Carson: Ecstatic Lyre*, 214.

57. Simone Weil, "The Love of God and Affliction," in *Waiting for God*, 117–136.

I highlight her use of this term 'affliction' advisedly, both because it was from Weil's point of view that Carson appears to consider it, and because it appears to be distinguished significantly from mere suffering.

This is one of the central themes in Derek Walcott's *Omeros*, to which I have already referred in relation to Carson's *Autobiography of Red*: "affliction is one theme/ of this work, this fiction" (*Omeros* Book I, V.ii, page 28). Affliction, Walcott suggests, may be healed—by poetry, if by nothing else. In his 1992 Nobel Address, he observes that "the fate of poetry is to fall in love with the world, in spite of History" (*The Antilles: Fragments of Epic Memory*, 28). "We shall all heal," Walcott tells us, at the conclusion of his epic (*Omeros*, Book VII, LXIII.ii, page 319). This rhetorical flow—from suffering, to affliction, to redemption—is one of the central preoccupations of all the spiritual writers whom Carson has in view here.

58. This is the final word in "The Gender of Sound," the last essay (and thus the final word) in *Glass, Irony and God*, 136–137.

59. Anne Carson, *Decreation*, 169.

60. Anne Carson, *Decreation*, 171–181.

61. Anne Carson, *Decreation*, 157.

62. Anne Carson, *Decreation*, 171.

63. For more on this paradox of self-effacing writing, see Johanna Skibsrud, "'To Undo the Creature': The Paradox of Writing in Anne Carson's *Decreation*," in Joshua Marie Wilkinson, ed., *Anne Carson: Ecstatic Lyre*, 132–137.

64. Anne Carson, *Decreation*, 171.

65. This comment appears in the Preface to Simone Weil, *The Need for Roots*, Arthur Wills, trans. (New York, NY: Octagon Books, 1984), vi.

66. Anne Carson, *Decreation*, 176. We will recall that in her initial Exemplum, Magurerite Porete emphasizes the great distance (*loing*) separating the maiden from her Lord, and how an image served to bring him near, but in a way that caused her pain. "The word is an image of [absent] things."

67. For a stunningly original reading of Marguerite Porete's spirituality and/as literary significance, see Amy Hollywood, "Reading as Self-Annihilation: Marguerite of Porete's *Mirror of Simple Souls*," in *Acute Melancholia and Other Essays: Mysticism, History, and the Study of Religion* (New York, NY: Columbia University Press, 2016), 129–145.

68. Carson had already anticipated much of what she says here in her Sappho translations, especially that of Fragment #2. See Anne Carson. *If Not, Winter: Fragments of*

Sappho, 7, 179, and Elizabeth Robinson, "An Antipoem That Condenses Everything: Anne Carson's Translations of the Fragments of Sappho," in Joshua Marie Wilkinson, ed., *Anne Carson: Ecstatic Lyre*, 181–187.

69. Anne Carson, *Decreation*, 179.
70. Anne Carson, *Decreation*, 177.
71. Anne Carson, *Decreation*, 179.
72. Plato, *Symposium* 206c–207a.
73. Anne Carson, *Decreation*, "Aria of the Flames," 222.
74. *The Notebooks of Simone Weil*, Arthur Wills, trans. (London and Boston: Routledge & Kegan Paul, 1956, 1976), II: 638–639.
75. Anne Carson, *Decreation*, 223.
76. Anne Carson dedicates concentrated attention to Joan of Arc's role as a translator of the divine voice in *Nay Rather*: "when her inquisitors asked 'What do your voices sound like?' and she answered 'Ask me next Sunday'" (14); "[r]ather like the silence that must have followed Joan of Arc's response to the theologians when they asked her, 'In what language do your voices speak to you?' and she answered: 'In better language than yours'" (26).
77. Caroline Walker Bynum, *Holy Feast and Holy Fast: The Religious Significance of Food to Medieval Women* (Berkeley, CA: University of California Press, 1986). It is instructive that the women who occupy much of Bynum's attention in this rich text (Hadewijch, Beatrice of Nazareth, Mechtild of Magdeburg, Marguerite of Oingt, Marie of Oignies, Agnes of Harcourt, Felipa of Porcelet, Marguerite of Navarre, and Teresa of Avila) are recalled as part of the same populist movement of spiritual nonconformism (often thought to be Free Spirited antinomians) known as *beguines*, the very association that led to Marguerite Porete's condemnation and execution in the spring/summer of 1310.

For more on this complicated and ambiguous movement, see Robert E. Lerner's Introduction to Marguerite Porete, *The Mirror of Simple Souls*, esp. 6–20.

78. This comment, from a remarkable recent book by Maggie Nelson, illustrates the worry eloquently in the context of contemporary queerness:

> Homonormativity seems to me a natural consequence of the decriminalization of homosexuality: once something is no longer illicit, punishable, pathologized, or used as a lawful basis for raw discrimination or acts of violence, that phenomenon will no longer be able to represent or deliver on subversion, the subcultural, the underground, the fringe, in the same way. That's why nihilist pervs like painter Francis Bacon have gone so far as to say that they wish the death penalty was still the punishment for homosexuality, or why outlaw fetishists like Bruce Benderson seek homosexual adventures in countries such as Romania, where one can still be imprisoned for merely hitting on someone of the same sex. . . .
>
> In the face of such a narrative, it's a comedown to wade through the planet-killing trash of a Pride parade, or to hear Chaz Bono cluck-clucking with David Letterman about how T[estaterone] has made him kind of an asshole to his girlfriend, who still annoyingly wants him to "process" for hours in that dreaded lesbian/womanly way.

[Maggie Nelson, *The Argonauts* (Minneapolis, MN: Graywolf Press, 2015), 73.]

I am grateful to my friend and colleague, Dr. Shannon Dunn, for this important reference.

79. Simone Weil in particular articulated a subtle worry about the limits of the erotic analogizing of spiritual aspiration and soulful extinction (perhaps including her own) in her "Iliad" essay: "a strange century indeed," she observes of the seventeenth century, "which took the opposite view from that of the epic period, and would only acknowledge human suffering in the context of love, while it insisted on swathing with glory the effects of force in war and in politics." [Simone Weil, "The *Iliad*, or, The Poem of Force" [1943] Mary McCarthy, trans. (Wallingford, PA: Pendle Hill Paperbacks, 1956), 37]

80. Anne Carson, *Decreation*, "L' (Ode to Monica Vitti)," 63–64.

81. William Carlos Williams, "Tribute to the Painters" (1955), in *William Carlos Williams: Selected Poems*, Charles Tomlinson, ed. (New York, NY: New Directions Publishing Corporation, 1985), 220–222.

82. Anne Carson, "Book of Isaiah," in *Glass, Irony and God*, 107–118, esp. 110.

83. Maya Deren, *Divine Horsemen: The Living Gods of Haiti* (London: Thames and Hudson, 1953), 249.

84. If he could be an intertextual influence on Dante, then why not on Anne Carson? See Madison U. Sowell, ed., *Dante and Ovid: Essays in Intertextuality* (Binghamton, NY: Center for Medieval & Renaissance Texts & Studies, 1991).

85. I am thinking of his *Metamorphoses* Book I, 452–567. I will have much more to say about this remarkable poem below.

86. The statue, carved between 1622 and 1625, is housed in the Villa Borghese in Rome. I am indebted to another contemporary museum exhibition, "*Ovidio: amori, miti e altre storie*," which I visited at the Scuderie del Quirinale in the fall of 2018, and which brought these and other stories freshly back to mind.

87. The history of reading Ovid's poetry, and of assessing his poetic importance (especially in comparison to Virgil), has been dominated by the question of whether and how to embrace his salacious and ironizing humor. Classical scholarship since the Second World War has witnessed a steady rise in the acceptance and appreciation of Ovid's winsome eroticism. Garth Tissol's *The Face of Nature: Wit, Narrative and Cosmic Origins in Ovid's Metamorphoses* (Princeton, NJ: Princeton University Press, 1997) offers an excellent survey of how Ovid's use of puns (Carson's favored erotic-rhetorical tool), and paradox (12–18), and syllepsis (18–26, where figurative and literal meanings are conjoined) are utilized *to display* metamorphosis—the instability and change built in to his very language choices, and hence his humor.

The way to avoid the humor had been to pursue allegorical readings instead: "one of the instruments by which old texts are accommodated to modern cultures, as when the Stoics allegorized Homer, or Alexandrian exegetes the Bible. A technique successful in moralizing Ovid found little difficulty with Virgil" [see Frank Kermode, *The Classic: Literary Images of Permanence and Change* (New York, NY: The Viking Press, 1975), 39].

For more on the history of Ovidian reception, see subsequent notes 94 and 107.

88. Later, Ovid returned to this text and added three new pairs of letters: Paris to Helen (16), Helen to Paris (17), Leander to Hero (18), Hero to Leander (19), Acontius

to Cydippe (20), and Cydippe to Acontius (21) . . . much as Carson has continued to add more "short talks" to her oeuvre.

89. Richard J. Tarrant. "The Authenticity of the Letter of Sappho to Phaon (Heroides XV)," *Harvard Studies in Classical Philology* 85 (1981): 133–153, begins with the observation that the "authenticity of no fewer than eleven of these letters has been impugned in the past fifteen years" (133). He makes the case that an internal analysis of the poem on the basis of "style and form" counts against Ovidian authorship (136). Tarrant focuses on three issues: a) the metrical peculiarities in the poem (137–138, only three in number and none definitive); b) the use of unusual or otherwise unattested words and phrases (139–142), concluding based on this lexicon that the poem was written in "the period between Seneca and Statius" (139); and c) suspect borrowing from Ovid's own later works (142–147). He concludes that the references in Ovid's *Amores* 2:18ff are later "interpolations" added to the poem (148–152), and that the Letter of Sappho was an imitative poetic exercise from a subsequent literary generation (148).

This third point is the critical one, but it relies upon a certain tone-deafness to Ovid's rich and self-referential irony, brilliantly analyzed by Vicky Rimell in "Epistolary Fictions: Authorial Identity in 'Heroides' 15," *Proceedings of the Cambridge Philological Society* 45 (1999): 109-135.

90. An excellent starting point is Albert R. Baca, "Ovid's Epistle from Sappho to Phaon (Heroides 15)," *Transactions and Proceedings of the American Philological Association* 102 (1971): 29–38, which admits that one manuscript, the *Codex Chisianus* (H 4.121) actually identifies Tibullus as the author of this letter (37n23). For Baca, the key is Ovid's own reference to the Sapphic letter in his *Amores* 2:18, 21–26 and 29–34 (29–30), coupled with the observation that his friend, Sabinus, wrote responses to six of these letters.

Baca makes sense of the manuscript history this way. Ovid published the original fifteen letters of the *Heroides* sometime between 19 and 2 BCE (30). Later, inspired by Sabinus's letter-and-response idea, and adopting a new meter he perfected in the *Metamorphoses*, he added Letters 16–21 and re-published the collection at some time between 4 and 8 CE (31). But Ovid removed the Sapphic letter from the collection then, after which it took on an independent life of its own (32). It was already an outlier, after all: Sappho was an historical, rather than a mythical, figure; the letter begins with rhetorical questions rather than a poetic prologue; and it is explicitly sexual in tone and content (34–37). In any event, a copy of the letter, now independent, ended up in the *Codex Tibullianum*, where it was re-discovered in the Renaissance (37). And that is when modern philologists like Daniel Heinsius (in 1629, possibly inspired by the earlier work of Joseph Scaliger) returned it to its proper place in the body of the *Heroides* (38n24).

See also Gianpiero Rosati, "Sabinus, the Heroides and the Poet-Nightingale: Some Observations on the Authenticity of the *Epistula Sapphus*," *Classical Quarterly* 46.1 (1996): 207–216.

91. Vicky Rimell, for her part, claims to be agnostic on the question ("Epistolary Fictions: Authorial Identity in 'Heroides' 15," 110–111), but her close study of the remarkably subtle poetic inter-referentiality seems to make more sense if Ovid were

its author. She reads the Sapphic letter in relation to Ovid's previous comments on the art of the love letter in *Ars Amatoria* 1, and the ironic death of elegy announced by the passing of the poet Tibullus in *Amores* 3:9. It is there that Ovid claims a certain divinity for the poet, a passage I will discuss in greater detail below.

92. See Grant Showerman, trans., and G. P. Gould, rev., *Ovid I: Heroides and Amores* (Cambridge, MA: Loeb Classical Library of Harvard University Press, 1977), 182–183 (translation emended):

> Neither the girls (*puellae*) of Pyrrha, nor Methymna,
>   nor any other Lesbian girls, move me now.
> Anactoria and Cydro mean nothing to me;
>   the sight of Atthis brings none of my prior joy (*grata*),
> nor the hundred more (*aliae centum*) that I scandalously loved (*crimine amavi*);
>   the love so many had is now yours alone (*unus habes*).
> (Ovid, *Heroides* XV, 15–20, translation emended)

As Vicky Rimell puts the conundrum, "[w]hat is Sappho doing, heterosexualized, at the end of a string of elegiac epistles written by women plucked straight from myth and each given their fifteen minutes of fame?" ("Epistolary Fictions: Authorial Identity in 'Heroides' 15," 109). Kate Gilhuly, utilizing Sara Lindheim's analysis [*Mail and Female: Epistolary Narrative and Desire in Ovid's Heroides* (Madison, WI: University of Wisconsin Press, 2003)], answers the question critically, noting that Ovid has deployed Sappho's many previous feminine loves only to normalize her in standard heterosexual terms: "it is her dying wish to be the object of male desire" ("Lesbians Are Not From Lesbos," 169).

93. Grant Showerman, trans., G. P. Gould, rev., *Ovid I: Heroides and Amores*, 196–197 (translation emended):

> If you wish to flee (*fugisse*) from Pelasgian Sappho—
>   though I give you no cause to wish to flee (*fugi*)—
> at least send me a cruel letter (*crudelis epistula*) in my misery,
>   that I may join my fate (*fata*) to Leucadian waters!
> (Ovid, *Heroides* XV, 217–220, translation emended)

94. For more on the transmission history of Ovid and of his literary legacy, see: Frank T. Coulson, "Bernardo Moretti, Biographer and Commentator on Ovid: The Manuscripts" (Spoleto: Presso la Sede del Centro, 1998); Frank T. Coulson, "Hitherto Unedited Medieval and Renaissance Lives of Ovid (I)," *Medieval Studies* 49 (1987): 152–207; Frank T. Coulson and Bruno Roy, *Incipitarium Ovidianum: A Finding Guide for Texts Related to the Study of Ovid in the Middle Ages and Renaissance* (Turnhout, Belgium: Brepols Publishers, 2000); Ralph J. Hexter, *Ovid and Medieval Schooling, Studies in Medieval School Commentaries on Ovid's Ars Amatoria, Epistulae ex Ponto, and Epistulae Heroidum* (München: Bei der Arbeo-Gesellschaft, 1986); John F. Miller and Carole E. Newlands, eds., *A Handbook to the Reception of Ovid* (West

Sussex: Wiley Blackwell, 2014); Ann Moss, *Ovid in Renaissance France: A Survey of the Latin Editions of Ovid and Commentaries Printed in France Before 1600*, Warburg Institute Surveys VIII (The Warburg Institute, University of London, 1982); A. N. L. Munby and Lawrence W. Towner, *The Flow of Books and Manuscripts, Papers Read at the Clark Memorial Library, March 30 1968* [Munby, "The Case of the 'Caxton' Manuscript of Ovid: Reflections on the Legislation Controlling the Export of Works of Art from Great Britain" and Towner, "Every Silver Lining Has a Cloud: The Recent Shaping of the Newberry Library's Collections"] (Los Angeles, CA: William Andrews Clark Memorial Library, University of California, 1969); and Madison U. Sowell, ed., *Dante and Ovid: Essays in Intertextuality*.

95. For the impact of the *Metamorphoses* in particular on Renaissance thought, one written in the midst of this contemporary Ovidian renaissance among literary scholars in the 1980s, see Leonard Barkan, *The Gods Made Flesh: Metamorphosis and the Pursuit of Paganism* (New Haven, CT: Yale University Press, 1986).

96. I am also trying to justify my juxtaposition of Ovid and Carson, since the connection may seem forced. After all, the Roman literary tradition played shamelessly with Sappho: Catullus heterosexualized her in his "translation" of the Love Triangle fragment, and Ovid did the same in his *Heroides*. Yet Carson confessed to a lifelong fascination with Catullus in *Nox*, and she has referred to Ovid, albeit rarely, as we shall see. Certainly they all inhabit the same rarified air of lyric-erotic poetry . . . but unique among them, Sappho was a woman.

We should recall Carson's own word of warning here: "It is always tricky, the question of whether to read an author's work in light of his life or not." (Anne Carson, *The Albertine Workout*, no. 56).

97. Carson, like Ovid, has arguably experienced all three, and for her the linkage of exile and transformation is a decidedly spiritual one.

98. For a brilliant glimpse into the sexual politics of Roman lyric, performed through a comparative examination of Livy's and Ovid's accounts of the so-called Rape of the Sabine Women, see Mary Beard, "The Erotics of Rape: Livy, Ovid and the Sabine Women," in Päivi Setälä and Liisa Savunen, eds., *Female Networks and the Public Sphere in Roman Society* (Rome: Acta Instituti Romani Finlandiae [Volume XXII], 1999), 1–10. Beard questions the standard reading which makes Ovid a poet sympathetic to the Sabines' distress, and therefore implicitly a critic of Roman patriarchy as it was inscribed in Livy's origin myth. The result is a *tour de force* criticism of Ovid's *Ars Amatoria*. The point is that Ovid's amorous verse is so riddled with paradox that reading it requires such a riddling.

99. Jane Alison, *The Love Artist* (New York, NY: Farrar Straus and Giroux, 2001).

Trained in Classics at Princeton University (where she read Ovid with Anne Carson), Alison is Director of the Creative Writing Program at the University of Virginia as well as the author of three stunningly original novels [*The Love Artist* (2001), *The Marriage of the Sea* (2003), *Natives and Exotics* (2005)], a memoir [*The Sisters Antipodes* (2009)], a translation of portions of Ovid's *Metamorphoses* [*Change Me* (2014)], a hybrid "autobiographical novel" [*Nine Island* (2016)], and most recently, a remarkable plea for non-linear story-telling [*Meander, Spiral,*

Explode: Design and Pattern in Narrative (2019)]. The wide range of Alison's genre-choices and classical influences are highly suggestive in relation to Carson's and Ovid's work, alike.

100. Jane Alison, *Change Me: Stories of Sexual Transformation from Ovid* (New York, NY: Oxford University Press, 2014).

Her novelistic memoir describing the creation of that remarkable neo-Ovidian text is *Nine Island* (New York, NY: Catapult, 2016).

101. See *Ovid I: Heroides and Amores*, Grant Showerman trans., and G. P. Gould rev. (Cambridge, MA: Loeb Classical Library of Harvard University Press, 1977).

102. See *Ovid II: The Art of Love and Other Poems*, J. H. Mozley, trans., and G. P. Gould rev. (Cambridge, MA: Loeb Classical Library of Harvard University Press, 1979), 12–233.

103. For this insight, I am indebted to the excellent introduction by Peter Green, for his translated edition of *Ovid: The Erotic Poems* (New York, NY: Penguin Books, 1982), esp. 22–25.

104. I recognize that this may seem an overly upbeat perspective on what are, in many cases, stories of hunted women transformed out of their desire to escape pursuit and assault. But there is more to it than that, some sort of psychic truth or cosmic principle—wanting, not wanting, not wanting to want, wanting anyway—that Ovid is after.

> Well, the transformations are logical. Ovid made that very clear. The transformations are fair. You become what you were bound to be; you become what you actually are.
>
> (Jane Alison, *Nine Island*, 186)

For more poetic reflection on this essentially mythic paradox, see Roberto Calasso, *The Marriage of Cadmus and Harmony*, Tim Parks, trans. (New York, NY: Viking, 1999), 1–24.

Fiona Cox reads Alison's use of Ovid as far "darker" than I do. "Alison is well aware of the horrors and dangers that lurk in the loveliest of Ovidian scenes, and she is sensitive to just how fragile Ovidian beauty is"; see Fiona Cox, *Ovid's Presence in Contemporary Women's Writing: Strange Monsters* (Oxford: Oxford University Press, 2018), 219–233, quote at 227.

105. For a fascinating early study of the lingering influence of Ovid in the Patristic period (especially on Prudentius and Lactantius), see Sister Marie Liguori Ewald, "Ovid in the *Contra Orationem Symmachi* of Prudentius," Ph.D. Dissertation, The Catholic University of America (1942), esp. 198–207.

For more contemporary work on these long-lingering Latin influences, see: Mary E. Barnard, *The Myth of Apollo and Daphne from Ovid to Quevedo: Love, Agon, and the Grotesque* (Durham, NC: Duke University Press, 1987), esp. 44–81; Peter Brown, *Through the Eye of a Needle: Wealth, the Fall of Rome, and the Making of Christianity in the West, 350–550 AD* (Princeton University Press, 2012), esp. xix–xxx, 103–109 (on the misnamed "Altar of Victory Controversy"), and 291-307; Peter Brown and Rita Lizzi Testa, eds., *Pagans and Christians in the Roman Empire: The Breaking of a Dialogue (IVth-VIth Century A.D.)* (Piscataway, NJ: Transactions

Publishers of Rutgers University, 2011), esp. 403–525; Ian Fielding, "A Poet Between Two Worlds: Ovid in Late Antiquity," in John F. Miller and Carole E. Newlands, eds., *A Handbook to the Reception of Ovid* (West Sussex: Wiley Blackwell, 2014), 100–113; Ian Fielding, *Transformations of Ovid in Late Antiquity* (New York, NY: Cambridge University Press, 2017); and Philip Rousseau and Manolis Papoutsakis, eds., *Transformations of Late Antiquity: Essays for Peter Brown* (Burlington, VT: Ashgate Publishing Company, 2009).

106. Ovid, *Ars Amatoria* II: 515–516; see J. H. Mozley, trans., G. P. Gould, rev., *Ovid: The Art of Love and Other Poems*, 100–101.

107. See *Ovid in Six Volumes*: *Ovid VI: Tristia, Ex Ponto*, A. L. Wheeler, trans., and G. P. Gould rev. (Cambridge, MA: Loeb Classical Library of Harvard University Press, 1988), 208–209, as Book V of the *Tristia* opens at V: 5–6.

For a sense of the historiography of Ovid's exile poetry, see: Hermann Fränkl, *Ovid: A Poet Between Two Worlds*, Sather Classical Lectures 18 (Berkeley, CA: University of California Press, 1945), 111–117ff; L. P. Wilkinson, *Ovid Recalled* (New York, NY: Cambridge University Press, 1955); E. J. Kenney, "The Poetry of Ovid's Exile," *Proceedings of the Classical Philological Society* 11 (1965): 37–49; Betty Roe Nagle, *The Poetics of Exile: Program and Polemic in the Tristia and Epistulae ex Ponto of Ovid*, Collections Latomus, Volume 170 (Bruxelles: Latomus Revue d'Études Latines, 1980); and Janet Levarie Smarr, "Poets of Love and Exile," in Madison U. Sowell, ed., *Dante and Ovid: Essays in Intertextuality*, 139–151.

108. Remarkably enough, this reprieve was finally granted, in a unanimous vote by the Roman City Council, on December 14, 2017. The virtues of *patientia* . . .

109. Ovid, *Tristia* II. 207–210; see *Ovid VI: Tristia Ex Ponto*, 70–71, translation emended.

The ambiguities of the case were laid out very well by Hermann Fränkel in his 1945 Sather Lectures at Berkeley, *Ovid: A Poet Between Two Worlds* (Berkeley, CA: University of California Press, 1969), 111–117 (see also 117–142 and 158–163).

For an interesting suggestion that it was Ovid's sexualized re-telling of the rites of Mars and Venus in the *Fasti* that was the poetic last straw, see Barbara Weiden Boyd, *Ovid's Homer: Authority, Repetition, and Reception* (New York, NY: Oxford University Press, 2017), 237–260, esp. 245n23. But see Fränkel, *Ovid: A Poet Between Two Worlds*, 142–151 for the ambiguities of such a chronology.

110. Ovid, *Tristia* IV.1.23–26; see *Ovid VI: Tristia Ex Ponto* 160–161, translation emended.

111. This issue is laid out nicely by Peter Green in *Ovid: The Erotic Poems*, 44–59, who builds on earlier work by John C. Thibault, *The Mystery of Ovid's Exile* (Berkeley, CA: University of California Press, 1964), 115–121.

112. Anne Carson, *Short Talks* (London, Ontario: Brick Books, 1992), 24.

113. Mary Louise Pratt offered the concept of "contact zones" as those ambivalent physical and cultural places in which two cultures meet, without necessarily being understandable to one another. She rehearses the tragic story of Guaman Poma, a bilingual Spanish-and-Quechua-speaking Andean who wrote an extraordinary chronicle of Spanish crimes that literally had no audience because he alone had the capacity to read his hybrid manuscript.

See her "Arts of the Contact Zone," *Profession* (1991): 33-40, later expanded in David Bartholomae, Anthony Petrosky and Stacey Waite, eds., *Ways of Reading: An Anthology for Writers,* 11th Edition (Bedford/St. Martin's Press, 2016), 512–532. Pratt returned to the story again in the Introduction to *Imperial Eyes: Travel Writing and Transculturation* (New York, NY: Routledge, 2007).

114. Ovid, *Tristia* III.14.45–52; see *Ovid VI: Tristia Ex Ponto* 154–157, translation emended.

115. For the Classical resonance and political implications of this idea, see Louis A. Ruprecht Jr., *Afterwords: Hellenism, Modernism and the Myth of Decadence* (Albany, NY: State University of New York Press, 1996).

116. Ovid, *Cures for Love,* 223–226, 241–244; see *Ovid II: The Art of Love and Other Poems,* 192–195, translation emended.

117. I have profited especially from Lauren Curtis, "Explaining Exile: The Aetiological Poetics of Ovid, *Tristia* 3," *Transactions of the American Philological Association* 145.2 (2015): 411–444; and K. Sara Myers, "Ovid's Self-Reception in His Exile Poetry," in John F. Miller and Carole E. Newlands, eds., *A Handbook to the Reception of Ovid* (West Sussex: Wiley Blackwell, 2014), 8–21.

118. There is another paradoxical virtue in Ovid's grief poetry, and that is the fact that he speaks in an openly autobiographical manner only here. This is the case most notably, and in the most concentrated fashion, in *Tristia* IV. 10; see *Ovid VI: Tristia Ex Ponto,* 196-207. The self-revelation has significant limits, of course, and is undertaken within careful forensic bounds. But there is enough here to warrant the conclusions I draw about his exile, I believe.

For more on the limits of such a reading, see John C. Thibault, *The Mystery of Ovid's Exile,* 20–32, and 130–133.

119. See Gareth Williams, *Banished Voices: Readings in Ovid's Exile Poetry* (New York, NY: Cambridge University Press, 1997).

120. See Peter Green, *Ovid: The Erotic Poems,* 38–40.

121. See David A. Campbell, ed., *Greek Lyric I: Sappho and Alcaeus,* 8–9:

From the time when Sappho sailed into exile [ἔπλευσε φυγοῦσα] from Mytilene to Sicily (? years): the earlier Critias was archon at Athens, and in Syracuse the "Gamoroi" (Landowners) held political power.

While the actual number of years is missing, these internal clues suggest dates roughly coinciding with 605/4–591/0 BCE.

122. See K. Sara Myers, "Ovid's Self-Reception in His Exile Poetry," 8–21.

123. Walter Benjamin, "The Task of the Translator," in *Illuminations,* 72.

124. Ovid, "To Carus" in *Ex Ponto* IV.13.19–23; *Ovid VI: Tristia, Ex Ponto,* A. L. Wheler, trans., G. P. Gould rev. ed. (Cambridge, MA: Loeb Classical Library of Harvard University Press, 1988), 476–477, translation emended.

125. Ovid, "To Carus" in *Ex Ponto* IV.13.17–18; *Ovid VI: Trista, Ex Ponto,* 476–477, translation emended.

126. In this same vein, we might recall the many literary examples of poets (Vladimir Nabokov, Joseph Conrad, Maya Deren) for whom the discovery of a new tongue unleashed new resonances in both, lending them new depth and brilliance.

127. Admittedly, this coy self-description shifts to "was born in Canada" later in her career, intensifying the question of her Canadian credentials among some scholars. I am more intrigued by her position as *a poet of self-exile*.

128. Ovid, *Ars Amatoria* I: 434–435; see *Ovid II: The Art of Love and Other Poems*, 42–43, translation emended.

129. Anne Carson, *The Beauty of the Husband: A Fictional Essay in 29 Tangos* (New York, NY: Alfred A. Knopf, 2001), 16.

Conclusion

Dreaming in the Night

> you used to say. "Desire doubled is love and love doubled is
> marriage."
> Madness doubled is marriage
> I added
> when the caustic was cool, not intending to produce
> a golden rule.
>
> —Anne Carson, *The Beauty of the Husband* (2001)

* * * * *

In one of her earlier and most influential essays, "The Anthropology of Water," which was first published in 1995, Carson offered this self-observation: "Water is something you cannot hold. Like men. I have tried. Father, brother, lover, true friends, hungry ghosts and God, one by one all took themselves out of my hands."[1] Reaching, grasping, madness, pain. . . . Carson has returned repeatedly to this constellation of ideas in many genres throughout the vast body of her published work. These same ruminations led her twenty years later to wonder whether "we need another language alongside our/ regular language to talk about the weird pain people do to/ one another."[2]

There is an old philosophical paradox, far more subtle than sophistical, which wonders whether there are two sorts of people in the world: those who think that there are two sorts of people in the world, and those who don't. Sappho's poetry, very much like Anne Carson's, seems to me to ponder the soulful question of whether there actually are two sorts of *lovers* in the world: those who sleep, peacefully and content, in the arms of a lover; and those who lie awake, incapable of such contentment, gazing at the lover's sleeping form, attempting to secure it in memory and poetic verse, against the inevitability of loss. Sappho was said to be one such wide-awake lover;[3] Anne Carson seems to me to be another, straining endlessly to escape such "sleepchains." That is the implicit message of Sappho's Pleiades fragment:

> The Moon has gone
> the way of the Pleiades.
> Midnight and time crawls.
> I lie alone.[4]

These latter poets know that love and lovers are very much like water and night time; they can slip through the fingers in an instant. You may indeed reach for them, but they will elude your grasp, somehow. This is an insight replete with spiritual resonance, as I tried to illustrate in the previous chapter with Sappho's, Marguerite Porete's, and Simone Weil's resuscitation of erotic imagery and the love triangle as a subtle translation of religious relation.

Loss—as Carson has reminded us over and over again in her essays, translations, and poetic verse—is the overarching theme of Greek lyric poetry, a literary tradition which has, not long after Homer invoked his Muse, tragically manned the barricades against the assaults of time and transformation. It is not accidental that in her most adventuresome and experimental hybrid works, God, the gods, and religion all make their appearance, perhaps most explicitly in *Decreation*, but not only there. The lover's re-creation is also necessarily a de-creation, and this is a stark religious truth worth pausing over, if (as I have already noted) we can permit our conception of religion to remain fluid.

Ovid may also seem an unpromising source of reflection on the religious resonances of the erotic life.[5] He often portrays himself, not simply as "Love's preceptor" (*praeceptor Amores*),[6] but also as an embittered, cynical, and world-weary combatant in the games of Venus. His views of the received Roman religion are often instrumental,

> The existence of gods is expedient (*expedit esse deos*) so let us expediently assume it,
>> offering wine and incense upon their ancient hearths (*antiquos focos*)—[7]

and even the newfangled "mystery religions" do not escape his lurid irony:

> Who would dare to profane (*vulgare profanis*) the rites of Ceres,
>> or to publish the sacred mysteries of Samothrace?
> To keep silent is but a prelude virtue (*virtus praestare*):
>> To speak what should be silent a vicious crime (*gravis culpa*). . . .
> Even if Venus's mysteries (*Veneris mysteria*) are not housed in a box (*cistis*),
>> nor resound to the clanging of bronze cymbals,
> yet they are so very popular among us (*inter nos*),

> that they demand silence between us (*inter nos*).
> That same Venus, when she casts her robes (*velamina*) aside, stoops
> to cover her secrets (*pubem*) with her left hand.⁸

Ovid's mockery of the imperial cult may well cause us to wonder how it took so long for his exile to be commanded:

> With the luck (*auspiciis*)—and the years (*annisque*)—of your father, my boy, you will make war,
> > with his years (*annis*)—and luck (*auspiciisque*)—you'll win. . . .
> May the Parthian cause be lost along with their arms;
> > may my prince add the wealth [and women] of the East to Latium.
> Father Mars and father Caesar, give him your aura (*numen*),
> > for one of you is a god (*deus*), and the other will be (*alter eris*).⁹

So much for the self-satisfied and cynical ennui of this luxuriating urban poet-lover, who leaves the real wars to other men, content with seducing their wives while they are away.

In the *Metamorphoses*, Ovid managed a self-transformation of uncanny poetic power. He had played with myths of cosmic creation in his earlier poems,¹⁰ but set the interest aside after this brief flirtation, in deference to his preferred topics of seduction, conquest, and withdrawal, followed inevitably by new assaults. But here, in this new work, creation—and re-creation—captures the interest of the love-poet anew. Even the poetic meter changes to capture the gravity of the change.

> My soul (*anima*) inclines to tell of bodies changed into new forms (*nova formas/ corpora*).
> You gods (*di*) (for you yourselves have wrought the changes) inspire my poem as it proceeds in flowing from
> the beginning of the world (*ab origine mundi*) to the present day.¹¹

As I noted, this quasi-epic poem will provide Ovid with far more than an occasion to display his dazzling creativity and encyclopedic knowledge of Greek mythology, though assuredly it does that. We should notice how a series of crucial religious concepts, all in relation—body (*corpora*), soul (*anima*), gods (*di*), creation (*origine mundi*), and transformation (*mutatas*)—have been artfully joined by the poet here in his proem. His soul wishes to speak of bodies, yet their transformations will effect the poetry and the soul. We may hear clear after-echoes of Marguerite Porete in this (and of Sappho, before her).

God, she boasts, has created her, and so she will create a book, and then she will read that book back to God. Similarly, in the *Metamorphoses*, the gods and the poets are imagined as co-creators of an epic hymn dedicated to the paradoxical eternity of flux and change.

Such an ambitious calling demands a significant elevation of the poet and his or her craft. Ovid had long insisted on the importance of poets, of course, but usually by way of humorous and ironic self-promotion.[12] And yet, as the *Ars Amatoria* comes to its inevitable close, and as Ovid's lyric attention turns sympathetically to women and their identical struggles to hold the soul together in the face of love's assaults, Ovid's promotion of the poets takes a decidedly less seductive turn. For there really are two kinds of lover in the world, he tells us now, the poets and the rest:

> Easy (*facile*) to catch us, as we burn with hot passions,
>   and we know all-too-well how to give it all away.
> The gentle art is what softens and conquers our spirits,
>   such that our beliefs and mores are of a piece.
> And so, my dear girls, be gentle with the poets:
>   they possess an aura (*numen*) and have the Muses' care.
> There is a god in us (*est deus in nobis*), and we communicate with
> the heavens (*commercia caeli*):
>   Our inspiration comes from a celestial throne (*sedibus aetheriis*).[13]

"There is a god in us, and we have contact with the heavens" . . . "our inspiration is celestial." These claims seem to be aiming at something more than mere seduction. And they announce a new line of enquiry, one that will transcend Ovid's earlier erotic interests, connecting this lyric tradition compellingly to Sappho's soaring hymn-craft. If anything, Ovid will expand upon these elevated claims for the poet's status, in the course of his exile.[14] The line between poet and priest has been blurred. Sex, once enfolded in the divinized embrace of eros, achieves the status of sacred ritual, and sexed bodies the status of religious conduit. There is much more to Cupid than cupidity. Love has earned its claim to transcendence. Moreover, what Sappho and Ovid can exploit in a way that Marguerite Porete and Simone Weil cannot, is a polyvalent and multiform conception of the divine, well-suited to a polytheistic cosmology. *Erôs* is a Greek name which spans the vast territory running from the overwhelming tidal wave of the heart to a divinely creative being and the entirety of his religious cult. Plato's *Symposium* and *Phaedrus* hinge on this vast and urgent semantic range; so does Sappho's poetry. Greek love contains multitudes. It begins necessarily with materiality, with bodies, and yet, as

Carson tells it, "Soul is what I kept watch on all that night" . . . her soul, we will recall, that was "stretched . . . between body and mind."

In the final chapters of this book, I have become interested in some of the religious resonances of Anne Carson's classical retrievals, retrievals which have as much to do with time, flux, and change (that is to say, metamorphosis) as they have to do with the immortal God or gods. Her poetic claims call for close attention to the subtle interface between genre, transgression, transformation and spirituality. Taken together, such things inscribe a world rather foreign to most of us.

These days, many tend to think of religion as a conservative force, as often as not violent and reactionary; we often make similar assumptions about the rigidity and conservatism of literary genres. Viewed this way, religions, like genres, establish rules of behavior and norms of conduct, and they jealously guard their perimeters (and their parameters) by punishing the transgressors.[15] Exile or prison is often the result of such creativity, if not something worse. What such a view overlooks is the profound role played by religion, and by genre, in inviting their own overturning—that is to say, in transgression and transformation. Religions actually *create* transgressive types[16]; literary genres do, too. You need a limit, after all, in order to have something to transcend.[17] Art without limits is not audacity; it is anarchy.

Religious adepts often tend to the transgressive, as I noted in the previous chapter.[18] We need only think of the blurry line separating the medieval saint from the heretic (or the witch), as well as those fluid and elusive figures who have been serially viewed as both—like Joan of Arc, or Marguerite Porete. This, I believe, accounts for much of Anne Carson's interest in them. Socrates was a religious transgressor; so was Jesus of Nazareth. Their transgressions created the possibility of new genres (philosophical dialogues, and gospels) and new norms (virtues and graces trumping the old laws). And it is in this sense that Carson's playful dance between various literary genres, as well as her scandalous heterodoxy in combining them, may involve transgressions of a sort, but ones offered in the service of poetic non-conformity intended to enact transformations, that is, new ways of seeing and experiencing the self in its (what? empty fullness? full emptiness?). This may well constitute the high religious calling of the poet and of poetry (and, by implication, all of their necessary translations), in the end. So Carson's work has consistently implied for more than thirty years.

I find it intriguing in this light that Anne Carson has returned to the traditional genres of the aphoristic essay and the poetic chapbook in several of her more recent publications: *The Albertine Workout*[19] and *Float*,[20] respectively. What poems promise, with their aphoristic and elusive means of presentation, is the gift of concentrated insight, those ah-ha moments that may give the self-soul-spirit back to itself with new and unexpected vision and texture.

"Nothing of him that doth fade/ But doth suffer a sea-change/ Into something rich and strange."[21]

In *The Albertine Workout*, a rather challenging text even by Carson's iconoclastic standards, she takes up her religious interests anew by linking the twinned topics of erotic longing and spirit conjuring. The occasion for this poetic meditation is Book 5 of Proust's 7-volume opus, entitled *La Prisonière*, and dismissed by Roger Shattuck as "the one volume of the novel that a time-pressed reader may safely and entirely skip."[22] The volume concentrates on an elusive—and therefore erotically intriguing—figure named Albertine, who "constitutes a romantic, psychosexual and moral obsession for the narrator of the novel mainly throughout volume 5."

> 8.
>
> The problems of Albertine are (from the narrator's point of view)
>
> a. lying
> b. lesbianism and (from Albertine's point of view)
> c. being imprisoned in the narrator's house.[23]

This novelistic situation, reminiscent of Nabokov's *Lolita* (or, as Carson sees it, of *Hamlet*'s Ophelia) provides Carson with the opportunity to extend her concerns over the sexualized male gaze which she has explored primarily in classical terms in her previous work.

> 24.
>
> The state of Albertine that most pleases Marcel is Albertine asleep.
>
> 25.
>
> By falling asleep she becomes a plant, he says.
>
> 26.
>
> Plants do not actually sleep. Nor do they lie or even bluff. They do, however, expose their genitalia.[24]

But the paradoxes of desire, of reaching and not grasping, are still Carson's primary poetic and existential concern.

> 17.
>
> Once Albertine has been imprisoned by Marcel in his house, his feelings change. It was her freedom that first attracted him, the way the wind billowed in her garments. This attraction is now replaced by a feeling of *ennui* (boredom). She becomes, as he says, a "heavy slave."

18.

This is predictable, given Marcel's theory of desire, which equates possession of another person with erasure of the otherness of her mind, while at the same time positing otherness as what makes another person desirable.

19.

And in point of fact, how can he possess her mind if she is a lesbian?

20.

His fascination continues.[25]

We should pause here, since the narrator's "theory of desire" is very much in line with the one Carson endorsed in *Eros the Bittersweet*. So there is more to this strange situation than an overmastering patriarchy or a sleepwalker's sexual gaze (though there is much of both here, to be sure).

The invocation of Albertine's lesbian desire provides us with one clue as to Carson's poetic interest, and here (now, again), as was the case in her first book, Carson sees lesbianism's revelatory qualities as fundamentally related to a kind of desire, rather than to sex or sexual identity. We may recall her spatial analysis of Sappho's Love Triangle Fragment. So, too, here: Albertine's alleged lesbianism makes her unreachable to the narrator, imprisoned or no. As, far more wrenchingly, does her premature death:

46.

Albertine's death in a riding accident on p. 642 of volume 5 does not emancipate Marcel from jealousy, it removes only one of the innumerable Albertines he would have to forget. The jealous lover cannot rest until he is able to touch all points in space and time ever occupied by the beloved.[26]

We have now been alerted to the fact that Carson is revisiting the theory of desire she first developed in *Eros the Bittersweet*. We have witnessed much of this before: desire occupying the space between reach and grasp; the erotic triangles; the ruses (or in this case, the bluffs); the concern with jealousy; the intense interest in space and time. So what is new here, apart from the shift in Greek to French, and an interest in the ancients giving way to the moderns?

One answer concerns what Carson will call the transposition theory, namely, that the figure of Albertine is "a disguised version of Proust's chauffeur, Alfred Agostinelli,"[27] using the narrator's explicit heterosexual desire as a cloak for Proust's more closeted homoerotic interests. The heart of this "transposition" is death: "53. There are four ways Albertine is able to avoid becoming entirely possessable in volume 5: by sleeping, by lying, by being a lesbian or by being dead. "54. Only the first three of these can she bluff."[28]

Agostinelli's death, Carson suggests, is clearly marked by Proust in a volume we can now see has been very aptly named, "The Prisoner" (since everyone in the story is imprisoned, in one way or another—by memory, if nothing else).

49.

> On May 30, 1914, French newspapers reported that Alfred Agostinelli, a student aviator, fell from his machine in the Mediterranean sea near Antibes and was drowned. Agostinelli, you recall, was the chauffeur whom Proust in letters to friends admitted that he not only loved but adored. Proust bought Alfred the aeroplane, which cost 27,000 francs, about $75,000, and had had it engraved on the fuselage with a stanza of Mallarmé. Proust also paid for Alfred's flying lessons and registered him at the flying school under the name Marcel Swann. The flying school was in Monaco. In order to spy on Alfred while he was there, Proust sent another favourite manservant, whose name was Albert.[29]

The connections to Albertine's novelistic demise are dramatic and suggestive. When Albertine first escapes her imprisonment, the narrator tries to bribe her back with the promise of a yacht he has just bought for her ("for 27,000 francs, about $75,000") and whose prow he has engraved with her favorite stanza from Mallarmé. That stanza tells the strange story of a swan that failed to migrate, and became imprisoned in winter ice. "Ice pleasure" is what Carson called such frozen forms of desire in her first book.[30]

The agonizing irony of purchasing a plane in which his lover was later to die is poignant enough, but the irony of dying *by drowning* in a plane crash takes us past irony to emotional catastrophe. There is a virtually mythic quality to this newspaper report, as Carson reads it, one that turns catastrophe to transcendence. For Agostinelli's death mimics the death of Icarus, as reported by none other than Ovid himself.[31] Ovid emphasized the rigors of Daedalus's imprisonment, his lying and his ruses, not to mention his invention of wings in order to escape Minos's overzealous grasp. Ovid was also careful to note that Icarus died, not from his fall, but by drowning, leaving an eloquent pile of (swan?) feathers floating in his wake.

When and why did Ovid report this sad tale? It appears in the second book of the *Ars Amatoria*, when Ovid turned to the daunting question of how to make love stay.

It is an erotic commonplace that losing a love is like losing a life, grief and mourning both running to excess. As Carson notes after the narrator's loss of Albertine, "[t]he jealous lover cannot rest until he is able to touch all the points in space and time ever occupied by the beloved."[32] The jealousy, we should recall, was prompted not by another lover in this instance, but by death itself—the ultimate erotic triangulation. How, then, to "touch all the points" touched by a lost lover? Some form of necromancy would be needed, if the lover is no more, and Carson gestures subtly to several processes of spirit-conjuring in this text. Three aspects of such conjuring stand out: photography; bluffing; and writing.

Carson's Albertine essay concludes with a moving meditation on "a small poorly reproduced 1907 photo of Proust and Alfred Agostinelli seated in their motor vehicle, dressed for a journey."[33] The photo itself is fairly nondescript, she tells us,[34] save for one compelling detail: Agostinelli's head is thrown back as if the car is hurtling forward at great speed. But of course they and the car were stock-still, as the exposure would have been long. The photograph of a dead man who was pretending to be moving swiftly while actually holding still is a haunting image, indeed, a living, spinning top captured through the pretense of being depicted photographically in mid-spin.[35] Such a photograph is also a still-life[36] pretending to capture real life—-a technological ruse, that is, or a bluff—though "[w]ho is bluffing whom is hard to say."[37]

> Proust avoids the verb *bluffer* but uses *le bluff* three times of interactions between Albertine and Marcel. He points out the difference between bluffing in poker and bluffing in love, namely, that a card game is played in the present tense and all that matters is victory. But love reaches into past and future and fantasy; its suffering consists in positing to those realms all that the bluff conceals.[38]

Love, or rather the loved one, plays his or her way across various tenses, dances lightly between points in time, conjures up a fantasy formed of equal parts past and future; the tense is (now, again). The lost beloved touches every emotional point, and the jealous lover who is left behind is also trapped in the necessity of trying to find a way to touch every such point again. But with death, that future has come to standstill, so it simply cannot be done.

And this, perhaps, is one reason lovers write so obsessively. Proust conjured the image of his lost lover, Alfred Agostinelli, in a fictional figure of his own creation: "Albertine." He conjured being with him still by imprisoning her, attempting to touch every poetic point of their relation. Tellingly, Proust was still at it, still working on the never-ending revision of his time with Alfred Agostinelli, "on his deathbed."[39] He did not know how to take his hand away (*manum de tabula*). The image is suggestive of themes that have become more prominent in Carson's poetic meditation in recent years: soul, spirit, transformation, the necromantic desire for the lost lover, even beyond the grave. But it displays a haughty, almost irreligious, preference for grasping over reaching.

In *Float*, these themes return in a new package (literally), born of Carson's increasingly extensive collaborations with visual and vocal artists. In point of fact, the materiality of the poetic packaging has become a prominent feature in Carson's work over the last decade: I am thinking particularly of the accordion-style collage that contains her necromantic meditations for a lost brother in *Nox*.[40] And I am thinking of another category whose religious valence may not be immediately evident: *luck*. The relation between fate and fortune was a significant preoccupation of Greek philosophy, long before the German Idealists made it a canon of modern historicism. Statues and sanctuaries dedicated to *Tychê* begin to populate the Hellenistic religious landscape, and gained new ground as *Fortuna* among the Romans. What, we are called to wonder, is *religious* about luck, whether good or bad?

Ovid put that question explicitly in his poetry, well before his own luck failed him.[41] Recall the snide couplet addressed to the young Augustus, playing the auspices and the years off of one another:

> With the luck—and the years—of your father, my boy, you will make war,
>   with his years—and luck—you'll win. . . .[42]

Plucky leaders do not like to hear of their pluck reduced to luck. And yet Ovid's repeated reference to the "auspices" serves to remind us how notoriously superstitious[43] both the Greeks and Romans were when it came to auguries before battle. Fortune is fickle, and her blessings are not evenly distributed, in love or in war.

Carson has attended to the poetic dimensions of luck in several recent works. In 2013, she elected to publish a poetic piece in which the individual lines were randomized by a computer and printed as such.[44] It makes for some strange reading. Pouring over the pages of *Float* creates a strange experience as well. Here, packaged inside a clear plastic container, are 22 assembled poems and essays printed separately as individual chapbooks. And yet, once they leave the box, they have a tendency to scatter like dead leaves, with that maddening tendency to blow their separate ways.[45] Carson suggests on the back cover that their "order is unfixed" and their "topics are various" such that "[r]eading can be freefall."[46] If there is an order to the reading, then it is as much a product of happenstance as of authorial intent. Or fate.

Perhaps the Greek character[47] who captures Carson's sympathy the most here is the Trojan princess-turned-priestess, Cassandra. The title of Carson's meditation on Cassandra, "Cassandra Float Can," alerts us to the fact that we are coming close to the central preoccupation of this entire chapbook series. Can Cassandra "float"? Will anyone let her? Floating normally means that we have managed to maintain our position on the surface of things, whether water or wind or whimsy. But Cassandra is plagued by depth, unplumbable depth. She is ultimately plagued by time itself. Like most women beloved of Apollo (and this was especially clear to Ovid), his divine attention exacts a terrible cost: "By crying out '*Apollon emos*,' Cassandra can designate the god as 'my Apollo' and 'my destroyer' at the same time in the same words," Carson observes. Apollo gives Cassandra the dubious gift of prophecy: the knowledge of the future, which is to say, the knowledge of fate. This divine gift also carries the flip-side curse of her never being believed. "Like space-time, [Cassandra] is nonlinear, nonnarrative and the most beautiful of Priam's daughters according to Homer who says that when she stood up to prophecy she shone like a lamp in a bomb shelter." In actual fact, Carson adds, Cassandra's prophetic trances "smell of a rip in spacetime." At this crucial point in her poetic conjuring of Cassandra, Carson seems to veer off, offering the following strange pronouncement.

> I only accidentally learned Greek, from a bored high-school Latin teacher who decided to teach me to read Sappho on my lunch hour. My entire career as a Classicist is a sort of preposterous etymology on the word *lunch*.

What kind of revelation is this? Who was this high-school Latin teacher, who preferred Sappho to Ovid? Why was she bored? Were the two lovers, or merely lunchmates? And how do you learn Sappho's Aeolic Greek over lunch?[48]

More to the point: what kind of accident was this? Was the high school teacher really an Apollonian (or Dionysian) apparition? After all, there is nothing accidental about Sappho's presence in Carson's life. If anything, Sappho is the singular lyric lodestar, the fatal focal point of Carson's entire writing life, from 1986 to now. If there is any poet whose verse has touched every point in Carson's universe, then surely it is Sappho.

The question thus becomes this: How is it that such an accident can be fatal? How is it that an accident can become a fate? Perhaps it is more apt to ask, "What kind of necessity is that?"[49] This is an eminently Greek question, one with profound religious overtones. We must remain alert, as Carson does, to the fact that "paganism" is one form of Greek religion; Christianity is another. Some of the most profound speculation on fate and fortune was born in that fascinating interstice, when the polytheistic Hellenic world was gradually becoming attracted, philosophically and culturally, to a particular kind of monotheism.

We see this most clearly, perhaps, in what was made of Plato's philosophy half a millennium after Socrates. In Plotinus's (204/5–270 CE) theo-philosophical reflections called the *Enneads* (they take this name ["The Nines"] from the way Plotinus's posthumous editor, Porphyry, organized the wide-ranging material into six books of nine [*ennea*] sections each), we meet philosophical speculation on divine principles at their densest and most difficult. In the last two sections of the final sixth volume,[50] we find the Neoplatonic philosopher grappling with themes that have long preoccupied Anne Carson (and Paul Celan) as well. The elusive answers to big questions—about the future, fate, and fortune—take us to the very limits of thought, of language, and potentially, to their breaking point. We do not know quite what to say, and so we are cast back (like Socrates in the *Phaedrus*) on metaphors, or images, or silence,[51] when we attempt to speak of God . . . and we can say "God" here, as well as "the Good," or "the One," without doing too much damage, I think, if only because Plotinus in this passage comes as close as he ever will to speaking of the divine principle (*archê*) within the metaphor of a living being with a personality and a will. This penultimate treatise, in fact, addresses the question of the relation between free will (*hekousia*) and the will (*thelêma*) of that One. Plotinus's approach is largely negative; we cannot say what the eternal divine principle is, only what it is not (later "apophatic" Christian mystics like Dionysius the Areopagite[52] would agree). But here, Plotinus dangles before us the intriguing next step of the enquiry, where we must "negate the negation" in order to glean some positive insight about the divine. Saying what something is not is still saying something, after all, sometimes something of the highest importance and illumination. I am not you, for instance, and my writing is not your reading anymore than your body is mine.

Here, then, is the question on which the treatise pivots: "If someone takes up the phrase 'it (just so) happened to be' (*sunebê*) [as applying to God], then we must not rest content with the term (*onoma*), but must also understand what the speaker has in mind (*noei*). What, then, has he in mind (*ti oun noei*)?" What, Plotinus appears to be asking, does a phrase like "it just so happened" really mean to say?

Essentially, he suggests, this phrase misconstrues the relationship between a primary cause (*archê*) and the things that it causes to be. People who think of the divine principle as "happening" (that is, "just so happening," in an arbitrary or accidental way) speak as if it could be otherwise. They falsely think that chance (*tychê*) or accident (*automaton*) can apply to God. They think that God, or the Good, is an ultimate cause (*archê*) because it has such-and-such a nature (*physin*) or such-and-such power (*dynamin*). But that comes close to putting the concepts backwards, Plotinus worries. God, or the Good, has the nature and power it has just because it is the *archê* (that almost gets to the point verbally, Plotinus suggests, but it is still not quite right). The problem lies partly in our language, and partly in the concepts toward which our language reaches: chance, accident, nature, and power. These terms involve a much-too-arbitrary way of speaking about God, and the Good. Such a thing cannot "just so happen to be" (*to tychon einai*); the best we can do is to imagine an utter uniqueness (*monachôs*), something to which our concepts of accident (*tychê*) and necessity (*anankê*) simply do not apply.

There are two ways to go with this strange line of thinking, and Anne Carson has traveled them both. In this treatise, Plotinus was especially interested in the relationship between the appearance of free human wills and this cosmic *archê* which we cannot even conceive of as a willful necessity. If human beings are to be understood in relation to that kind of God, or that kind of will, or that kind of Good,[53] then what precisely is the relation: "what kind of with-ness is it?"[54] This is a line of enquiry which Carson has not yet published, to my knowledge. But the question has certainly been with her for a very long time.

The second line of thinking pursues a more explicitly erotic trajectory. Anne Carson did not just so happen to learn to read Sappho, after all; she came to adore Sappho, with a passion that has been evident from her first book to her most recent ones. To be sure, this line of thinking and feeling can, unless we are very careful, turn the beloved into a god—much as Juliet solemnly surmised, when referring to Romeo as "the god of my idolatry."[55]

But this Romantic temptation misses the classical dimension of Carson's subtle (and holy) conception of erotic desire. Eros is the god, after all, not the beloved—eros creates the hole through which light may pour in. There are those who can experience change of self in the face of another's presence in their lives as transformation, as metamorphosis, rather than simply as a loss. There are those who can experience the presence of the divine as ravishing, as ravishment, as many medieval women came to feel it. Marguerite Porete's lyrical and consuming final vision makes the eroticism of this nearly scandalous intimacy very apparent:

> Therefore his eye beholdeth me: that he loveth none more than me. This is the substance of my heart.
> Therefore his eye beholdeth me, he may not suffer nor will, but that he be conjoint with me.
> Therefore his eye beholdeth me, that he loveth none more than me; my necessity requireth it.
> Therefore his eye beholdeth me. I will nothing that he willeth not. Such power hath love over me.
> Therefore his eye beholdeth me, that he loveth none more than me. Ah, ah, fine love of my heart.
> Therefore his eye beholdeth me, thou makest of two wills one will. Such is the nature of thee.
> Therefore his eye beholdeth me, that he loveth none more than me. Now—Amen.
> Here endeth the book that Love calleth THE MIRROR OF SIMPLE SOULS.[56]

Not Reason, not Virtue, not Sacrament, not Holy Church, not even Soul,[57] but Love and Love alone does this spirit-work. Some modern mystics, like Simone Weil, have attested to this same erotic self-sundering, what she called "decreation." There are those who can render such experiences lyrically, as a kind of poetic "un-losing." In short, there are those who find transcendence in erotic love, and approach it as sacred mystery.

Anne Carson just so happens to be one of those who do. And we are very fortunate that this is so.

> Something about the laundry chute down which we tumbled—this
> mineshaft,
>   cataract,
>   toboggan-slide (waterslide, landslide),
>   plummet,
>   sheer descent,
>   amnesia drop,
>   vertical dive
>   this fast rainpipe,
>   this precipitance,
>   this parachute,
>   headlong fall, this
>   streaming
>   downspout
>   of vodoo pine—
>   cried out to be addressed
>   as
>   *thine.*[58]

Or to say it in a different way, since she has been meditating on Proust of late:

> Proust says memory is of two kinds.
> There is the daily struggle to recall
> where we put our reading glasses
>
> and there is a deeper gust of longing
> that comes up from the bottom
> of the heart
>
> involuntarily.
> At sudden times.
> For surprise reasons.[59]

"Surprise reasons" seems a more auspicious term than "fate" or "fortune"; it certainly comes closer to what Carson seems to have been pondering over the past forty years. For the spirited lover, the beloved is an utterly singular, utterly unique entity, that single other being who has touched every point in our space and time, one who cannot be thought of as either an accidental or a necessary presence. If we imagine the lover as "necessary," then we're grasping them too tightly, like a spinning top we inadvertently stop cold. If we imagine the lover as an "accident" which life has brought near us, an event which just so happens, then we're not even reaching.

NOTES

1. Anne Carson, "The Anthropology of Water," in *Plainwater: Essays and Poetry* (New York, NY: Vintage Books, 1995, 2000), 113-260 (quote at 117).

2. Anne Carson, "Hack Gloss," in Roni Horn, *Hack Wit* (Göttingen: Steidl, 2015), no page numbers.

3. In the charming words of William Mason, "Cupid, well thou know'st the tender soul, / That poesy inspires, is very wax / To beauty's piercing ray. . . . She was the very soul of Poesy; / Form'd by Apollo's self: her tuneful frame / Was the rich lyre, whence all his rapture flow'd."
See William Mason, "Sappho: A Lyric Drama in Three Acts" (London: W. Bulmer & Co., 1797, 1809), 6, 53.

4. Sappho, Fragment 168B, translation mine.

5. Though I note that, even two generations ago, a landmark edition dedicated to Ovid, N. I. Herescu's *Ovidiana: Recherches sur Ovide* (Paris: Société d'Édition "Les Belles Lettres," 1958) contained two successive sections entitled "Le Poète de l'Amour" and "Le Poète des Dieux."

6. Ovid, *Ars Amatoria* I: 17; *Ovid II: The Art of Love and Other Poems*, 26–27, translation emended.

7. Ovid, *Ars Amatoria* I: 637–638; see *Ovid II: The Art of Love and Other Poems*, 56–57, translation emended.

8. Ovid, *Ars Amatoria* II: 601–604, 608–614; see *Ovid II: The Art of Love and Other Poems*, 106–109, translation emended.

9. Ovid, *Ars Amatoria* I: 191–192, 201–204; see *Ovid II: The Art of Love and Other Poems*, 26–27, translation emended.

10. Ovid, *Ars Amatoria* II: 467–492.

11. Ovid, *Metamorphoses* I: 1–4, translation mine.

12. For a suggestion as to the far more serious point Ovid is making here, see Ellen Oliensis, "The Paratext of *Amores* I: Gaming the System," in Laura Jansen, ed., *The Roman Paratext: Frame, Texts, Readers* (Cambridge: Cambridge University Press, 2014), 206–223.

13. Ovid, *Ars Amatoria* III: 543–550; see *Ovid II: The Art of Love and Other Poems*, 156–157, translation emended.

14. Matthew M. McGowan, in *Ovid in Exile: Power and Poetic Redress in the Tristia and Epistulae ex Ponto* [Mnemosyne Supplements 309] (Leiden: E. J. Brill, 2009), does an excellent job of drawing out two brilliant poetic ambiguities which Ovid exploits for his own defense in exile: the verbal echo between crime (*crimina*) and song (*carmina*) (55–62); and the juxtaposition of Augustus's claim to divinity versus Ovid's claim for the poet's immortality in continuing to be read (63–92, 203–216). McGowan traces an aggressive subtext within these exilic writings, one in which the *carmina* are not *crimina*, because they are the source of the poet's immortality, that will outlast even that of an absolutist prince's pretensions to the same.

15. I have profited enormously from conversations about genre, its expectations and its demands, in and beyond the bounds of philosophy with my good friend and colleague, Timothy Engström.

See his "Foundational Standards and Conversational Style: The Humean Essay as an Issue of Philosophical Genre," *Philosophy & Rhetoric* 30.2 (1997): 150–175.

16. The Gifford Lectures which Jeffrey Stout delivered in Edinburgh in May 2017 focused on this crucial idea, posing the critical question to any proponent of modern theories of secularization: "How would our understanding of religion and politics have to change if the religious voices of egalitarian freedom movements were given their due?" His *tour de force* survey of such movements, from Cicero, through Las Casas and Machiavelli, through Milton and Emerson, to Martin Luther King Jr., concluded on a note of rare lyricism (which may be accessed online at *https://www.giffordlectures.org/lecturers/jeffrey-stout*):

> Another thread running through the history of religion-talk is the idea of becoming an example of something *for* others—the power, importance, and price of standing *for* something *before* others. Writing a gospel, venerating a saint, emulating a philosopher, initiating a movement, addressing a council, a court, a congregation, or an audience in Edinburgh—all of these acts have to do with exemplarity. Standing *for* something—however fallibly—in the face of catastrophic harm, a cloud of witnesses has conveyed a venerable heritage to us. In so far as they *meant* well, they also meant *well*. They took pains to make their lives legible to an observant eye. By standing for something, they acquired foes as well as friends.
>
> When new Caesars rule for private gain, or for a faction's sake against the rest, they are tyrants. When they seek and acquire powers that leave others at their mercy, they are oppressors. Is not their due then the concerted and courageous opposition of all upright human beings—until the day when our hope for reconciliation on proper terms can be fulfilled? The just have long been called to strip off every encumbrance and rise up. They who have striven with idols and masters have at times prevailed. The past is where the precedents are. The present is where we shall make of them what we *will*.

In my notebook from that occasion, I transcribed the last lines thusly:

> A cloud of witnesses has borne something to us. They took pains to become legible to us. By standing, they made enemies as well as friends. The past is where the precedents are. The present is where we will decide what to make of them.

For more on these ideas, see his *Democracy and Tradition* (Princeton, NJ: Princeton University Press, 2004) and *Blessed Are the Organized* (Princeton, NJ: Princeton University Press, 2010). Stout's influence on what I have argued in the last chapter and again here is obvious, I hope, and I am deeply grateful for his work as I am for his friendship.

17. For more on this idea, see Louis A. Ruprecht Jr., "The Ethos of Olympism: The Religious Meaning of the Modern Olympic Movement," *Soundings* 81.1/2 (1998): 267–302, and "Sport Matters: On Art, Social Artifice and the Rules of the Game, or, The Politics of Sport," in Vassiliki Rapti and Eric Gordon, eds., Ludics: Play As Humanistic Inquiry (New York, NY: Palgrave Press, 2021), 47–72.

18. While I have not treated Ovid's complicated late work, the *Fasti*, I am intrigued by the reading of that work offered by Carole E. Newlands in *Playing with Time: Ovid and the Fasti* (Ithaca, NY: Cornell University Press 1995). Newlands suggests that the *Fasti*, an incomplete treatment of six of the twelve months in the new Julian calendar, may be read as a profoundly modern document in which the novelty of the calender (and many other Augustan innovations, like the *imperium* itself) are identified as such and deployed to give the lie to a stable, traditional and unchanging regime that was backward-looking rather than Janus-faced. She even notes Ovid's blurring of traditional generic expectations there:

> When the elegiac meter is harnessed to Roman religious and historical themes, it remains a creative tool by which Ovid can question and even undermine the orthodoxies of his day.... Indeed, the expansion of this new, audacious elegiac genre to encompass imperial as well as erotic themes permits a broader and more thorough play with Roman values and ideas about the past and invites us to look at them in constantly shifting lights. The range of tones which this new form of elegy encompasses—from exegetical to bawdy, from sorrowful to grand—puts into question any authoritarian view of the past as a repository of values crucial in shaping Roman identity and worthy of imitation. Ovid's *Fasti* offers a more chaotic view of the past as a patchwork of brutality and nobility, licence and dignity.... Finally, the *Fasti* overall has, I believe, a planned structure that reflects a general movement from optimism to disillusionment. (15–16, 18)

For more on the political intent of the new calendar, see Mary Beard, "A Complex of Time: No More Sheep on Romulus' Birthday," *Proceedings of the Classical Philological Society* 33 (1987): 1–15.

19. Anne Carson, *The Albertine Workout* (New Directions Poetry Pamphlet #13, 2014).

20. Anne Carson, *Float* (New York, NY: Alfred A. Knopf, 2016).

21. William Shakespeare, *The Tempest* I.ii.

It is worth noting that this line is inscribed on Shelley's tombstone in the *Acattolica* Cemetery in Rome.

22. Quoted at Anne Carson, *The Albertine Workout*, 6.

23. Anne Carson, *The Albertine Workout*, 6.

24. Anne Carson, *The Albertine Workout*, 10.

25. Anne Carson, *The Albertine Workout*, 8-9.

26. Anne Carson, *The Albertine Workout*, 16.

27. Anne Carson, *The Albertine Workout*, 6.
28. Anne Carson, *The Albertine Workout*, 19.
29. Anne Carson, *The Albertine Workout*, 17.
30. Anne Carson, *Eros the Bittersweet*, 111–116. This is also, instructively, the chapter where she first announces her shift in interest, from space to time.
31. Ovid, *Ars Amatoria* II: 21–98.
32. Anne Carson, *The Albertine Workout*, 16.
33. Anne Carson, *The Albertine Workout*, 38.
34. Naturally, one source of Carson's poetic brilliance is that she considers no visual image to be "nondescript." She confesses to a striking personal connection of visual and verbal representation in the context of the publication of her *Short Talks*. They were originally intended to be verbal supplements to a series of sketches which she hoped to display, but since "[n]obody liked the drawings . . . I expanded the titles into talks." The story is rehearsed by Ian Rae in *From Cohen to Carson: The Poet's Novel in Canada* (Montreal: McGill-Queen's University Press, 2008), 227, and by Monique Tschofen in "First I Must Tell about Seeing," 31.

Tschofen concludes with great insight that Carson here offers "a dense meditation on two related terms–*vision and revision*" (31, italics mine), which serves as a helpful way of entering into her creative engagement with the Classics and the entirety of its visual field.

35. Proust would later remark that "[a] photograph acquires something of the dignity which it ordinarily lacks when it ceases to be a reproduction of reality and shows us things that no longer exist" [*Remembrance of Things Past*, C. K. Scott Moncrieff and Stephen Hudson, trans. (Wordsworth Classics of World Literature, 2006), II: 693.
36. One quasi-classical linguistic irony is relevant here: in both Modern Italian and Modern Greek the term for "still life" is "dead nature" (*natura morte* or *nekrê physê*).
37. Anne Carson, *The Albertine Workout*, 15.
38. Anne Carson, *The Albertine Workout*, 37.
39. Anne Carson, *The Albertine Workout*, 19.
40. Of the sister-in-law she did not know she had, she says this: she died in April 2010 of alcohol, grief, and longing ["Powerless Structures Fig. II (Sanne)," in *Float*].
41. See Carson's oblique reflections on "fortune," "arrangements," and "promises," in "108 (flotage)" in *Float*.
42. Ovid, *Ars Amatoria* I: 191–192.
43. The contrast between right *religio* and false *superstitio* enjoyed a long rhetorical life among the Roman moralists, an insight I have also taken from Jeffrey Stout's 2017 Gifford Lectures in Edinburgh. The Greek term, *deisidaimonia*, possesses a far more complex lexical register, good or bad depending on the context, and very often possessing shades of both, as in Paul's usage, as depicted in *Acts of the Apostles* 17.

For more on this Greek religious notion, see Dale Martin, *Inventing Superstition: From the Hippocratics to the Christians* (Cambridge, MA: Harvard University Press, 2007).

44. Anne Carson, "By Chance the Cycladic People," from *Nay Rather*, which was reprinted in 2016 in *Float*.

45. I am indebted to my friend, Laura McKee, herself a gifted poet and novelist, for this insight. Note that it also makes citation by page numbers again impossible. In reflecting on the challenges of working with a fragmentary Greek lyric tradition (i.e., Sappho, Mimnermus, Stesichorus, and the rest), Carson observes:

> The fragments of the *Geryoneis* itself read as if Stesichorus had composed a substantial narrative poem then ripped it to pieces and buried the pieces in a box with some song lyrics and lecture notes and scraps of meat. The fragment numbers tell you roughly how the pieces fell out of the box.

(Anne Carson, *Autobiography of Red*, 6–7)

46. Admittedly, there is a one-page table of content, but it too is separate and may wander, in which case all bets are off. And in any case, the order on the Content page does not match the randomized order in the box.

47. Carson also performs a bravura reading of the Hebrew biblical character of Jezebel in "Stacks," from *Float*, one which plays out her mischaracterization and mistreatment by the so-called prophets with rich poetic sympathy.

48. In a 2011 interview with Eleanor Wachtel, published in *Brick: A Literary Journal 71*, Carson is more specific:

> I owe my career and happiness to Alice Cowan in Port Hope High School. . . . [S]he was a very unusual person. She smelled of celery all the time. And after that year she disappeared. Quit, I guess, and somebody told me she ended up in Africa. Some decades later when I did a reading somewhere—I think Montreal—and mentioned her because I read some Greek stuff, a woman came up to me afterward and said, "Alice Cowan's my mother and she now lives on a farm in northern Ontario. She's kind of a hermit. She'd probably like to hear from you but she won't answer." So I wrote her a letter and indeed she didn't answer. So that's all I know about Alice Cowan.

49. Carson poses precisely this question just one stanza prior to the poetic passage that serves as the frontispiece to this book. See "The Glass Essay, in *Glass, Irony and God*, 11.

50. I am using the text by A. H. Armstrong, *Plotinus VII* (Cambridge, MA: Loeb Classical Library of Harvard University Press, 1988), focusing particularly on *Ennead* VI.9, pages 252–257. Of great additional interest are two sections in Book III: section 1 "On Destiny" (*Peri Eimarmenês*), and section 5 "On Love" (*Peri Erôtos*).

51. See the marvelous lines in Anne Carson, "Sonnet on Addressing Oscar Wilde," in "Possessive Used as Drink (Me): A Lecture on Pronouns in the Form of 15 Sonnets," in *Float*.

52. See *The Writings of Dionysius the Areopagite*, Rev. John Parker, trans. (Aeterna Press, 2014) and, for more on the modern renderings of such apophatic thinking, Thomas A. Carlson, *Indiscretion: Finitude and the Naming of God* (Chicago, IL: University of Chicago Press, 1999).

53. "I am what I am," God told Moses in *Exodus*, which is an apt statement, as far as it goes, but one that leaves little room for argument or further discussion, thereby

undercutting the possibilities of Greek philosophy, and foreclosing our delight in further understanding.

54. Anne Carson, *Economy of the Unlost*, viii. Or, to connect Carsons's prose to Plotinus's: What kind of *necessity* is that?

55. William Shakespeare, *Romeo and Juliet* II.ii

56. Marguerite Porete, *The Mirror of Simple Souls*, 294–295.

The Latin text of the *Librum [capit] speculum simplicitum anima* (*Vat.lat.* 4355, ff54v–55r, and *Rossiani* 4, ff156v–158r) appears to conclude without this ending, but rather with that "Approval" which was taken to be the Author's Preface in the anonymous English edition of 1927 (*io creatura a create conduti mediante qua creator de se fecit hiic librii pro quibus nescio nec sare nolo. quia hoc non debeo nel le . . .*). The *Chigiani* text (96r–143r) possesses a difficult final page whose ending is uncertain. For more on the translation-and-transmission history of this troubled text, see Field, *The Beguine, the Angel, and the Inquisitor*, 204–207.

The Italian critical edition of the Old French manuscript (2018, pages 452–453) and the modern English translation by Ellen Bandinsky (1993, pages 220–221) say this rather differently, and far less poetically: "And thus I say to you, in conclusion, as God has given you highest creation and excellent light and singular love, be fertile and increase this creation without deficiency, for His two eyes always see you. And so ponder and consider that this seeing makes the Soul Simple" [*Et pource vous dis je, pour conclusion, se Dieu vous a donnee haulte creacion et excellente lumiere et singuliere amour, comprolissez et multipliez sans deffaillance ceste creacion; car ses deux yeulx vous regardent tousdis; et se bien considerez et regardez, ce regart fait estre l'Ame simple*].

Here is another clue as to which version of *The Mirror* Carson consulted, namely the Middle English version, and by which she was inspired. Curiously, Robert Lerner suggests that this might have been "an independent creation of the Middle English translator" rather than Marguerite's own hymnic refrain ("New Light on *The Mirror of Simple Souls*," 101).

57. The anonymous English translator captures Marguerite's paradoxes with some elegant punning of his or her own: the "sole" being of God makes even the "soul" irrelevant; and this "naughting of herself" has moved the author well past any naughtiness (290–295).

58. Anne Carson, "Drop't Sonnet" in "Possessive Used as Drink (Me): A Lecture on Pronouns in the Form of 15 Sonnets," in *Float*.

59. Anne Carson, "Wildly Constant," in *Float*.

Epilogue
Six Questions and an Afterword

> The sorcerer who pricks his thumb as he calls up the shades of the dead (*les ombres*) knows that they will heed his call because they can indulge in (*lapent*) his own blood. He also knows, or he should know, that the voices who speak with him are wiser (*plus sages*) and more worthy of attention (*plus dignes d'attention*) than his own clamorous outcries.
>
> —Marguerite Yourcenar, "Reflections on the Composition of the *Memoirs of Hadrian*" (1957)

* * * * *

Here, I offer some final aphoristic reflections in the form of six questions, answers to which are made more difficult by Anne Carson's studied refusal to deliver standard academic fare, even when writing in her most scholarly voice about decidedly scholarly topics. The relevant questions, many readers have informed me, are these:

What form of Classics has Anne Carson been performing?
The Greek lyric tradition, in the main, with some important Roman offshoots.
Does Anne Carson have comparable contemporaries?
Not really, unless you are willing to count Friedrich Nietzsche a contemporary.
May we anticipate Anne Carson's approach having successors?
It is difficult to say; her work, much like her voice, really is sui generis.
What Classical wisdom emerges from Anne Carson's unique line of vision?
That eros is concerned with desire (reach), not sex (grasp). And that's not as simple as it sounds.
What has Anne Carson added to the Classical repertoire?
In an important and undervalued way, religion. Eros is a god.
Does that god have a body?

So long as we do, yes.

* * * * *

In my attempts to make sense of Anne Carson's demanding corpus, I have done more than utilize the predictable classical Greek repertoire, though I have made extensive use of that. I have also turned to three rather unexpected sources of erotic and spiritual insight: Ovid, Marguerite Porete, and Simone Weil. All three were writers who sought to make and unmake the standard self in deference to an erotic god who is the lord of transformation. In a final gesture of appreciation, I would like to add one final author, and one more book, to the corpus, one that links Ovid's elusive Roman world, and its deeply fleshed spirituality, to the French tradition of sacred letters.

That text is Marguerite Yourcenar's *Memoirs of Hadrian*,[1] published in French the year after Anne Carson was born, translated into English three years later, and essaying a brilliant literary re-creation of a Roman world quite possibly lost to us after the triumphs of a more Christian culture. In some remarkable "Reflections on the Composition of the *Memoirs of Hadrian*"[2] that she composed after completing this historical novel, Yourcenar identified her interest in those times this way:

> Retrieved from a volume of Flaubert's correspondence, intensely read and heavily underlined by me in roughly 1927, is this remarkable passage: "The gods were no more, and the Christ was not yet: there was a unique historical moment, from Cicero to Marcus Aurelius, when man was alone (*l'homme seul a été*)." A large part of my life would be spent in trying to define (*à essayer de définir*), and then to portray, that man existing alone (*cet homme seul*) and yet also intimately related to everything.[3]

The artistic pretense of the book is that it is a letter written by the Roman emperor Hadrian (76–138 CE) to his adoptive grandson and future emperor, Marcus Aurelius (121–180 CE). Hadrian is sixty years old and "about to die of an edemic heart"; Marcus is seventeen. Little by little, the letter,

> begun in order to inform you of the progress of my illness (*mon mal*) has become . . . the written meditation of a sick man (*d'un malade*) who grants an audience to his memories (*ses souvenirs*). I now propose something more: I have now determined to recount my life to you. . . . I do not expect your seventeen years to understand everything. I desire, nonetheless to instruct (*instruire*) you, and to shock (*choquer*) you, as well. Your tutors (*précepteurs*), whom I have chosen myself, have given you your severe education, . . . I offer you here, in the guise of a corrective, a recitation stripped of preconceived ideas and

of abstract principles, derived from the experience of a single man (*d'un seul homme*) who is myself.⁴

Why this book-length memoir is addressed to Marcus Aurelius is not explained, but the discerning reader will see the rationale clearly enough. Marcus is arguably the most famous exemplar of late Roman Stoicism the empire produced. His *Meditations*⁵ is a textbook of Stoic duty and Stoic virtue, notable for its rigor and severity. By contrast, Hadrian is rigorous, but not severe. These Memoirs, then, offer an alternative type of Stoicism for the young philosopher to consider. Stoicism is not a *disembodied* philosophy, after all; no philosophy can be that, if it aspires to be human.

As we have seen throughout this book, a central preoccupation of the classical world lay in coming to a proper philosophical understanding of the relationship between body, mind, soul, and spirit. That rich vocabulary haunts the *Memoirs of Hadrian*, from the first page to the last. At the outset, the emperor has just been visited at his villa in Tivoli by his physician, Hermogenes. The doctor sees only his crude matter: humors, blood, lymph. Hadrian, a self-styled philosopher, thinks in more holistic terms of soul and body. "I love my body (*J'aime mon corps*); it has served me well, and in every way, and I do not begrudge it the care it now needs."⁶ This may sound very much like a mindful philosopher, observing his own body as if from above, as if from outside. Grave illness and physical discomfort can create that out-of-body perspective, to be sure, but we soon learn that this is how Marcus conceives of things, not Hadrian. For what follows in the first section of this epistolary memoir is a long meditation on various bodily matters, bodily pleasures primarily, and their appropriate enjoyment. Speaking in terms reminiscent of what Foucault would later describe as "care for the self" (*le souci de soi-même*)," Hadrian ticks off his various and varying attitudes toward exercise, food, drink, even rest and sleep.

In all of this, the emperor sounds reasonable, moderate, and decidedly self-controlled . . . until, that is, he comes to the subject of erotic desire.⁷

> The cynics and the moralists are in agreement, placing the erotic pleasures (*les voluptés de l'amour*) among the delights (*les jouissances*) termed gross . . . I shall believe in this classification of the erotic (*l'amour*) among the purely physical delights (supposing that such a thing exists) on the day when I may see a gourmet sobbing with joy before his favorite dish like a lover (*un amant*) gasping on a young shoulder. Of all our games (*jeux*), love's play is the only one (*le seul*) which threatens to unsettle the soul (*l'âme*), and is also the only one (*le seul aussi*) in which the player must necessarily abandon himself to the body's ecstasy (*délire du corps*). To abdicate reason (*raison*) is not indispensable for the drinker (*le buveur*), but the lover (*l'amant*) who leaves reason in control does not follow his god to the end (*au bout*).

This will be surprising, and perhaps unwelcome, news for a teenager committed to a rigorist version of Stoic virtue. Stoic reason traditionally is characterized as willing the minimization of bodily pleasures in order to eliminate potential perturbations of the soul. What possible benefit, then, might come of Hadrian's surprising recommendation of a decidedly erotic therapy? Remarkably, Hadrian has a compelling answer to this question, and it is related to the Stoic commitment to one's fellow rational beings. Hadrian reminds Marcus (and us) that these rational beings are more than simply rational; they are unique and therefore they must remain a mystery.

> Abstinence or excess involve but a single person (*l'homme seul*) . . . every sensual step we take places us in the presence of the Other (*l'Autre*) . . . That mysterious play (*jeu mystérieux*) which extends from the love of a body (*l'amour d'un corps*) to the love of a whole person (*l'amour d'une personne*) has seemed to me noble (*beau*) enough to consecrate one part of my life to it . . .
>
> And I admit that reason (*la raison*) stands utterly confounded in the presence of the veritable prodigy that love is, and of the strange obsession which makes this same flesh (*cette même chair*) . . . inspire us with such a passion of caresses simply because it is animated by an individuality different from our own, and because it presents certain lineaments of beauty to us, though the best judges may continue to disagree about what they are. Here human logic grinds to a halt, as before the revelations of the Mysteries. . . .

In a word, duty to another calls for the sundering of self. We have heard this demand many times in the guise of the lyric poets and spirited women whom Carson admires, perhaps Sappho most notably. And yet Hadrian (and Yourcenar) combine these lyric flights of rhetoric with deep philosophical awareness, much as Carson brought Sappho into conversation with Plato in her first book.

> I have sometimes dreamed of constructing a system of human knowledge which would be based on the erotic (*un système de connaissance humaine basé sur l'érotique*), a theory of contact wherein the mystery and the dignity of others consists precisely in offering to Me (*au Moi*) just that point of view which another world affords. Pleasure (*La volopté*), in such a philosophy, would be a more complete and also a more specialized means of approach to the Other, one more technique placed in the service of coming to know that which is not ourselves. . . . [W]hen these contacts persist and multiply about one unique creature, to the point of embracing him completely, when each portion of a body (*parcelle d'un corps*) becomes laden for us with meaning as overpowering as the features of a face (*traits d'un visage*), when this one being (*un seul être*) haunts us like music and torments us like a problem, . . . when he passes from the periphery of our universe to its very center, and finally becomes for

us more indispensable than our very own selves, then that astonishing prodigy takes place in which I perceive more an invasion of the flesh (*un envahissement de la chair*) by the spirit (*par l'esprit*) than a simple game for the flesh alone (*un simple jeu de la chair*).

What Hadrian here enunciates is the erotic dynamic whereby the adventure presented by one unique other nullifies the Stoic distinction between pleasure and perturbation, between body and mind. And it is here that the language of "spirit" comes to the fore. Spirit combined with flesh is what constitutes a body. We have touched this point before.

I present this remarkable discussion as a commentary on Carson's entire literary corpus, or, if we prefer to obey chronology, then I have presented Carson's remarkable oeuvre as a commentary on this remarkable passage from the fictional memoirs of a dying Roman ruler. The chronology scarcely matters. "Soul is the place."[8]

NOTES

1. Marguerite Yourcenar, *Mémoires d'Hadrien* (Paris: Librairie Plon, 1951); *Memoirs of Hadrian*, translated by Grace Frick in collaboration with the author (New York, NY: Farrar Straus & Giroux, 1954, 1957, 1963). The following translations are my own emendations.

2. For a critical analysis of these "Reflections," see Louis A. Ruprecht Jr., "Clio and Melpomene: In Defense of the Historical Novel," *Historical Reflections/Réflections Historiques* 23.3 (1997): 389–418.

3. Yourcenar, *Mémoires d'Hadrien*, 321; *Memoirs of Hadrian*, 319–320, translation emended.

4. Yourcenar, *Mémoires d'Hadrien*, 29; *Memoirs of Hadrian*, 20–21, translation emended.

5. I am using the Greek and English text edited by C. R. Haines, ed., *Marcus Aurelius* [Antoninus, The Emperor to Himself] (Cambridge, MA: Loeb Classical Library, 1930, 1999).

6. Yourcenar, *Mémoires d'Hadrien*, 11–12; *Memoirs of Hadrian*, 4, translation emended. *J'aime mon corps*, calls for a stronger verb than "like," which is the word Grace Frick chose.

7. The following quotations are all taken from Yourcenar, *Mémoires d'Hadrien*, 20–23; *Memoirs of Hadrian*, 12–15, translations emended.

8. It is perhaps worth noting that we possess a poem composed by Hadrian and addressed to his own soul, one with which Yourcenar concludes her book:

>   Anima vagula, blandula,
>   hospes comesque corporis,
>   quae nunc abibis in loca

pallidula, rigida, nudula,
nec, ut soles, dabis iocos . . .

Little soul, delicate and drifting,
guest and companion of my own body,
you will now reside in an abode
that is pallid, stark and bare,
leaving your child's play behind . . . (translation mine)

Appendix

THE MAJOR WORKS OF ANNE CARSON

Eros the Bittersweet: An Essay (Princeton University Press, 1986)
Short Talks (Brick Books, 1992)
Glass, Irony and God (New Directions, 1995)
    Short-listed for the Forward Prize
Plainwater: Essays and Poetry (Alfred A. Knopf, 1996)
Autobiography of Red (Alfred A. Knopf, 1998)
    Short-listed for the National Book Critics Award and the T.S. Eliot Prize for Poetry
Economy of the Unlost: Reading Simonides of Keos with Paul Celan (Princeton University Press, 1999)
Elektra (Oxford University Press, 2001)
Men in the Off Hours (Alfred A. Knopf, 2001)
    Winner of the Griffin Poetry Prize
The Beauty of the Husband: A Fictional Essay in 29 Tangos (Alfred A. Knopf, 2001)
    Winner of the T.S. Eliot Prize for Poetry
If Not, Winter: Fragments of Sappho (Alfred A. Knopf, 2002)
Decreation: Poetry, Essays, Opera (Alfred A. Knopf, 2005)
Grief Lessons: Four Plays by Euripides (New York Review Books, 2006)
An Oresteia: Agamemnon, Elektra, Orestes (Faber and Faber, 2009)
NOX (New Directions Publishing Company, 2010)
Antigonick (New Directions Publishing Company, 2012)
Red Doc> (Alfred A. Knopf, 2013)
    Short-listed for the Folio Prize and winner of the Griffin Poetry Prize
Nay Rather (American University of Paris: The Cahier Series No. 21, 2013)

Iphigeneia among the Taurians (University of Chicago Press, 2014)
The Albertine Workout (New Directions Poetry Pamphlet #13, 2014)
Bakkhai, Euripides: A New Version by Anne Carson (Oberon Books, 2015)
Antigone (Oberon Books, 2016)
Float (Alfred A. Knopf, 2016)
Norma Jeane Baker of Troy (Oberon Books Ltd., 2019)
Euripides: The Trojan Woman, a Comic, with Rosanna Bruno (New Directions Publishing Company, 2021)
H of H Playbook (New Directions Publishing Corporation, 2021)

SCHOLARLY ARTICLES AND SHORT ESSAYS

"The Justice of Aphrodite in Sappho Fr. 1," *Transactions of the American Philological Association* 110 (1980): 135–142.
"Wedding at Noon in Pindar's *Ninth Pythian*," *Greek, Roman and Byzantine Studies* 23 (1982): 121–128.
"Putting Her in Her Place: Women, Dirt, Desire," in David Halperin, John J. Winkler and Froma Zeitlin, eds., *Before Sexuality: The Construction of Erotic Experience in the Ancient Greek World* (Princeton, NJ: Princeton University Press, 1990), 135–169.
"The Justice of Aphrodite in Sappho I," in Ellen Greene, ed., *Reading Sappho: Contemporary Approaches* (Berkeley, CA: University of California Press, 1996), 226–232.
"Hack Gloss," in Roni Horn, *Hack Wit* (Göttingen: Steidl, 2015), no page numbers.
"We've Only Just Begun," *Harper's Magazine* (January 2016): 69–73
"1=1," *The New Yorker*, Volume 91, Issue 43 (January 11, 2016)
"Back the Way You Went," *The New Yorker*, Volume 92, Issue 35 (October 31, 2016)
"Stacks," *PAJ: A Journal of Performance & Art* 39.2 (May 2017): 89–108
"Flaubert Again," *The New Yorker*, Volume 94, Issue 33 (October 22, 2018)
"Lakes," *Brick: A Literary Journal* 100 (Winter 2018): 75–80
"Short Talk on Homer and John Ashbery," *The New Yorker*, Volume 94, Issue 42 (December 24, 2018)
"Short Talk on Kafka on Hölderlin," *The New York Review of Books* (May 28, 2020)

Bibliography

Sidney Abbott and Barbara Love, *Sappho Was a Right-On Woman: A Liberated View of Lesbianism* (New York, NY: Stein and Day, 1972).
Sarah LaChance Adams, Caroline Lundquist, and Christopher Davidson, eds., *New Philosophies of Sex and Love: Thinking Through Desire* (London: Rowman & Littlefield, 2017).
John D'Agata, "A____ with Anne Carson," *The Iowa Review* 27.2 (1997): 1–22 [https://ir.uiowa.edu/cgi/viewcontent.cgi?article=4868&context=iowareview].
———, "A Talk with Anne Carson," *Brick: A Literary Journal* 57 (1997): 14–22.
———, "Review of Men in the Off Hours by Anne Carson," *Boston Review* 25.3 (Summer 2000) [http://bostonreview.net/BR25.3/dagata.html]
Will Aitken, "Anne Carson, The Art of Poetry No. 88," *Paris Review* 171 (Fall 2004) https://www.theparisreview.org/interviews/5420/the-art-of-poetry-no-88-anne-carson.
———, *Antigone Undone: Juliette Binoche, Anne Carson, Ivo van Hove and the Art of Resistance* (Saskatchewan: University of Regina Press, 2018).
Jane Alison, *Change Me: Stories of Sexual Transformation from Ovid* (New York, NY: Oxford University Press, 2014).
———, *The Love Artist* (New York, NY: Farrar Straus Giroux, 2001).
———, *The Marriage of the Sea: A Novel* (New York, NY: Farrar Straus and Giroux, 2003).
———, *Meander, Spiral, Explode: Design and Pattern in Narrative* (New York, NY: Catapult, 2019).
———, *Natives and Exotics* (New York, NY: Harcourt Mifflin Harcourt Publishing Company, 2005).
———, *Nine Island* (New York, NY: Catapult, 2016).
———, *The Sisters Antipodes: A Memoir* (New York, NY: Houghton Mifflin Harcourt Publishing Company, 2009).
"Anne Carson," *Current Biography* 67.5 (2006): 93–96.

Emily Apter, *Against World Literature: On the Politics of Untranslatability* (London: Verso, 2013).

A. H. Armstrong, trans., *Plotinus VII* (Cambridge, MA: Loeb Classical Library of Harvard University Press, 1988).

William Arrowsmith, trans., *Euripides: Alcestis* (New York, NY: Oxford University Press, 1974).

———, ed., *Nietzsche: Unmodern Observations* (New Haven, CT: Yale University Press, 1990).

Apostolos N. Athanassakis, trans., *Hesiod: Theogony, Works and Days, Shield* (Baltimore, MD: Johns Hopkins University Press, 1983).

Albert R. Baca, "Ovid's Epistle from Sappho to Phaon (Heroides 15)," *Transactions and Proceedings of the American Philological Association* 102 (1971): 29–38

Leonard Barkan, *The Gods Made Flesh: Metamorphosis and the Pursuit of Paganism* (New Haven, CT: Yale University Press, 1986).

Mary E. Barnard, *The Myth of Apollo and Daphne from Ovid to Quevedo: Love, Agon, and the Grotesque* (Durham, NC: Duke University Press, 1987).

Ian Baucomb, *Specters of the Atlantic: Finance Capital, Slavery and the Philosophy of History* (Durham, NC: Duke University Press, 2005).

Mary Beard, "A Complex of Time: No More Sheep on Romulus' Birthday," *Proceedings of the Classical Philological Society* 33 (1987): 1–15.

———, "The Erotics of Rape: Livy, Ovid and the Sabine Women," in Päivi Setälä and Liisa Savunen, eds., *Female Networks and the Public Sphere in Roman Society* (Rome: Acta Instituti Romani Finlandiae [Volume XXII], 1999), 1–10.

Walter Benjamin, *Illuminations: Essays and Reflections*, Hannah Arendt, ed. (New York, NY: Shocken Books, 1968).

———, *The Origin of German Tragic Drama*, John Osborne, trans. (New York, NY: Verso, 1977).

———, *Ursprung des deutschen Trauerspiels* (Frankfurt am Main: Suhrkamp Verlag, 1963).

Ruby Blondell, *Helen of Troy: Beauty, Myth, Devastation* (New York, NY: Oxford University Press, 2013).

———, "Refractions of Homer's Helen in Archaic Lyric," *American Journal of Philology* 131 (2010): 349–391.

———, "'Third Cheerleader from the Left': From Homer's Helen to Helen of Troy," *Classical Reception Journal* 1 (2009): 4–22.

Ruby Blondell and Kirk Ormand, eds., *Ancient Sex: New Essays* (Columbus, OH: The Ohio State University Press, 2015).

Anton Bierl and André Lardinois, The Newest Sappho (P. Sapph. Obbink and P. GC inv. 105, frs. 104): *Studies in Archaic and Classical Greek Song*, Volume 2 (Leiden and Boston: E. J. Brill, 2016).

John Boswell, *Christianity, Homosexuality and Social Tolerance: Gay People in Western Europe from the Beginning of the Christian Era to the Fourteenth Century* (The University of Chicago Press, 1980).

Barbara Weiden Boyd, *Ovid's Homer: Authority, Repetition, and Reception* (New York, NY: Oxford University Press, 2017).

William Brockliss, Pramit Chaudhuri, Ayelet Haimson Lushkov and Katherine Wasdin, eds., *Reception and the Classics: An Interdisciplinary Approach to the Classical Tradition* (New York, NY: Cambridge University Press, 2012) [Yale Classical Studies 36].

Peter Brown, *Through the Eye of a Needle: Wealth, the Fall of Rome, and the Making of Christianity in the West, 350–550 AD* (Princeton, NJ: Princeton University Press, 2012).

——— and Rita Lizzi Testa, eds., *Pagans and Christians in the Roman Empire: The Breaking of a Dialogue (IVth–VIth Century A.D.)* (Piscataway, NJ: Transactions Publishers of Rutgers University, 2011).

Jacob Burckhardt, *The Civilization of the Renaissance in Italy*, S. G. C. Middlemore trans. (New York, NY: Penguin Books, 1990).

Katherine Burkett, *Literary Form as Postcolonial Critique* (London: Ashgate Publishing, 2012).

Simon Burris, Jeffrey Fish, and Dirk Obbink, "New Fragments of Book 1 of Sappho," *Zeitschrift für Papyrologie und Epigraphik* 189 (2014): 1–28.

Shane Butler, ed., *Deep Classics: Rethinking Classical Reception* (London: Bloomsbury Academic, 2016).

Stefano Buzzi and Antonio Alioni, eds., *Nuove acquisizione di Saffo e delle lirica greca: per il testo di P. Köln inv. 21351* (Alexandria: 2008).

Caroline Walker Bynum, *Holy Feast and Holy Fast: The Religious Significance of Food to Medieval Women* (Berkeley, CA: University of California Press, 1986).

Roberto Calasso, *The Marriage of Cadmus and Harmony*, Tim Parks, trans. (New York, NY: Viking, 1999).

David A. Campbell, ed., *Greek Lyric I: Sappho and Alcaeus* (Cambridge, MA: Harvard University Press, 1982).

———, *Greek Lyric III: Stesichorus, Ibycus, Simonides, and Others* (Cambridge, MA: Loeb Classical Library of Harvard University Press, 1991).

Thomas A. Carlson, *Indiscretion: Finitude and the Naming of God* (Chicago, IL: University of Chicago Press, 1999).

Barbara Cassin, ed., *Vocabulaire européen des philosophies: Dictionnaire des intraduisibles* 26.2 (Paris: Seuil, 2004).

Israel Chalfin, *Paul Celan: A Biography of His Youth*, Maximilian Bleyleben, trans. (New York, NY: Persea Books, 1991).

Elizabeth Coles, "The Sacred Object: Anne Carson and Simone Weil," *Acta Poetica* 34.1 (2013): 127–154.

Robert Coles, *Simone Weil: A Modern Pilgrimage* (Reading, MA: Addison-Wesley Publishing Company, Inc., 1987).

Amy Colin, *Paul Celan: Holograms of Darkness* (Bloomington, IN: University of Indiana Press, 1991).

Giorgio Colli and Mazzino Montinari, eds., *Nietzsche Briefwechsel: Kritische Gesamtausgabe in 8 Bänden* (Berlin: Walter de Gruyter, 1975).

———, *Friedrich Nietzsche: Sämtliche Werke, Kritische Studienausgabe in 15 Bänden [KSA]* (Berlin: Walter de Gruyter, 1967–1977).

W. Robert Conner, "Women Poets and the Origin of the Greek Hexameter," *Arion*, Third Series 27.2 (2019): 85–110.

Frank T. Coulson, "Bernardo Moretti, Biographer and Commentator on Ovid: The Manuscripts" (Spoleto: Presso la Sede del Centro, 1998).

———, "Hitherto Unedited Medieval and Renaissance Lives of Ovid (I)," *Medieval Studies* 49 (1987): 152–207.

———, and Bruno Roy, *Incipitarium Ovidianum: A Finding Guide for Texts Related to the Study of Ovid in the Middle Ages and Renaissance* (Turnhout, Belgium: Brepols Publishers, 2000).

Fiona Cox, *Ovid's Presence in Contemporary Women's Writing: Strange Monsters* (Oxford: Oxford University Press, 2018).

Paul Curtis, *Stesichoros's Geryoneis [Mnemosyne Supplements 333]* (Leiden, Boston: E. J. Brill, 2011).

Guy Davenport, "Introduction" to *Glass, Irony and God* (New Directions, 1995). vii–x.

Malcolm Davies and Patrick J. Finglass, *Stesichorus: The Poems* (New York, NY: Cambridge University Press, 2014).

Gregson Davis, special ed., "The Poetics of Derek Walcott: Intertextual Perspectives," *South Atlantic Quarterly* 96.2 (1997).

Andrea Deagon, "The Twelve Double-Hours of Night: Insomnia and Transformation in 'Gilgamesh'," *Soundings* 81.3/4 (1998): 461–489.

Maya Deren, *Divine Horsemen: The Living Gods of Haiti* (London: Thames and Hudson, 1953).

Jacques Derrida, *Sovereignties in Question: The Poetics of Paul Celan*, Thomas Dutoit and Outi Pasanen, eds. and trans. (New York, NY: Fordham University Press, 2005).

Dan Disney, "Sublime Disembodiment? Self-as-Other in Anne Carson's *Decreation*," *Orbis Litterarum* 67.1 (2012): 25–38.

E. R. Dodds, ed., *Euripides Bacchae, 2nd Edition* (Oxford: Clarendon Press, 1960).

Carol L. Dougherty, "Why Does Aphrodite Have Her Foot on That Turtle?," *Arion*, Third Series 27.3 (2020): 25–47.

Sir Kenneth Dover, *Greek Homosexuality* (Cambridge, MA: Harvard University Press, 1979).

Timothy Engström, "Foundational Standards and Conversational Style: The Humean Essay as an Issue of Philosophical Genre," *Philosophy & Rhetoric* 30.2 (1997): 150–175.

Sister Marie Liguori Ewald, "Ovid in the Contra Orationem Symmachi of Prudentius," Ph.D. Dissertation, The Catholic University of America (1942).

Sean L. Field, *The Beguine, the Angel, and the Inquisitor: The Trials of Marguerite Porete and Guiard of Cressonessart* (Notre Dame, IN: University of Notre Dame Press, 2012).

———, Robert E. Lerner et Sylvain Piron, *Marguerite Porete et Le Miroir des Simples Âmes: Perspectives Historiques, Philosophiques et Littéraires* (Paris: Librairie Philosophique J. Vrin, 2013).

Ian Fielding, *Transformations of Ovid in Late Antiquity* (New York, NY: Cambridge University Press, 2017).
Henry Leroy Finch, *Simone Weil and the Intellect of Grace* (New York, NY: Continuum, 1999).
P. J. Finglass and Adrian Kelly, eds., *Stesichorus in Context* (Cambridge: Cambridge University Press, 2015).
Leah Flack, *Modernism and Homer: The Odyssey of HD, James Joyce, Osip Mandalstam and Ezra Pound* (New York, NY: Cambridge University Press, 2015).
Joan Fleming, "'Talk (Why?) With Mute Ash': Anne Carson's Nox as Therapeutic Biography," *Biography: An Interdisciplinary Quarterly* 39.1 (Winter 2016): 64–78.
Michel Foucault, *Histoire de la sexualité; Vol. I, La volonté de savoir* (Paris: Editions Gallimard, 1976).
———, *Histoire de la sexualité; Vol. II, L'usage des plaisirs* (Paris: Editions Gallimard, 1984).
———, *The History of Sexuality, Volume 1: An Introduction*, Robert Hurley, trans. (New York, NY: Vintage Books, 1978).
———, *The History of Sexuality, Volume 2: The Use of Pleasure*, Robert Hurley trans. (New York, NY: Vintage Books, 1985).
Barbara Hughes Fowler, "The Archaic Aesthetic," *The American Journal of Philology* 105.2 (1984): 119–149.
Hadrien France-Lanord, *Paul Celan et Martin Heidegger, le sens d'un dialogue* (Paris: Fayard, 2004).
Hermann Fränkl, *Ovid: A Poet Between Two Worlds, Sather Classical Lectures 18* (Berkeley, CA: University of California Press, 1945, 1969).
Andre Furlani, "Reading Paul Celan with Anne Carson: 'What Kind of Withness Would That Be?'," *Canadian Literature* 176 (Spring 2003): 84–104.
Henry Fuseli, *Lectures on Painting to the Royal Academy in London* (London: Henry G. Bohn, 1848).
Kay Gabriel, "Specters of Dying Empire: The Case of Carson's Bacchae," *Tripwire: A Journal of Poetics* (2018): 315–323
Hans-Georg Gadamer, *Gadamer on Celan*, Richard Heinemann and Bruce Krajewski, eds. (Albany, NY: State University of New York Press, 1997).
Douglas E. Gerber, ed., *Greek Elegiac Poetry from the Seventh to Fifth Centuries BC* (Cambridge, MA: Loeb Classical Library of Harvard University Press, 1999).
Kate Gilhuly, "Lesbians Are Not from Lesbos," in Ruby Blondell and Kirk Ormand, eds., *Ancient Sex: New Essays* (Columbus, OH: The Ohio State University Press, 2015), 143–176.
Dina Giorgis, "Discarded Histories and Queer Affects in Anne Carson's Autobiography of Red," *Studies in Gender and Sexuality* 15 (2014): 154–166.
Nahum N. Glatzer, ed., *Franz Kafka: The Complete Stories* (New York, NY: Shocken Books, 1971).
Jerry Glenn, *Paul Celan* (New York, NY: Twayne Publishers, Inc., 1973).
Barbara Graziosi and Emily Greenwood, eds., *Homer in the Twentieth Century: Between World Literature and the Western Canon* (New York, NY: Oxford University Press, 2005).

Peter Green, trans., *Ovid: The Erotic Poems* (New York, NY: Penguin Books, 1982).
Ellen Greene, ed., *Reading Sappho: Contemporary Approaches* (Berkeley, CA: University of California Press, 1996).
———, *Re-Reading Sappho: Reception and Transmission* (Berkeley, CA: University of California Press, 1996).
Emily Greene and Marilyn B. Skinner, eds., *The New Sappho on Old Age: Textual and Philosophical Issues* (Washington, DC: Hellenic Foundation Publications, 2009).
Michael Gronewald and Robert W. Daniel, "Ein neuer Sappho-Papyrus," *Zeitschrift für Papyrologie und Epigraphik* 147 (2004): 1–8.
———, "Nachtrag zum neuen Sappho-Papyrus," *Zeitschrift für Papyrologie und Epigraphik* 149 (2004): 1–4.
Karlfried Gründer, ed., *Der Streit um Nietzsches "Geburt der Tragödie"* (Hildesheim: Georg Olms Verlag, 1989).
Romana Guarnieri, "Quando si dice, il caso!" *Bailamme: Rivista di spiritualità e politica* 8 (1990): 45–55.
C. R. Haines, ed., *Marcus Aurelius [Antoninus, The Emperor to Himself]* (Cambridge, MA: Loeb Classical Library, 1930, 1999).
Johanna Hanink, *The Classical Debt: Greek Antiquity in an Era of Austerity* (Cambridge, MA: Harvard University Press, 2017).
Lorna Hardwick, *Reception Studies [New Surveys in the Classics No. 33]* (Oxford University Press, 2003).
———, "Thinking with Classical Reception: Critical Distance, Critical License, Critical Amnesia?" in Edmund Richardson, ed., *The Edges of Classical Reception* (London: Bloomsbury Academic, 2019), 13–25.
———, *Translating Words, Translating Cultures* (London: Gerald Duckworth & Co., Ltd., 2000).
John Hellman, *Simone Weil: An Introduction to Her Thought* (Philadelphia, PA: Fortress Press, 1984).
Jeet Here, "Poet or 'Prize-Reaping Machine'?" *National Post* 31 (January 2002): B5+.
N. I. Herescu's *Ovidiana: Recherches sur Ovide* (Paris: Société d'Édition "Les Belles Lettres," 1958).
Ralph J. Hexter, *Ovid and Medieval Schooling, Studies in Medieval School Commentaries on Ovid's Ars Amatoria, Epistulae ex Ponto, and Epistulae Heroidum* (München: Bei der Arbeo-Gesellschaft, 1986).
Ben Hjorth, " 'We're Standing in the Nick of Time': The Temporality of Translation in Anne Carson's Antigonick," *Performance Research* 19.3 (2014): 135–139.
Friedrich Hölderlin, *Sophokles: Antigone* (Altenmünster: Jazzybee Verlag and North Charleston, SC: Createspace, 2017).
Amy Hollywood, *Acute Melancholia and Other Essays: Mysticism, History, and the Study of Religion* (New York, NY: Columbia University Press, 2016).
Richard Hunter, *On Coming After: Studies in Post-Classical Greek Literature and its Reception* (Berlin: Walter de Gruyter Verlag, 2008).
Pauline Jaccon, "'A Strange New Kind of/Inbetween': Anne Carson et l'impulsion créative en traduction," *Ticontre. Teoria Testo Traduzione* 12 (2019): 449–467.

———, "Reflective Voices: Peering into Anne Carson's Translational Writing through Marguerite Porete's *Mirror of Simple Souls*," *Palimpsestes* 36 (2022): forthcoming.

Laura Jansen, ed., *The Roman Paratext: Frame, Texts, Readers* (Cambridge: Cambridge University Press, 2014).

Chris Jennings, "The Erotic Poetics of Anne Carson," *University of Toronto Quarterly* 70.4 (2001): 923–936.

Ruven Karr, *Die Toten im Gespräch: Trialogische Strukturen in der Dichtung Paul Celans* (Hannover: Wehrmann Verlag, 2015).

E. J. Kenney, "The Poetry of Ovid's Exile," *Proceedings of the Classical Philological Society* 11 (1965): 37–49.

Frank Kermode, *The Classic: Literary Images of Permanence and Change* (New York, NY: The Viking Press, 1975).

Theresa M. Krier, "Sappho's Apples: The Allusiveness of Blushes in Ovid and Beaumont," *Comparative Literature Studies* 25.1 (1988): 1–22.

Kathleen Kuiper, "Anne Carson," *Encyclopedia Brittanica*, https://www.britannica.com/biography/Anne-Carson.

Glenn Kurtz, "What Remains: Sappho and Mourning," *Southwest Review* 95.1/2 (2010): 246–254.

Philippe Lacoue-Labarthe, *Poetry as Experience*, Andrea Tarnewski, trans. (Palo Alto, CA: Stanford University Press, 1999).

Adam Lecznar, "Shut Your Eyes and See: Digesting the Past with Nietzsche and Joyce," in Shane Butler, ed., *Deep Classics: Rethinking Classical Reception* (London: Bloomsbury Academic, 2016), 127–143.

Claudio Leonardi and Birger Munk Olsen, eds., *The Classical Tradition in the Middle Ages and the Renaissance* (Spoleto: Centro Italiano di Studi sull'Alto Medioevo, 1995).

Robert E. Lerner, "New Light on The Mirror of Simple Souls," *Speculum* 85 (2010): 91–116.

Maya Linden, "'Metaphors of War': Desire, Danger, and Ambivalence in Anne Carson's Poetic Form," *Women's Studies* 43 (2014): 230–245.

Sara Lindheim, *Mail and Female: Epistolary Narrative and Desire in Ovid's Heroides* (Madison, WI: University of Wisconsin, 2003).

Christopher Logue, *War Music* (New York, NY: Farrar Straus and Giroux, 1981, 1987).

James K. Lyon, *Paul Celan and Martin Heidegger: An Unresolved Conversation, 1951–1970* (Baltimore, MD: Johns Hopkins University Press, 2001).

Sarah T. Mace, "Amour, Encore! The Development of δηὖτε in Archaic Lyric," *Greek, Roman and Byzantine Studies* 34 (1993): 335–364.

Bonnie MacLachlan, "What's Crawling in Sappho fr. 130," *Phoenix* 43.2 (1989): 95–99.

Dale Martin, *Inventing Superstition: From the Hippocratics to the Christians* (Cambridge, MA: Harvard University Press, 2007).

Chris Mason, "Bright Lyre Becomes Voice: Translating Sappho Into Songs," *The Antioch Review* 67.1 (2009): 109.

William Mason, "Sappho: A Lyrical Drama in Three Acts" (n.p., 1797).
Mary Maxwell, "Questions & Comments from the Audience," *Arion*, Third Series 21.1 (2013): 175–192.
Thomas McEvilley, *Sappho* (Putnam, CT: Spring Publications, 2008).
Matthew M. McGowan, *Ovid in Exile: Power and Poetic Redress in the Tristia and Epistulae ex Ponto [Mnemosyne Supplements 309]* (Leiden: E. J. Brill, 2009).
Oran McKenzie, "Spillage and Banditry: Anne Carson's Derivatives," in Martin Leer and Genoveva Puskás, eds., *Economies of English* (Tübingen: Narr Francke Attempto Verlag, 2016), 225–242.
Kevin McNeilly, special ed., "Anne Carson," *Canadian Literature* 176 (Spring 2003): 1–104.
Richard Methley, *Speculum Animarum Simplicium, A Glossed Latin Version of the Mirror of Simple Souls* (Salzburg: Institüt für Anglistik und Amerikanstik, 2010), two volumes.
Carlo Michelstaedter, *Persuasione e la rettorica* (Milano: Adelphi Edizione, 1982).
———, *Persuasion and Rhetoric*, Russell Scott Valentino, Cinzia Sartini Blum, and David J. Depew, trans. (New Haven, CT: Yale University Press, 2004).
John F. Miller and Carole E. Newlands, eds., *A Handbook to the Reception of Ovid* (West Sussex: Wiley Blackwell, 2014).
Ann Moss, *Ovid in Renaissance France: A Survey of the Latin Editions of Ovid and Commentaries Printed in France Before 1600, Warburg Institute Surveys VIII* (The Warburg Institute, University of London, 1982).
Glenn W. Most, "Reflecting Sappho," *Bulletin of the Institute of Classical Studies* 40 (1995): 15–38.
J. H. Mozley, trans., and G. P. Gould rev., *Ovid II: The Art of Love and Other Poems*, (Cambridge, MA: Loeb Classical Library of Harvard University Press, 1979).
A. N. L. Munby and Lawrence W. Towner, *The Flow of Books and Manuscripts, Papers Read at the Clark Memorial Library, March 30 1968 [Munby, "The Case of the 'Caxton' Manuscript of Ovid: Reflections on the Legislation Controlling the Export of Works of Art from Great Britain" and Towner, "Every Silver Lining Has a Cloud: The Recent Shaping of the Newberry Library's Collections"]* (Los Angeles, CA: William Andrews Clark Memorial Library, University of California, 1969).
Stuart J. Murray, "The Autobiographical Self: Phenomenology and the Limits of Narrative Self-Possession in Anne Carson's Autobiography of Red," *English Studies in Canada* 31.4 (2-0-5): 101–122.
Betty Roe Nagle, *The Poetics of Exile: Program and Polemic in the Tristia and Epistulae ex Ponto of Ovid, Collections Latomus, Volume 170* (Bruxelles: Latomus Revue d'Études Latines, 1980).
Alexander Nehamas, *The Art of Living: Socratic Reflections from Plato to Foucault* (Berkeley, CA: The University of California Press, 1998).
———, *Nietzsche: Life as Literature* (Cambridge, MA: Harvard University Press, 1985).
Maggie Nelson, *The Argonauts* (Minneapolis, MN: Graywolf Press, 2015).
Carole E. Newlands, *Playing with Time: Ovid and the Fasti* (Ithaca, NY: Cornell University Press 1995).

Friedrich Nietzsche, *Beyond Good and Evil*, Walter Kaufmann, trans. (New York, NY: Vintage Books, 1967).
———, *The Birth of Tragedy and The Case of Wagner*, Walter Kaufmann, trans. (New York, NY: Vintage Books, 1967).
———, "David Strauss: The Confessor and the Writer," Herbert Golder, trans., in Arrowsmith, ed., *Nietzsche: Unmodern Observations*, 3–72.
———, Die fröhliche Wissenschaft [18], in Giorgio Colli und Mazzino Montinari, eds., *Friedrich Nietzsche: Sämtliche Werke, Kritische Studienausgabe in 15 Bänden* (Berlin: Walter de Gruyter, 1967–1977), III: 343–651.
———, *The Gay Science*, Walter Kaufmann, trans. (New York, NY: Vintage Books, 1967).
———, Die Geburt der Tragödie [1872], in Giorgio Colli und Mazzino Montinari, eds., *Friedrich Nietzsche: Sämtliche Werke, Kritische Studienausgabe in 15 Bänden* (Berlin: Walter de Gruyter, 1967–1977), I: 11–156.
———, *Philosophy in the Tragic Age of the Greeks*, Marianne Cowan, trans. (Washington, DC: Regnery Publishing, Inc., 1962).
———, "On the Use and Abuse of History in the Service and Disservice of Life," in William Arrowsmith, ed., *Unmodern Observations* (New Haven, CT: Yale University Press, 1990), 75–145.
———, *Twilight of the Idols*, trans. (Indianapolis, IN: Hackett Publications, 1997).
———, "We Classicists," William Arrowsmith, trans., in William Arrowsmith, ed., *Unmodern Observations* (New Haven, CT: Yale University Press, 1990), 307–387.
———, Wir Philologen [1875], in Giorgio Colli und Mazzino Montinari, eds., *Friedrich Nietzsche: Sämtliche Werke, Kritische Studienausgabe in 15 Bänden* (Berlin; Walter de Gruyter, 1967–1977), VIII: 1–120.
Brent Nongbri, *God's Library: The Archaeology of the Earliest Christian Manuscripts* (New Haven, CT: Yale University Press, 2018).
Martha C. Nussbaum, *Aristotle's De motu animalium* (Princeton, NJ: Princeton University Press, 1978).
———, *The Fragility of Goodness: Luck and Ethics in Greek Tragedy and Philosophy* (New York, NY: Cambridge University Press, 1986).
———, "Love and the Individual," in *Love's Knowledge* (New York, NY: Oxford University Press, 1990), 314–334.
———, *Upheavals of Thought: The Intelligence of Emotions* (New York, NY: Cambridge University Press, 2001).
Dirk Obbink, "Two New Poems by Sappho," *Zeitschrift für Papyrologie und Epigraphik* 189 (2014): 32–49.
Ellen Oliensis, "The Paratext of Amores I: Gaming the System," in Laura Jansen, ed., *The Roman Paratext: Frame, Texts, Readers* (Cambridge: Cambridge University Press, 2014), 206–223.
Jessi O'Rourke-Suchoff, "'Near and Unlost': Reading Paul Celan with Anne Carson," *The Germanic Review* 93 (2018): 76–83.
Fulvio Orsini, *Carmina Novem Illustrium Feminarum [Songs of Nine Illustrious Women Poets]* (Antwerp: Ex officina Christophori Plantini, 1568).

Alice Oswald, *Memorial: A Version of Homer's Iliad* (New York, NY: W. W. Norton & Company, 2011).

Cynthia B. Patterson, *The Family in Greek History* (Cambridge, MA: Harvard University Press, 1998).

Rachael Peckham, "What Binds Them Together," *New Ohio Review* 22 (2017): 150–153.

Francine du Plessix Gray, *Simone Weil* (New York, NY: Penguin Books, 2001).

Mark Polizzotti, *Sympathy for the Traitor: A Translation Manifesto* (Cambridge, MA: MIT Press, 2018).

Margherita Porete, *Lo Specchio delle Anime Semplici, testo medio francese a fronte*, Giovanna Fozzer, trans. (Firenze: Le Lettere, 2018).

Marguerite Porete, *The Mirror of Simple Souls* (London: Burns Oates and Washburne Ltd., 1927).

———, *The Mirror of Simple Souls*, Ellen L. Babinsky, trans. (Mahwah, NJ: Paulist Press, 1993).

Robert Potts, "Neither Rhyme nor Reason," *Guardian UK* (26 January 2002): 1–3.

A. C. Quatremère de Quincy, *Canova et ses ouvrages, ou Mémoires Historiques sur la vie et les travaux de ce célèbre artiste* (Paris: Adrien le Clere et C.ie Imprimeurs-Libraires, Quai des Augustins, No. 35, 1834).

———, *Considérations Morales sur la Destination des Ouvrages de l'Art, ou De l'Influence de leur Emploi* (Paris: De L'Imprimerie de Crapelet, 1815).

———, De l'état de l'architecture Égyptiennes, considérée dans son origine, ses principes et son goût, et comparée sous les mêmes rapports à l'Architecture Greque. Dissertation qui a remporté, en 1785, le Prix par l'Académie des Inscriptions et Belles-Lettres (Paris: Chez Barrois l'aîné e Fils, Libraires, rue de Savoye, No. 23, An XI--1803).

———, *Le Jupiter Olympien, ou, L'Art de la Sculture Antique considéré sous un nouveau point de vue* (Paris: De l'Imprimerie de Firmon Didot, 1815).

———, *Letters to Miranda and Canova on the Abduction of Antiquities from Rome and Athens*, Chris Miller and David Gilks, trans., with David Poulot (Malibu, CA: Getty Research Foundation, 2012).

———, *Lettres au Générale Miranda sur le Préjudice qu'Occasionneraient aux Arts & à la Science le Déplacement des Monuments de l'Art de l'Italie, le Démembrement de ses Écoles, & la Spoliation de ses Collections, Galeries, Musées, etc.* (n.p., 1796).

———, *Lettres écrites de Londres à Rome, et adressées à M. Canova; sur les Marbres d'Elgin, ou les Sculptures du Temple de Minerve à Athènes* (Rome, n.p., 1818).

———, *Lettres sur l'enlèvement des ouvrages de l'art antique a Athènes et a Rome* (Paris: Adrien le Clere et C.ie, Quai des Augustins, No. 35, 1836).

———, *Sur la Statue Antique de Vénus Découverte dans l'Ile de Milo en 1820, Transporte a Paris par M. Le Marquis de Rivière, Ambassadeur de France a la Cour Ottomane* (Paris: Chez Debure Frères, Libraires du Roi; de l'Imprimerie de Firmin Didot, Imprimeur du Roi, 1821).

Ian Rae, "'Dazzling Hybrids': The Poetry of Anne Carson," *Canadian Literature* 166 (2000): 17–41.

———, *From Cohen to Carson: The Poet's Novel in Canada* (Montreal: McGill-Queen's Press, 2008).

———, "Verglas: Narrative Technique in Anne Carson's 'The Glass Essay'," *English Studies in Canada* 37.3/4 (2011): 163–186.

Tatiani G. Rapatzikou, "Anne Carson's *NOX*: Materiality and Memory," *Book 2.0* 7.1 (2017): 57–65.

Diane Rayor, trans., *Sappho's Lyre: Archaic Lyric and Women Poets of Ancient Greece* (Berkeley, CA: University of California Press, 1991).

Elizabeth Reeder, "What a Thirst It Was: Longing Excess and the Genre-Bending Essay," *Journal of Writing in Creative Practice* 10.1 (2017): 27–47.

Melanie Rehak, "Things Fall Together," *New York Times Magazine* (26 March 2000): 36–39.

Edmund Richardson, ed., *Classics in Extremis: The Edges of Classical Reception* (Bloomsbury Academic, 2019).

Vicky Rimell, "Epistolary Fictions: Authorial Identity in 'Heroides' 15," *Proceedings of the Cambridge Philological Society* 45 (1999): 109–135.

Robin Robertson, trans., *Euripides Bacchae, with a Preface by Daniel Mendelsohn* (New York, NY: HarperCollins Publishers, 2014).

Pablo Oyarzun Robles, *Entre Celan y Heidegger, 2nd Edition* (Santiago: Ediciones/ Metales Pesados, 2013).

Gianpiero Rosati, "Sabinus, the Heroides and the Poet-Nightingale: Some Observations on the Authenticity of the Epistula Sapphus," *Classical Quarterly* 46.1 (1996): 207–216.

Philip Rousseau and Manolis Papoutsakis, eds., Transformations of Late Antiquity: Essays for Peter Brown (Burlington, VT: Ashgate Publishing Company, 2009).

Louis A. Ruprecht Jr., *Afterwords: Hellenism, Modernism and the Myth of Decadence* (Albany, NY: State University of New York Press, 1996).

———, *Classics at the Dawn of the Museum Era: The Life and Times of Antoine Chrysostome Quatremère de Quincy (1755–1849)* (New York, NY: Palgrave, 2014).

———, "Clio and Melpomene: In Defense of the Historical Novel," *Historical Reflections/Réflections Historiques* 23.3 (1997): 389–418.

———, "The Ethos of Olympism: The Religious Meaning of the Modern Olympic Movement," *Soundings* 81.1/2 (1998): 267–302.

———, "Finding and Losing One's Way: Eros and the Other in Greek Tragedy and Philosophy," in Sarah LaChance Adams, Caroline Lundquist and Christopher Davidson, eds., *New Philosophies of Sex and Love: Thinking Through Desire* (London: Rowman & Littlefield, 2017), 15–34.

———, "Sport Matters: On Art, Social Artifice and the Rules of the Game, or, The Politics of Sport," in Vicki Rapti and Eric Gordon, eds. *Ludics: Play As Humanistic Inquiry* (New York, NY: Palgrave Macmillan, 2021), 47–72.

———, *Symposia: Plato, the Erotic and Moral Value* (Albany, NY: State University of New York Press, 1996).

———, *This Tragic Gospel: How John Corrupted the Heart of Christianity* (San Francisco, CA: Jossey-Bass, 2008).

———, *Tragic Posture and Tragic Vision: Against the Modern Failure of Nerve* (New York, NY: Continuum, 1994).

———, *Was Greek Thought Religious? On the Use and Abuse of Hellenism, From Rome to Romanticism* (New York, NY: Palgrave Macmillan, 2002).

———, "Who Owes What to Whom? Some Classical Reflections on Debt, Greek and Otherwise," a review of Johanna Hanink, *The Classical Debt: Greek Antiquity in an Era of Austerity* (Cambridge, MA: Harvard University Press, 2017), in *Arion*, Third Series 26.1 (2018): 165–194.

———, "Wilamowitz versus Winckelmann: On the Romantic Roots of Nietzsche's Birth of Tragedy," *New Nietzsche Studies* 10.3/4 (2017, 2018): 169–186.

———, *Winckelmann and the Vatican's First Profane Museum* (New York, NY: Palgrave, 2011).

Clarise Samuels, *Holocaust Visions: Surrealism and Existentialism in the Poetry of Paul Celan* (Columbia, SC: Camden House, Inc., 1993).

Phil Sapirstein, "The First Doric Temple in Sicily, Its Builder, and IG XIV 1," *Hesperia* 90 (2021): 411–477.

Susan Scheinberg, "The Bee Maidens of the Homeric Hymn to Hermes," *Harvard Studies in Classical Philology* 83 (1979): 1–28

Roy Scranton, "Estranged Pain: Anne Carson's *Red Doc>*," *Contemporary Literature* 55.1 (2014): 202–214.

Robert Shorrock, *The Myth of Paganism: Nonnus, Dionysus and the World of Late Antiquity* (London: Bloomsbury Academic, 2011, 2013).

Grant Showerman, trans., and G. P. Gould, rev., *Ovid I: Heroides and Amores* (Cambridge, MA: Loeb Classical Library of Harvard University Press, 1977).

Jane McIntosh Snyder, *Lesbian Desire in the Lyrics of Sappho* (New York, NY: Columbia University Press, 1997).

Sam Solecki, ed., S*pider Blues: Essays on Michael Ondaatje* (Montreal: Vdhicule, 1985).

David Solway, "The Trouble with Annie," *Books in Canada* 30.1 (July 2001): 24–26.

Madison U. Sowell, ed., *Dante and Ovid: Essays in Intertextuality* (Binghamton, NY: Center for Medieval & Renaissance Texts & Studies, 1991).

Eric O. Springsted, *Christus Mediator: Platonic Mediation in the Thought of Simone Weil* (Chico, CA: American Academy of Religion Series No. 41, 1983).

George Steiner, "Anne Carson Translates Antigone," *Times Literary Supplement* (1 August 2012).

———, *Antigones* (New York, NY: Oxford University Press, 1984).

Jeffrey Stout, *Democracy and Tradition* (Princeton, NJ: Princeton University Press, 2004).

———, *Blessed Are the Organized* (Princeton, NJ: Princeton University Press, 2010).

Gillian Sze, "The Consolatory Fold: Anne Carson's Nox and the Melancholic Archive," *Studies in Canadian Literature* 44.1 (2019): 66–80.

Peter Szondi, *On Textual Understanding and Other Essays*, Harvey Mendelsohn, trans. (Minneapolis, MN: University of Minnesota Press, 1986).

Richard J. Tarrant. "The Authenticity of the Letter of Sappho to Phaon (Heroides XV)," *Harvard Studies in Classical Philology* 85 (1981): 133–153.

Megan Terry, "Approaching Simone: A Drama in Two Acts" (Samuel French, Inc., 1970).
John C. Thibault, *The Mystery of Ovid's Exile* (Berkeley, CA: University of California Press, 1964).
Peter Thomson, *Shakespeare's Theatre, 2nd Edition* (New York, NY: Routledge, 1992).
Thea S. Thorsen, "Corinna and Colleagues in Ancient Rome. Tatian's Catalogue of Statues (Oration ad Graecos 33-4) Reconsidered," *Mnemosyne, Fourth Series* 65.4/5 (2012): 695–715.
———, "The Newest Sappho (2016) and Ovid's Heroides 15," in Thea S. Thorsen and Stephen Harrison, eds., *Roman Receptions of Sappho* (New York, NY: Oxford University Press, 2019), 249–264.
Thea S. Thorsen and Stephen Harrison, eds., *Roman Receptions of Sappho* (New York, NY: Oxford University Press, 2019).
Garth Tissol, *The Face of Nature: Wit, Narrative, and Comic Origins in Ovid's Metamorphoses* (Princeton, NJ: Princeton University Press, 1997).
Monique Tschofen, "'First I Must Tell about Seeing': (De)monstrations of Visuality and the Dynamics of Metaphor in Anne Carson's Autobiography of Red," *Canadian Literature* 180 (2004): 31–50.
Lee Upton, *Defensive Measures: The Poetry of Niedecker, Bishop, Glück, and Carson* (Lewisburg, PA: Bucknell University Press, 2005).
Helena Van Praet, "Recalibrating Categorisation: A Semiological Reading of Anne Carson's Decreation," *English Text Construction* 12.2 (2019): 167–195.
Eleanor Wachtel, "Interview with Anne Carson," *Brick: A Literary Journal* 71 (2011).
Derek Walcott, *The Antilles: Fragments of Epic Memory* (New York, NY: Farrar Straus and Giroux, 1992).
———, *Omeros* (New York, NY: Farrar Straus Giroux, 1990).
Abraham Wasserstein and David J. Wasserstein, *The Legend of the Septuagint: From Classical Antiquity to Today* (New York, NY: Cambridge University Press, 2006).
Simone Weil, *Gateway to God*, David Raper, ed. (New York, NY: Crossroad, 1982).
———, *Gravity and Grace*, Arthur Wills, trans. (New York, NY: Octagon Books, 1983).
———, *"The Iliad, or, the Poem Force" [1943]*, Mary McCarthy, trans. (Wallingford, PA: Pendle Hill Paperbacks, 1956).
———, "The Iliad, Poem of Might," in *Intimations of Christianity among the Ancient Greeks* (London: Routledge & Kegan Paul, 1957), 24–55.
———, *Intimations of Christianity among the Ancient Greeks* (London: Routledge & Kegan Paul, 1957).
———, *Lectures on Philosophy*, Hugh Price, trans. (New York, NY: Cambridge University Press, 1978).
———, *The Need for Roots*, Arthur Wills, trans. (New York, NY: Octagon Books, 1984).
———, *The Notebooks of Simone Weil*, Arthur Wills, trans. (London and Boston: Routledge & Kegan Paul, 1956, 1976).

———, *Oppression and Liberty*, Arthur Wills & John Petrie, trans. (Amherst, MA: University of Massachusetts Press, 1973).

———, *Waiting for God*, Emma Crauford, trans. (New York, NY: Harper & Row, Publishers, 1951).

Daniel Weissbort and Astradur Eysteinsson, eds., *Translation—Theory and Practice: A Historical Reader* (New York, NY: Oxford University Press, 2006).

A. L. Wheeler, trans., and G. P. Gould rev., *Ovid VI: Tristia, Ex Ponto* (Cambridge, MA: Loeb Classical Library of Harvard University Press, 1988).

Christine Wiesenthal, "The 'Impossible Truth' of Writing Off the Subject: Anne Carson's Decreation Poetics and 'The Glass Essay,'" *TEXT*, Special Issue 50 (2018): 1–10.

Ulrich von Wilamowitz-Möllendorff, "Future Philology!" Gertrude Postl, trans. and Babette Babich, ed., *New Nietzsche Studies* 4.1/2 (2000): 1–32.

Joshua Marie Wilkinson, ed., *Anne Carson: Ecstatic Lyre* (Ann Arbor, MI: University of Michigan Press, 2015).

L. P. Wilkinson, *Ovid Recalled* (New York, NY: Cambridge University Press, 1955).

Thomas Willard, "Anne Carson," in Rosemary M. Canfield Reisman, ed., *Critical Survey of Poetry: British, Irish, and Commonwealth Poets* (Ipswich, MA: Salem, 2010), Volume 1, 225–228.

C. K. Williams, trans., *The Bacchae of Euripides*, with an Introduction by Martha Nussbaum (New York, NY: Farrar Straus and Giroux, 1990).

Gareth Williams, *Banished Voices: Readings in Ovid's Exile Poetry* (New York, NY: Cambridge University Press, 1997).

William Carlos Williams: *Selected Poems*, Charles Tomlinson, ed. (New York, NY: New Directions Publishing Corporation, 1985).

Johann Joachim Winckelmann, *Gedancken über die Nachahmung der Griechischen Wercke in der Mahlerey und Bildhauer-Kunst* (Friedrichstadt, gedruckt bey Christian Heinrich Hagenmüller, 1755).

———, *Gedanken über die Nachahmung der griechischen Werke in der Mahlerey und Bildhauer Kunst, zweite vermehrte Auflage* (Dresden und Leipzig: Im Verlag der Waltherischen Handlung, 1756).

———, *Geschichte der Kunst des Alterthums* (Dresden: In der Walterischer Hofbuchhandlung, 1764).

———, *The History of Ancient Art*, G. Henry Lodge, trans. (Boston: James R. Osgood and Company, 1880).

———, *History of the Art of Antiquity*, Harry Francis Mallgrave, trans., Alex Potts, ed. (Malibu, CA: Getty Foundation Publications, 2006).

———, *Reflections on the Imitation of Greek Works in Painting and Sculpture*, Elfriede Heyer and Roger C. Norton, eds. (La Salle, IL: Open Court Publishing Company, 1987).

———, *Monumenti Antichi Inediti*, spiegati ed illustrati da Giovanni Winckelmann, Prefetto delle Antichità di Roma (Roma, 1767).

———, *Johann Joachim Winckelmann: Monumenti Antichi Inediti, Volume I e II*, Maria Elisa García Barraco e Laurentino García y García, eds. (Roma: Arbor Sapientiae Editore, 2018).

Christopher S. Wood, "Reception and the Classics," William Brockliss, Pramit Chaudhuri, Ayelet Haimson Lushkov, and Katherine Wasdin, eds., [*Yale Classical Studies* 36] *Reception and the Classics: An Interdisciplinary Approach to the Classical Tradition* (New York, NY: Cambridge University Press, 2012).

Kiene Brillenburg Wurth, "Re-vision as Remediation: Hypermediacy and Translation in Anne Carson's *Nox*," *Image & Narrative* 14.4 (2013): 20–33.

The Writings of Dionysius the Areopagite, Rev. John Parker, trans. (Aeterna Press, 2014).

Dimitrios Yatromanolakis, *Sappho in the Making: The Early Reception* (Cambridge, MA: Center for Hellenic Studies at Harvard University Press, 2007).

Marguerite Yourcenar, *Mémoires d'Hadrien* (Paris: Librairie Plon, 1951).

———, *Memoirs of Hadrian*, translated by Grace Frick in collaboration with the author (New York, NY: Farrar Straus and Giroux, 1954, 1957).

Robert Zaretsky, "The Logic of the Rebel: On Simone Weil and Albert Camus," *Los Angeles Review of Books* (March 7, 2020).

Index

Achilles, 25n13, 56, 136n46
Aeschylus (c525–c456 BCE),
 Aeschylean, 8, 11, 70n38;
 Agamemnon (458 BCE),
 50–52, 70n38
Alison, Jane, 123–125, 144nn99–100,
 144n104, 177
Archilochus (fl.c650 BCE), 80, 91,
 102n66, 108, 129
Aristophanes (c446–c386 BCE),
 Aristophanic, 11, 81
Aristotle (384–322 BCE), 8, 71n46;
 katharsis in, 55
 lost works, xv
 Nicomachean Ethics, 91, 101n63
 Poetics, 71
 Rhetoric, 91, 101n63

Benjamin, Walter (1892–1940), 22, 178;
 "The Image of Proust"
 (1929), 105
 *On the Origin of German Tragic
 Drama* (1925), 8, 24nn4–6
 "The Task of the Translator"
 (1923), 42, 68–69n21, 101n59,
 128, 147n123
Boswell, John (1947–1994):
 *Christianity, Social Tolerance
 and Homosexuality* (1980), 22,
 32n70, 178
Buber, Martin (1878–1965), 92
Butler, Judith, 73n64

Camus, Albert (1913–1960),
 107, 132n13
Catullus [Gaius Valerius Catullus]
 (c84–c54 BCE), 2, 11, 41, 106,
 131n7, 143n96
Celan, Paul (1920–1970), 90, 92, 93,
 101n59, 103n73 103n84, 119, 160
Deren, Maya (1917–1961), 121,
 140n83, 147n126
Dionysus, 63, 64, 75n77, 159, 160
Dover, Sir Kenneth (1920–2010):
 Greek Homosexuality (1979), 22,
 32n69, 180
Duncan, Isadora (1877–1927), 60

Eco, Umberto (1932–2016), xiii–
 xvi, xviin1
Emerson, Ralph Waldo (1803–
 1882), 7, 132n14
Erato, 78

Euripides (c484–406 BCE), Euripidean,
53, 60, 64, 65, 70nn38–39, 71n46,
88, 98n28;
  Alkestis (438 BCE), 72n60
  The Bacchae (c406 BCE), 60–65,
  70n41, 74nn73–76
  Hekabe (c425 BCE), 56–57
  Herakles (c416 BCE),
  55–56, 100n54
  Hippolytus (428 BCE), 57–59
  in exile, 72n59
  Iphigeneia Among the Taurians
  (c413 BCE), 59–60, 70n40, 72n61
  Orestes (408 BCE), 50, 53, 70n38
  psychological depth in, 53–54
  rewriting myth in, 84
  The Trojan Women (415 BCE), 51

Foucault, Michel (1926–1984):
  The History of Sexuality (1976–
  1984), 22, 32n71, 181

Gide, Andre (1869–1951), 107
Gnosticism, 113–114

Heidegger, Martin (1889–1976), 86, 92,
  100n43, 103n73
Hesiod (fl.c750 BCE), 81–82
Hölderlin, Friedrich (1770–1843),
  63, 74n71, 78
Horton, Kristin, 73n64

Jaccon, Pauline, xx, 32n65,
  66n3, 182–183
Jezebel, 167n47
Joan of Arc (1412–1431), 118, 119,
  139n76, 153

Kafka, Franz (1883–1924), 9–10, 15,
  25, 30n42, 85, 116
kletic hymn, 116–117

Lombardo, Stanley, 130n1
(Pseudo)Longinus (c213–273 CE),
  80, 93, 114;

  On the Sublime, 12, 98n22
Lord Chamberlain's Men, 2

Marguerite (of) Porete (c1250–1310),
  xvi, 109–110, 114–119, 129,
  134nn30–31, 138nn55–56, 138–
  139nn66–67, 150, 152–153, 170;
  as *beguine*, 139n77
  The Mirror of Simple Souls,
  133–134nn29, 135–136nn35–
  39, 161, 186
Maximus of Tyre (2nd century CE), 21,
  22, 31n62, 32n66
McKee, Laura, xx, 167n45
Michelstaedter, Carlo (1887–1910), 22;
  Persuasion and Rhetoric
  (1910), 8, 184
Michelangelo [Buonarroti]
  (1475–1564), 64
Mimnermus (fl.c630–600 BCE),
  101n55, 167n45
Montaigne, Michel Eyquem de (1533–
  1592), 3, 6n8, 107, 131–132n11
Mozart, Wolfgang Amadeus
  (1756–1791), 65

Nelson, Maggie, 139–140n78, 184
Nietzsche, Friedrich (1844–1900),
  xiii–xvi, xviin1, 9, 22, 40, 50, 66,
  100n52, 101n57, 185;
  The Birth of Tragedy (1872), 7,
  10, 24nn2–3, 67n13
  as classicist, xv, 41, 169
  We Classicists [Wir Philologen]
  (1876), 67n13
Nussbaum, Martha C., 9, 22, 185;
  Aristotle's De Motu Animalium
  (1979), 24n9
  The Fragility of Goodness
  (1986), 8, 24n8
  "Love and the Individual", 31n47
  Upheavals of Thought
  (2001), 135n35

Orsini, Fulvio (1529–1600), 27n19;

Carmina Novem Illustrium Feminarum (1568), 69n23, 185
Ovid [Publius Ovidius Naso] (43 BCE–17 CE), Ovidian, 3, 109, 121, 124, 128, 129, 143n98, 150, 158, 159, 170;
    Art of Love (*Ars Amatoria*), 123, 125, 144nn102–103, 145n106, 146n111, 146n116, 147n128, 152, 156, 163nn6–10, 164n13, 166n31
    banishment of, 125, 127
    Cures for Love (*Remedia Amores*), 123
    Fasti, 145n109, 165n18
    Heroides, 122, 125, 141–142nn88–90, 143n96, 144n101
    Loves (*Amores*), 123
    Medea, 123
    Metamorphoses, 122, 123, 126, 140n85, 143n95, 151, 152, 163n11
    Poems from Exile (*Tristia* and *Ex Ponto*), 124, 145nn107–110, 146n114, 146n117, 147nn124–125
    reception history of, 140–141n87, 143n94, 144–145n105, 145n107
    self–exile in, 126
Oxyrhynchus, xvi, xviin3, 43

Palinode, 17, 18, 80, 89
Plato (c428–c423 BCE), Platonic, xiv, 2, 15, 19, 26, 38, 54, 114, 159, 172;
    Crito, 112, 136nn42–43, 136n45
    Middle Period of, 32n68, 71n47
    Phaedo, 30n46
    Phaedrus, xv, 10–11, 17–21, 30n46, 30–31n47, 31n53, 77, 80, 85, 131n11, 152, 160
    Philebus, 30n46
    Republic, 30n46, 71n47
    Symposium, 1, 81, 110, 117, 135n35, 152
Porete. *See* Marguerite (of) Porete
Proust, Marcel (1871–1922), 105, 154–157, 162, 166n35

Quatremère de Quincy, Antoine Chrysostome (1755–1849), ii, 186

Sappho (c630–c570 BCE), Sapphic, xi, xiv, 10, 11, 16, 17, 22, 28–29n23, 39, 51, 54, 58, 62, 65, 79, 89, 94, 96n2, 108, 110, 111, 114, 115, 129, 138n56, 150, 152, 159, 167n45, 172, 175;
    as Archaic, 14
    as fragmentary, xvi, 15, 27n19, 37, 39, 40, 41, 45, 49, 98n25, 117
    as lover, 30n45, 149–150
    as lyric poet, 4, 33n72, 40, 78, 113, 122, 152
    as musician, 77
    as priestess/religious, 3, 105
    as a riddler, 29n34
    as virtuoso, 12, 21
    Bittersweet Fragment (#130), 11, 12, 13, 15, 25–26n14, 42
    Fragment #16, 43–44
    Fragment #105A–B, 47–49, 82–83
    Fragment #146, 46–47
    in exile, 109, 119, 127, 146n121
    in translation, 42, 121, 175
    irony in, 44–45, 57, 79
    "Letter to Phaon", 122, 141–142nn89–96
    Love Triangle Fragment (#31), 12, 14, 16, 26–27n19, 29n23, 36, 38–39, 41, 42, 155
    Ode (Hymn) to Aphrodite (#1), 12, 15, 16, 26n18, 26–27n19, 29n39, 32n67, 39–40, 41, 42, 105
    Pleiades Fragment (#168B), 12, 43, 69n23, 149–150, 163n4
    suicide of, 122
Sappho Was a Right–On Woman (1972), 22, 33n72, 177
Septuagint, 65, 75n81, 96, 103n85

Shakespeare, William (1564–1616), 2, 4nn1–2, 56, 57, 71n53, 71n55, 165n21;
  Romeo and Juliet, 161, 168n55
Simonides of Keos (c556–c468 BCE), 80, 89–96, 98n24, 101n59, 102n69, 105, 107, 111, 115
Socrates (469–399 BCE), 10, 17, 18, 19, 20, 21, 22, 31n59, 112, 153, 159, 160
Sophocles (c496–406 BCE), 65;
  Antigone (c441 BCE), 60–63, 65, 71n43, 73n64, 74nn67–70,
  Elektra (c420–414 BCE), 50, 52–53, 70n38
Spirit:
  in the New Testament, 137–138n53
Steiner, George, 60–61, 73n63, 73n65, 188
Stesichorus (c630–c555 BCE), 79–80, 81, 87, 89, 97n12, 97n14, 98nn24–27, 167n45;
  as fragmentary, 82–83
  "interviewed", 99n35
Stout, Jeffrey, 188;
  Gifford Lectures, 164–165n16, 166n43

Suda, 79

Thermopylae, 95

Da Vinci, Leonardo (1452–1519), 64
Vulgate, 66

Walcott, Derek (1930–2017), 78, 96n4, 97n5, 138n57
Weil, Simone (1909–1943), 108, 111, 114, 115, 119, 129, 132nn14–15, 133n17, 138n57, 138n65, 150, 152, 162, 168nn56–57, 170, 189–190;
  arrogant humility, 116
  "The *Iliad*, or, The Poem of Force" (1943), 107, 132n16, 140n79
  The Notebooks of, xii, 117–118, 139n74
Williams, William Carlos (1883–1963), 120

Yourcenar, Marguerite (1903–1987), 169–173, 173n1, 173nn3–4, 107nn6–7, 191

Zeno of Citium (c334–262 BCE), 25n13

About the Author

Louis A. Ruprecht Jr. is the inaugural William M. Suttles Professor of Religious Studies in the Department of Anthropology at Georgia State University, where he also serves as Director of the Center for Hellenic Studies. His work examines the artistic, cultural, ethical, and political interface between Greek antiquity, Christian antiquity, and the contemporary world.

His most recent books include: *Quatremère de Quincy's Moral Considerations on the Place and Purpose of Works of Art: Introduction and Translation* (2020); *An Elemental Life: Mystery and Mercy in the Work of Father Matthew Kelty, OSCO* (2018); *Report on the Aeginetan Sculptures with Historical Supplements* (2017); *Policing the State: Democratic Responses to Police Power Gone Awry, in Memory of Kathryn Johnston, 2nd Edition* (2015); *Classics at the Dawn of the Museum Era: The Life and Times of Antoine Chrysostome Quatremère de Quincy* (2014); *Winckelmann and the Vatican's First Profane Museum* (2011).

www.ingramcontent.com/pod-product-compliance
Lightning Source LLC
Chambersburg PA
CBHW020119010526
44115CB00008B/886